22 ⁹⁵

International
Ethics

International Ethics

A *Philosophy & Public Affairs* Reader

Edited by CHARLES R. BEITZ, MARSHALL COHEN, THOMAS SCANLON, and A. JOHN SIMMONS

Contributors

LAWRENCE A. ALEXANDER

CHARLES R. BEITZ

MARSHALL COHEN

ROBERT K. FULLINWIDER

GREGORY S. KAVKA

DOUGLAS P. LACKEY

DAVID LUBAN

GEORGE I. MAVRODES

THOMAS NAGEL

ONORA O'NEILL

PETER SINGER

MICHAEL WALZER

Princeton University Press
Princeton, New Jersey

Published by
Princeton University Press,
41 William Street,
Princeton, New Jersey 08540
In the United Kingdom:
Princeton University Press,
Chichester, West Sussex
Copyright © 1985 by
Princeton University Press

First Princeton Paperback
printing, 1985
First hardcover printing, 1985
Fourth printing, 1990

9 8

LCC: 84-42938
ISBN: 0-691-07683-9 (cloth)
ISBN: 0-691-02234-8 (paper)

Princeton University Press
books are printed on acid-free
paper, and meet the guidelines for permanence and
durability of the Committee
on Production Guidelines for
Book Longevity of the Council
on Library Resources

Printed in the United States
of America

Most of the essays in this book appeared originally in the quarterly journal *Philosophy & Public Affairs*, published by Princeton University
Press. Some essays include minor corrections.

Marshall Cohen, "Moral Skepticism and International Relations," *P&PA* 13, no. 4 (Fall 1984),
copyright © 1984 by Princeton University Press;
Thomas Nagel, "War and Massacre," *P&PA* 1,
no. 2 (Winter 1972), copyright © 1972 by
Princeton University Press; George I. Mavrodes,
"Conventions and the Morality of War," *P&PA* 4,
no. 2 (Winter 1975), copyright © 1975 by
Princeton University Press; Robert K. Fullinwider, "War and Innocence," *P&PA* 5, no. 1
(Fall 1975), copyright © 1975 by Princeton University Press; Lawrence A. Alexander, "Self-De-
fense and the Killing of Noncombatants: A Re-
ply to Fullinwider," *P&PA* 5, no. 4 (Summer
1976), copyright © 1976 by Princeton University
Press; Douglas P. Lackey, "Missiles and Morals:
A Utilitarian Look at Nuclear Deterrence,"
P&PA 11, no. 3 (Summer 1982), copyright ©
1982 by Princeton University Press; Gregory S.
Kavka, "Doubts About Unilateral Disarmament,"
P&PA 12, no. 3 (Summer 1983), copyright ©
1983 by Princeton University Press; Douglas P.
Lackey, "Disarmament Revisited: A Reply to
Kavka and Hardin," *P&PA* 12, no. 3 (Summer
1983), copyright © 1983 by Princeton University
Press; Michael Walzer, excerpts from *Just and
Unjust Wars*, pp. 51–63, 86–101, 106–108, 339–
42. Copyright © 1977 by Basic Books, Inc., Publishers. Reprinted by permission of the pub-
lisher. David Luban, "Just War and Human
Rights," *P&PA* 9, no. 2 (Winter 1980), copyright
© 1980 by Princeton University Press; Michael
Walzer, "The Moral Standing of States: A Response to Four Critics," *P&PA* 9, no. 3 (Spring
1980), copyright © 1980 by Princeton University
Press; David Luban, "The Romance of the Nation-State," *P&PA* 9, no. 4 (Summer 1980),
copyright © 1980 by Princeton University Press;
Peter Singer, "Famine, Affluence, and Morality,"
P&PA 1, no. 3 (Spring 1972), copyright © 1972
by Princeton University Press; Onora O'Neill,
"Lifeboat Earth," *P&PA* 4, no. 3 (Spring 1975),
copyright © 1975 by Princeton University Press;
Charles R. Beitz, "Justice and International Relations," *P&PA* 4, no. 4 (Summer 1975), copyright © 1975 by Princeton University Press.

CONTENTS

Part V. International Humanitarianism and Distributive Justice

INTRODUCTION

Political events of the last twenty years have brought into relief several important moral issues in international affairs. For example, the Vietnam War and the intensification of the nuclear arms race focused concern on the philosophical basis of rules for the conduct of war. Interventionary warfare as well as evidence of growing international interdependence raised both old and new problems about the moral significance of national boundaries and the nature of a state's right not to be interfered with by outsiders. Famines, rapid population growth, and pressure from the third world for a "new international economic order" gave rise to questions about the moral foundations of international property rights and the requirements of international distributive justice.

Philosophers have paid less attention to these issues than their political importance warrants. Perhaps the reason is that they have wondered whether these political problems involve elements of genuine philosophical perplexity. Or they may have doubted that philosophers were in a position to contribute constructively to political debate about these matters. The editors believe that the selections collected in this volume (most of which appeared originally in *Philosophy & Public Affairs*) will lay to rest doubts on both scores, while suggesting numerous directions for further exploration.

The collection opens with an essay by Marshall Cohen. Cohen's paper serves as an introduction to those that follow by exploring the first problem likely to confront the theorist of international ethics—pervasive skepticism that moral judgment in international affairs is meaningful at all. Skepticism about international ethics has a long history in modern moral philosophy, especially in the work of Hobbes and Hume, and it has been influential in recent Anglo-American international thought in the guise of "political real-ism." Cohen examines these and other forms of international skepticism and argues that, for all that can be learned from the more sophisticated versions of the doctrine, none supplies any reason in principle for abstaining from moral judgment about international affairs.

The articles in Part II take up the question of the moral basis of the rules of war, in particular the rule of noncombatant immunity normally thought to prohibit the intentional taking of innocent life. Thomas Nagel describes the basic philosophical conflict as one between absolutist and utilitarian justifications of the rule, and notes how the interpretation of the rule will change depending upon which type of justification is adopted. He explores absolutist views at some length and argues that they provide a better account of the moral importance of innocence than utilitarian views.[1]

George Mavrodes' contribution presents a criticism of several versions of the absolutist doctrine of noncombatant immunity deriving from traditional just war theory. He argues that the traditional understanding of noncom-batant status, which associates it with innocence, will not stand up to careful scrutiny. In place of absolutism, Mavrodes supplies an alternative theory of noncombatant immunity based on a view of warfare as a convention-de-pendent activity in which the parties agree to respect noncombatant im-munity as a kind of damage-limitation device. Mavrodes' theory is the subject of the exchange between Robert Fullinwider and Lawrence Alexander pre-sented in the brief papers that conclude this section of the collection.

We turn in Part III to moral questions about the justifiability of the system of nuclear deterrence. The main selection is an essay by Douglas Lackey outlining a utilitarian argument for unilateral nuclear disarmament. Lack-ey's position differs from standard philosophical versions of unilateralism in not relying on controversial claims about the impermissibility of threatening civilian lives; instead, he is concerned to minimize the expected overall costs of nuclear armament strategy.

Lackey's case for unilateralism depends in part on speculative estimates of the probable Soviet response to nuclear disarmament by the United States. In the next selection, Gregory Kavka claims that these estimates are im-

1. For two utilitarian replies to Nagel, see R. B. Brandt, "Utilitarianism and the Rules of War," and R. M. Hare, "Rules of War and Moral Reasoning," both in *Philosophy & Public Affairs* 1, no. 2 (Winter 1972), pp. 145–65 and 166–81. These and other articles on the morality of war have been collected in the *Philosophy & Public Affairs* Reader, *War and Moral Re-sponsibility*, ed. Marshall Cohen, Thomas Nagel, and Thomas Scanlon (Princeton: Princeton University Press, 1974).

plausibly optimistic; Kavka advances several other criticisms of Lackey's position as well. The section concludes with Lackey's replies to these criticisms.[2]

The subject of Part IV is the moral status of the nation-state. The debate begins with excerpts from Michael Walzer's *Just and Unjust Wars*.[3] This book is a comprehensive study of the moral dilemmas of warfare. We can present here only a small portion of Walzer's rich and suggestive text. In these selections, he sets forth his argument that (with important exceptions) states have a right of communal integrity that prohibits unprovoked military intervention. This right derives from the rights of persons to live in their own historic communities, in which conflict and controversy about political and social arrangements are appropriately worked out by the members themselves according to their own traditions. The argument is significant for two reasons. First, its foundation in consent theory involves some of the most basic and controversial issues of political philosophy. Second, the thesis of communal integrity bears on a much wider range of problems in international relations than those connected with military intervention; indeed, in an interdependent world where states have a variety of nonmilitary as well as military means for interfering in one another's affairs, the communal integrity thesis might be seen as the main regulative principle for international politics.

In "Just War and Human Rights," David Luban takes issue with Walzer's derivation of states' rights from individual rights. Luban claims that the derivation actually yields a far more limited form of the nonintervention principle than Walzer recognizes. On Luban's view, states that systematically violate their citizens' human rights cannot justifiably claim to be protected against outside interference by a right of communal integrity, and other states may justifiably intervene (in fact, may have a *duty* to intervene) when intervention would improve respect for human rights.

Luban's criticism goes to the heart of Walzer's theory by questioning the idea that states are analogous to persons in having rights of autonomy. Similar criticisms have been voiced by several other commentators.[4] In his

2. Further criticisms of Lackey's position are advanced by Russell Hardin in "Unilateral Versus Mutual Disarmament," *Philosophy & Public Affairs* 12, no. 3 (Summer 1983), pp. 236–54.

3. New York: Basic Books, 1977.

4. See, for example, Charles Beitz, "Bounded Morality: Justice and the State in World Politics," *International Organization* 33, no. 3 (Summer 1979), pp. 405–24; Gerald Doppelt, "Walzer's Theory of Morality in International Relations," *Philosophy & Public Affairs* 8, no. 1

reply to these critics, Walzer provides an expanded account of the derivation of states' rights from individual rights, and defends his version of the non-intervention principle against that set forth by Luban. In a brief rejoinder, Luban explains why he finds Walzer's reply unconvincing.[5]

The essays in the concluding section of this volume take up the subject of international humanitarianism and distributive justice, certainly the most neglected of the important moral issues in international affairs. Peter Singer's contribution asks how much those in the affluent world are obligated to give in order to help relieve suffering, and in the extreme but not unlikely case, to prevent death, associated with food shortages and famine in the poor countries. The answer, he claims, is that they should give *at least* until, by giving more, they would have to sacrifice something as important morally as the suffering that their gift would relieve.[6]

Singer's question presupposes that the affluent have a responsibility to help relieve suffering elsewhere. Some people would deny this; they might argue, for example, that not having *caused* food shortages elsewhere, the affluent have no obligation to help avoid them or minimize their human costs. In "Lifeboat Earth," Onora O'Neill argues that such a position involves too narrow a view of one's responsibilities to others; in particular, it fails to take seriously the implications of the common belief that everyone has a right not to be killed. By not helping to avoid situations of extreme scarcity when it is in our power to do so, we commit the moral equivalent of murder.

In the last article in this volume, Charles Beitz considers whether principles of social justice widely acknowledged to apply within the nation-state should also be applied globally. He argues that the theory of justice set forth by John Rawls[7] should, on Rawls's own premises, be given a global interpretation. The import of Beitz's argument transcends the context of debate about Rawls's theory of justice, for it raises the question of why the re-

(Fall 1978), pp. 3–26; Richard Wasserstrom, Review of *Just and Unjust Wars, Harvard Law Review* 92, no. 2 (December 1978), pp. 536–45.

5. Rejoinders by Beitz and Doppelt appear in *Philosophy & Public Affairs* 9, no. 4 (Summer 1980), pp. 385–91 and 398–403.

6. For Singer's further thoughts on the view set forth in this article, see his "Postscript" in *World Hunger and Moral Obligation*, ed. William Aiken and Hugh LaFollette (Englewood Cliffs, NJ: Prentice-Hall, Inc., 1977), pp. 33–36; "Reconsidering the Famine Relief Argument," in *Food Policy: The Responsibility of the United States in the Life and Death Choices*, ed. Peter G. Brown and Henry Shue (New York: Free Press, 1977), pp. 36–53; and *Practical Ethics* (Cambridge: Cambridge University Press, 1979), chap. 8.

7. In *A Theory of Justice* (Cambridge, MA: Harvard University Press, 1971).

quirements of *any* theory of distributive justice should be limited to the area within national boundaries. If such a limitation cannot be defended morally, Beitz claims, then the affluent have more extensive and far-reaching international obligations than most people have recognized.[8]

8. A substantially revised and extended version of Beitz's article appears as Part III of his book, *Political Theory and International Relations* (Princeton: Princeton University Press, 1979). For further comments on this argument, see his "Cosmopolitan Ideals and National Sentiment," *Journal of Philosophy* 80, no. 10 (October 1983), pp. 591–600.

PART I

The Challenge
of Skepticism

MARSHALL COHEN   Moral Skepticism
and International
Relations

To an alarming degree the history of international relations is a history
of selfishness and brutality. It is a story in which spying, deceit, bribery,
disloyalty, ingratitude, betrayal, exploitation, plunder, repression, subjection, and genocide are all too conspicuous. And it is a history that may
well culminate in the moral catastrophe of nuclear war. This situation
has elicited a number of very different reactions from those who discourse
on international relations. For some the moral quality of international
relations from the Athenians at Melos to the Soviets in Poland is so
deplorable that they question whether moral standards in fact apply to
the international realm. George Kennan remarks, for instance, that the
conduct of nations is not "fit" for moral judgment.[1] This ambivalent way
of putting the matter betrays a nostalgia for moral assessment while
announcing a skepticism about its very possibility. Benedetto Croce is
beyond ambivalence or nostalgia. This self-professed disciple of Machiavelli boldly proclaimed that in the realm of international politics lies are
not lies, or murders murders.[2] Moral categories and judgments are simply
out of place in the realm of international affairs. The first task of this
article will be to examine this extreme form of moral skepticism about

I am grateful to Jonathan Bennett, Charles Beitz, Michael Doyle, Thomas Scanlon, John
Simmons, Barry Stroud, Judith Thomson and Susan Wolf for extremely helpful comments,
and to the Society for Ethical and Legal Philosophy and the Yale Legal Theory Workshop
for very useful discussion. Sections of this article were written at The Institute for Advanced
Study in the academic year 1981–1982 on a grant from the National Endowment for the
Humanities.

1. George Kennan, *American Diplomacy 1900–1950* (New York: New American Library,
1951), p. 87.

2. Benedetto Croce, *Politics and Morals*, trans. Salvatore J. Castilione (New York: Philosophical Library, 1945), pp. 3–4.

international relations, first in its realist, and then in its Hobbesian, form.

The realists argue that international relations must be viewed under the category of power and that the conduct of nations is, and should be, guided and judged exclusively by the amoral requirements of the national interest. Sometimes they argue, as writers since Spinoza have argued, that if a statesman fails to pursue the national interest (and submits to some other, perhaps ethical, standard) he acts improperly and violates his contract with those he represents.[3] On this view, the only proper question to ask of him is whether his actions and policies advance the national interest and increase his nation's power. But the suggestion that the statesman has a moral obligation to do for his constituency whatever he has implicitly undertaken to do (on a contract, or as trustee or agent) is no better than the argument that the corporation president has an overriding obligation to sell thalidomide for the benefit of his shareholders, or that the Mafia hitman has an overriding obligation to kill for his employers.[4] And, in any case, these are not the terms a responsible constituency can be understood to have exacted from those who conduct its affairs. Often a democratic people will wish its affairs to be conducted in a morally acceptable fashion and it is, in any case, entirely appropriate to judge both a nation's, and its statesmen's, conduct by pertinent moral standards. A more tempting argument for the realist view that international conduct is improperly guided or judged by moral standards supposes that actions which seem to be politically acceptable in the international realm appear to be condemned by morality, and that morality must, therefore, be irrelevant to the judgment of international conduct. I argue that this view of the realists is founded on an overly simple conception of the structure of morality, one that they share with the naive moralists who are the main object of their attack. Once a more complex account of morality is provided, the realist view that international relations can only be measured against political standards of power and the national interest loses its plausibility. The substance of that more complex morality is, I believe, non-utilitarian, and I employ it to provide a moral assessment of the realist doctrine of the balance of power.

Hobbesian skepticism about international relations also rests on an

3. Spinoza, *Tractatus Theologico-Politicus*, in *The Political Works of Spinoza*, ed. A. G. Wernham (Oxford: Clarendon Press, 1958), p. 141.

4. Thomas Nagel, "Ruthlessness in Public Life," in *Public and Private Morality*, ed. Stuart Hampshire (Cambridge: Cambridge University Press, 1978). p. 80.

*Moral Skepticism
and International
Relations*

inadequate view of morality. But here the problem is less with the Hobbesian account of the structure of morality than with the Hobbesian view of the conditions under which morality applies. For, in Hobbes's view, issues of justice and injustice do not arise in the state of nature even as, in the view of Treitschke and Bosanquet, ethical issues do not arise in the absence of "community" or outside the realm of Hegelian *Sittlichkeit*.[5] I argue, however, that ethical principles apply in the state of nature even as they apply in the absence of the common life that allegedly characterizes national communities. Besides, the actual situation of states is very different from that of individuals in the state of nature.

In contrast to the realists and Hobbes, a second group of theorists grants that international relations are subject to moral requirements. Some of them argue that these requirements differ from the requirements of common morality and constitute a special "political" morality or even a peculiarly "international" one. Others like David Hume think the requirements are those of common morality but argue that they apply to princes with less force than they do to private persons.[6] Those who speak of a special "political," or "international," morality often contrast private or common or Christian morality with an incompatible pagan morality (as in Isaiah Berlin's Machiavelli), or with a disillusioned ethic of "responsibility" (Weber), or with an ethic of nationalism or of national self-assertion.[7] I argue against them that when the requirements of these alternative "moralities" are indeed legitimate they can be shown to follow from the application of standard moral principles to the unusual circumstances of international conduct. All too often, however, these special moralities sanction unlimited violence as a political means or unrestrained national self-aggrandizement as a political end, and they must then simply be rejected as morally insupportable. There is little to choose between the view that international conduct is exempt from moral assessment and the view that it is governed by a morality which sanctions and even encourages the most objectionable practices of international life. Indeed, the difference between them is sometimes merely verbal, and when it is

5. Hobbes, *Leviathan*, ed. C. B. McPherson (Middlesex, England: Penguin Books, 1968), p. 188; Heinrich von Treitschke, *Politics*, trans. Blanche Dugdale and Torben de Bille (London: Constable and Co., 1916), p. 94; Bernard Bosanquet, *The Philosophical Theory of the State* (London: Macmillan and Co., 1958), p. 325.

6. Hume, *A Treatise of Human Nature*, ed. L. A. Selby-Bigge (Oxford: Clarendon Press, 1946), p. 568.

7. Isaiah Berlin, "The Originality of Machiavelli," in *Against the Current* (New York: The Viking Press, 1980), pp. 45ff.; Max Weber, *Politics as a Vocation*, trans. H. H. Gerth

more than this the realists are probably correct in thinking their amor-
alism less dangerous because it is less inflammatory and self-righteous.
For reasons of space, and because the doctrine that there is a special
morality of international relations has not, in my view, been given an
intellectually impressive defense, I shall not discuss it here. I will, however, discuss the much more plausible and brilliantly elaborated view of
David Hume. But I argue that Hume's view, according to which ordinary
moral rules apply with less force to international affairs, derives from his
false identification of the conventions of international conduct with the
actual requirements of justice. Those conventions are often unjust, and
demonstrating that they are in every nation's interest does not establish
their justice. I conclude that international conduct is open to moral assessment. Furthermore, these assessments rest on principles that govern
every domain of human conduct and govern them all with equal rigor.

REALISM AND POWER POLITICS

Realist writings display many serious misunderstandings of the nature
of morality and, as I have suggested, these misunderstandings contribute
to the realists' skepticism about the role of morality in international affairs.
The post-World War II realists, for instance, often fail to distinguish
between the moral and the "moralistic" or between the legal and the
"legalistic." All too often the realists suggest that because "moralistic" or
"legalistic" attitudes and policies are irrelevant, and even dangerous, in
international affairs, morality and law are irrelevant and dangerous as
well. This is, of course, a non sequitur. There is no reason why the genuine
moralist cannot agree with the realist that "moralistic" politicians often
claim to discern moral issues where doing so is inappropriate and self-
defeating. The moralist may acknowledge, for instance, that the diplomatic recognition of a Communist regime does not imply moral approval
and that it is often both permissible and politically prudent to extend
such recognition to regimes whose moral principles we nevertheless reject.[8] Again, the genuine moralist can agree with the realist that a "mor-

---

and C. Wright Mills (Philadelphia: Fortress Press, 1965), pp. 46ff.; Arnold Wolfers, "Statesmanship and Moral Choice," in *Discord and Collaboration* (Baltimore: The Johns Hopkins
Press, 1962), p. 59.

8. Hans J. Morgenthau, *Politics Among Nations*, 2d ed. (New York: Alfred A. Knopf,
1959), pp. 11–12.

alistic" foreign policy, one founded on utopian ideals and sentimental
slogans designed to win elections or to galvanize the passions of a democratic populace in time of war, is often hypocritical, obtuse, and self-
defeating. But the moralist is not required to endorse a foreign policy
because it invokes moral-sounding formulas that call on us to conquer
the forces of evil, to exact war "reparations" because justice requires it,
or to make the world safe for democracy come what may. He can agree,
for instance, that morality did not require the Allies to demand total victory
or to impose a humiliating peace on Germany after World War I. Even
if Germany's actions gave the Allies the right to impose such a peace,
morality did not require them to exercise it. We do not think we are
morally obliged to punish children or criminals as severely as their conduct justifies if giving them another chance, issuing a moderate rebuke,
or devising a rehabilitative regime is likely to produce better results. When
Kennan condemns the vindictive reparation requirements imposed on
Germany, or criticizes the humiliating attitude of the Western powers
toward the Weimar Republic, he is not deploring something that morality
or a moral attitude requires.[9] Indeed, the sensible moralist will doubtless
agree with the realists that imposing a moderate peace of the sort Metternich and Castlereagh imposed on France after the Napoleonic wars
would have been better than the Versailles approach. Similarly, morality
did not require that we pursue a policy of unconditional surrender during
World War II. Kennan himself admits that faced with an enemy like
Hitler there may have been no practical alternative to this policy.[10] However that may be, the moral, as distinguished from the purely strategic,
arguments against inviting the Red Army into the heart of Europe would
surely have outweighed the argument that Germany must be rendered
helpless and put utterly at our mercy.

The realist's critique of "moralism" is, then, often politically acute and
salutary. But "moralism" is not morality, and showing that "moralistic"
attitudes and policies have a pernicious influence on foreign policy does
not show that morality itself must be banished from the realm of international affairs. Certainly, it does not show that a moral point of view
must be replaced by a realistic one that takes the national interest to
provide what Morgenthau calls "the one guiding star, one standard of

9. Kennan, *American Diplomacy*, pp. 57, 71.
10. Ibid., p. 76.

thought, one rule of action" in the international sphere.[11] Power politics is not the only alternative to a muddled moralism. ·

If the confusion of "moralism" with morality provides one source of skepticism about the role of morality in international affairs, confusions about the structure of morality provide others. For many who speak in favor of a moral approach to international politics identify morality with the simple rules that in their opinion govern the conduct of ordinary life. R. W. Mowat, for instance, sees the Ten Commandments and the Golden Rule as central and remarks that they are "universal propositions without reservations, without exceptions."[12] Mowat's book is entitled *Public and Private Morality* and it is characteristic of writers of his persuasion to insist that the rules and principles which apply in private life apply in the public realm as well. Often, like Mowat, and like the realists' *bête noire*, Woodrow Wilson, they deplore the standard of conduct that prevails in the relations of states and look forward (in the words of Wilson's address to Congress on declaring war in 1917) to "the beginning of an age in which it will be insisted that the same standards of conduct and of responsibility for wrong shall be observed among nations and their governments that are observed among the individual citizens of individual states."[13]

But we do not need to invoke the special circumstances of international life to see that Mowat's position is untenable. Breaking a promise in order to aid the victim of an accident, lying to the Gestapo about the Jew in the attic, or killing a ruthless attacker in self-defense or to save a third party all constitute justifiable exceptions to the rules that Mowat and other simple moralists have in mind. If this is the case in domestic life, it is reasonable to expect that there will be exceptions to the rules forbidding promise breaking, lying, and killing in the circumstances of international life as well, and on occasion, at least, we can share Treitschke's scorn for the statesman who warms his hands over the smoking ruins of his fatherland comforting himself with the thought that he has never lied.[14] As Treitschke's remark suggests, the realists are correct in thinking

11. Morgenthau, *In Defense of the National Interest* (New York: Alfred A. Knopf, 1952), p. 242.

12. R. B. Mowat, *Public and Private Morality* (Bristol: Arrowsmith, 1933), p. 40.

13. Quoted by Morgenthau in *Scientific Man vs. Power Politics* (Chicago: University of Chicago Press, 1974), p. 180.

14. Treitschke, *Politics*, p. 104; R. M. Hare, "Reasons of State" in *Applications of Moral Philosophy* (Berkeley and Los Angeles: University of California Press, 1972), p. 19.

*Moral Skepticism
and International
Relations*

that at least some of the actions simple moralists deplore are in fact necessary, defensible, and even admirable. But since realists all too often share the simple moralist's view that these actions are proscribed by morality, they are compelled to adopt the untenable position that international conduct cannot and should not be judged by moral standards. We have here the familiar phenomenon of the skeptic or realist who is a disappointed absolutist. But this inversion of the simple moralist's view is theoretically unsound and encourages a cynicism that is, if anything, even more dangerous than the naiveté and utopianism it is meant to supplant. It is necessary, therefore, to question this inadequate view of morality and to replace it with a more complex conception that will dissipate some of the tension between the often reasonable political positions of the realists and the demands of morality as the simple moralist sees them.

We must agree, then, that any reasonably accurate account of our moral view will acknowledge that moral rules often have exceptions and that we do nothing wrong when we act within an exception. (This is, indeed, what we mean when we speak of an exception.) But we need to complicate our conception of morality still further if we are to guard against more sophisticated skepticisms that feed on what is, even with this amendment, an overly simple view of morality.

For a more sophisticated realist may argue that even a morality which admits exceptions to its rules (as his does) will not be able to accept as legitimate actions that he (and sometimes that we) nevertheless consider legitimate. For many such actions, far from falling within the recognized exceptions to moral rules, actually require us to default on our moral obligations, to violate the rights of others, or to do other things that are objectionable from a moral point of view. For instance, Britain and France unquestionably defaulted on their legal (and in this case on their moral) obligations under the Covenant of the League of Nations when they failed to impose sanctions on Italy in response to her invasion of Abyssinia.[15] And the Jews violated the right of the Palestinian people to live where and how they reasonably wished when they established the State of Israel. But these more sophisticated realists may argue that despite these moral infractions, what Britain and France did, and what the Jews did, was legitimate. And, since these actions were legitimate they must have been

15. I owe the example to Michael Howard.

legitimate from a "political," even if they were illegitimate from a "moral," point of view. Therefore, the realists conclude once again that in international affairs the political point of view is the appropriate or, at least, the overriding one.

But analyses of this sort are nevertheless misguided. They are flawed by their failure to appreciate the phenomenon of moral conflict. And this is a phenomenon that any adequately complex morality must acknowledge.[16] For it is often the case, and many would argue it is the case in the examples just mentioned, that those who violate a moral obligation do so in obedience to a weightier or a more compelling moral obligation. Thus, Britain and France failed to fulfill their duties under the League Covenant but they did so because they feared that honoring them would seriously impair their ability to defend either themselves or the fundamental values of a liberal civilization in what they could see was the coming struggle against fascism. In acting on these weightier obligations Britain and France acted not simply with political realism but in what was, from a moral point of view, the better way. Similarly, it can be argued, the Jews in asserting their religious and historical rights, and in doing what was required to secure the very existence of the Jewish people, acted on morally justifiable grounds. It is because the realist fails to appreciate the fact of moral conflict, or to understand that we are sometimes morally justified in defaulting on our obligations, in violating the rights of others, or, more generally, in doing dark and terrible things, that he develops a "political" justification for doing them. From this "realistic," political point of view he often criticizes the naiveté of the moralist's political thinking. But the fault lies rather in the simplicity of his own view of morality. For, as we have seen, that view fails to provide an adequate account of moral conflict and lacks an adequate understanding of moral tragedy.

But while stressing complexity we must avoid complicity, and it is therefore important to emphasize that many of the wrongs which so unhappily disfigure the history of international relations are wholly unjustifiable from a moral point of view. We must resist those theorists (and apologists) who discern imponderable moral conflict or inescapable moral tragedy in every act of aggression or exploitation. If the British and the

16. Bernard Williams, "Ethical Consistency," in *Problems of the Self* (Cambridge: Cambridge University Press, 1973), pp. 166–86; Ruth Barcan Marcus, "Moral Dilemmas and Consistency," *Journal of Philosophy* 17 (March 1980):121–36.

French were justified in defaulting on their legal obligations to the League, the same cannot be said of the German failure to honor Belgian neutrality. If the Jews were justified in violating the rights of the Palestinians, the same cannot be said of the Italian assault on the rights of the Abyssinians. All too often the atmosphere of international relations is precisely as objectionable as the simple moralist says it is. The actions of a Kaiser Wilhelm or a Mussolini must not be rationalized from a "political" point of view or romanticized as cases of "tragic" necessity.

Although we cannot accept the simplicities of a moral theory like Mowat's, we should endorse his view that the history of international conduct is to an alarming degree the history of unconscionable insolence, greed, and brutality. Napoleon addressing his troops suggests what is all too often its moral atmosphere: ". . . Soldiers, you are naked, [and] ill nourished . . . I will lead you into the most fertile plains in the world. Rich provinces, great cities, will be in your power. There you will find honour, glory, riches."[17] On sentiments like these it is not difficult to pass moral judgment. If the realist is to persuade us that such judgments are inappropriate or impossible, this will require more forceful arguments or considerations than we have so far examined.

Many realists would claim that the tradition of political theory which stretches from Machiavelli to Croce and culminates in the main line of present-day thinking about international relations provides arguments and considerations of the required sort. According to this tradition, international relations occupies an autonomous realm of power politics exempt from moral judgment and immune to moral restraint. Unquestionably, this ubiquitous school of thought displays an amazing vitality, but a systematic presentation of its views is not easy to find. Perhaps the most notable in recent times is Hans Morgenthau's classic work, *Politics Among Nations*, and it will be useful to examine it here.

A main objective of Morgenthau's book, and of the realist school, is to show that Wilsonian hopes for a moral alternative to power politics is at very least naive and sentimental. Morgenthau asserts, for example, that it is an illusion to think that "men have the choice between power politics and its necessary outgrowth, the balance of power, on the one hand, and a different, better kind of international relations on the other."[18] It is, therefore, surprising to discover that Morgenthau does not argue directly

17. Quoted by Mowat in *Public and Private Morality*, p. 59.
18. Morgenthau, *Politics Among Nations*, p. 155.

that this better kind of international politics is impossible. Rather, he argues more generally that since all politics is ultimately power politics the desire for a better kind of international politics is, at best, utopian.[19]

In defending the claim that all politics is "power" politics Morgenthau illicitly stretches this phrase beyond its traditional meaning and offers implausible biopsychological and quasi-Marxist arguments to show that domestic politics, and even that family relations, are really disguised forms of the struggle for power. It is unnecessary to examine these arguments here because even if Morgenthau were correct of thinking that all politics is power politics, these argumentative strategies would not help him. If the operation of power politics is compatible with the felicities of family life and the moderation and legal character of the most fortunate national communities, then the operation of power politics does not preclude the possibility of that "better kind" of international politics that the liberal hopes for and works toward. To the contrary, showing that all relations are infected with power politics in this sense shows that international relations do not present a unique problem or an impossible terrain for ethical conduct or ethical judgment.

If Morgenthau wishes to demonstrate that this better kind of international politics is impossible, he will have to show that international politics is power politics in a narrower sense—one that fails to characterize at least some forms of municipal politics and family life. Power politics in the required sense must be incompatible with ethical conduct and impervious to ethical judgment.

Morgenthau tries to make plausible the claim that international politics is power politics in this appropriately narrower sense by suggesting, to begin with, that at least some international activities are not political at all.[20] Since they are nonpolitical he does not need to show that they characteristically display a struggle for power. The fact is, however, that if (as he says) the exchange of scientific information, famine and disaster relief, cultural and trade relations, and even much diplomatic activity are free from the struggle for power, the thesis that all international politics is power politics, opaque to moral assessment, loses much of its bite. Indeed, the claim threatens to reduce to the uninformatively circular observation that the aspect of international relations which is pure power politics is the aspect of international relations which is pure power politics—assuming there is one. But what, if anything, is that aspect? Morgenthau further dilutes the claim that all international politics is power politics by conceding that some nations, like Monaco, are politically inactive on the international scene or are, like Switzerland, only minimally active. Morgenthau insists, however, that unlike Monaco and Switzerland some nations, in particular, the United States and the U.S.S.R., are maximally active and their relations (again, he does not say which of their relations) constitute the paradigm of international political relations. These nations are engaged in a straightforward struggle for power, and their conduct confirms the view that international politics is best understood as an autonomous realm of power in which the actions of nations are neither motivated by ethical considerations nor subject to ethical judgment. But even Morgenthau's paradigm case is far from persuasive, and no one has stated the main objection to it more forcefully than Morgenthau himself. In another, less theoretical work, he writes that "Washington and Moscow are not only the main centers of power, they are also the seats of hostile and competing political philosophies. . . . [We have here] a conflict between two kinds of moral principles, two types of moral conduct, two ways of life."[21] This is, in a sense, quite true, but it suggests that we shall not understand even Morgenthau's paradigm case of international politics unless we acknowledge that the parties involved are in part ethically motivated and that their actions are subject to moral assessment. I would argue that despite alarming lapses Washington often acts in conformity with moral requirements, even in its conflicts with Moscow. After all, Washington refrained from attacking Moscow at a time when the United States enjoyed a monopoly of nuclear weapons. And, surely, moral restraint, and sometimes something more attractive, often characterizes Washington's political relations with many other, more amicable nations. Whether or not this is so, however, the way of life we are defending is founded on moral principles that are plainly incompatible with the amoral pursuit of power, for any such policy must systematically ignore the rights and fundamental interests of others. If in certain extreme circumstances a struggle for power can be justified on grounds of, say, self-defense, this will itself be a morally grounded defense. In other circumstances an unrestrained pursuit of power will be condemned by the moral principles we ourselves acknowledge.

21. Morgenthau, *In Defense of the National Interest*, p. 62.

Morgenthau might argue that, while this seems to be so, the moral principles that nations announce are simply ideological counters employed in the struggle for power. But Morgenthau has given no reason to think this is true of moral language in its international applications alone, and if the claim is meant to follow from an account of the ideological nature of moral discourse in general, it implies a broader moral skepticism than Morgenthau wants to embrace, or than we are examining here. Morgenthau also suggests that from the point of view of the political scientist seeking to predict the behavior of nations they are best viewed as entities inhabiting an autonomous realm of power. But even if this were plausible (as I think it is not), it would not follow that statesmen and citizens should view themselves as occupying an autonomous realm in which the only appropriate grounds for action and judgment are assessments of power. In Morgenthau's view

> the political realist maintains the autonomy of the political sphere, as the economist, the lawyer, and the moralist maintain theirs. He thinks in terms of interest defined as power, as the economist thinks in terms of utility; the lawyer, of the conformity of action with legal rules; the moralist, of the conformity of action with moral principles. The economist asks: "How does this policy affect the welfare of society, or a segment of it?" The lawyer asks: "Is this policy in accord with the rules of law?" The moralist asks: "Is this policy in accord with moral principles?" And the political realist asks: "How does this policy affect the power of the nation?" . . . The political realist is not unaware of the existence and relevance of standards of thought other than the political one. As a political realist, he cannot but subordinate these other standards to the political one. And he parts company with other schools when they impose standards of thought appropriate to other spheres upon the political one. It is here that political realism takes issue with the "legalistic-moralistic approach" to international politics.[22]

Plainly, however, morality has no discrete sphere of its own (a sphere of moral "fact") parallel to, but separate from, the main areas of human activity. It is not only appropriate, but characteristic and necessary, to apply its standards to economic, legal, and political phenomena. If the economist asks which of two policies produces greater utility, the moralist

22. Morgenthau, *Politics Among Nations*, pp. 10–11.

should ask of those policies, is the distribution of utility they propose morally acceptable? If the lawyer asks of an action, does it conform to the legal rules, the moralist should ask, are those rules just? Similarly, then, if the political realist asks, how does this policy affect the power of the nation, the moralist must ask of that policy, does this increase in the nation's power, or the method of achieving it, violate the rights of others, or unfairly threaten their security, or is it, rather, within the permissible limits of autonomous action? Moral standards can and must be applied to the same phenomena that are also judged by economic, legal, and political standards. Often, too, moral standards will have to prevail over those more special standards. As we cannot accept the extreme realist view that moral concepts and judgments do not apply in the political realm, so we must also reject the less extreme, but still insupportable, view that these judgments must always be subordinated to political ones. For this requires that the decisive considerations always be considerations of power, and even its most celebrated proponents like Morgenthau cannot adhere to that deplorable doctrine unambiguously, consistently, or plausibly.

It will be useful to note briefly the related topic of the balance of power, for this central idea of Western political thinking is itself morally problematic. Morgenthau spoke of power politics and of "its inevitable outgrowth," the balance of power. And if one means by "the balance of power" any outcome the struggle for power produces, then a balance of power is necessarily, and trivially, the inevitable consequence of power politics. It will be recalled that Morgenthau also remarked that no different, better kind of politics is possible. This view is, however, highly questionable and has, in fact, been questioned by those in the mainstream of balance-of-power theorizing. For writers in this central tradition, a balance of power is not just any consequence of the struggle for power but a specific result of the exercise of power, one that displays "equilibrium."[23] Different writers have different conceptions of what constitutes an equilibrium. For some, an equilibrium exists when power is so arranged that its very distribution prevents the hegemony of any state over any other, or over all others, or when the distribution of power is such that the essentials of the status quo are maintained. Some writers like Rousseau think that power politics (at least European power politics) has

23. Edward Vose Gulick, *Europe's Classical Balance of Power* (New York: W. W. Norton, 1967), pp. 42ff.

a natural tendency to result (or that it inevitably results) in equilibrium. Rousseau remarked that if the balance were broken "for a moment" it would soon reestablish itself so that, "if the Princes who are accused of aiming at universal monarchy were in reality guilty of any such project, they gave more proof of ambition than genius."[24] But it is implausible to believe that every disturbance of an equilibrium will soon right itself (this assumption may have been encouraged by contemporary laissez-faire theories of the market), and the illusions of theorists like Rousseau were soon dispelled by Napoleon's attempt to emulate the achievements of Caesar and Charlemagne. Plainly, then, at least some states will need to reject pure power politics and practice moderation and restraint if an equilibrium is to be achieved. Balance-of-power politics in the sense of equilibrium politics is, undoubtedly, different and better than pure power politics. And those who have proposed it as a norm for international politics have certainly supposed it to be a possible form of politics. But balance-of-power politics, in the sense of equilibrium politics, nevertheless permits, and even requires, actions that are morally objectionable, and the restraints it imposes are not, in general, those that morality requires.

It has often been felt that the successful conduct of a policy of this sort is incompatible with the political morality of democratic institutions.[25] If a balance-of-power policy is to be pursued, foreign affairs will have to be placed in the hands of those who are adept at scrutinizing and manipulating the ebb and flow of power. In addition, those who conduct foreign policy will have to divert national resources from domestic uses (even from morally urgent ones) and evade or ignore popular sentiment. This is why realists so often profess admiration for the procedures of classical diplomacy and express irritation at democratic demands for publicity ("open covenants openly arrived at"), consultation, and popular support. It explains, in part, their objection to the moralizing tendencies of the foreign policies of democratic nations. For nations practicing balance-of-power politics will have to respond to the demands of the balance

24. Rousseau, *Abstract of the Abbé de Saint Pierre's Project for Perpetual Peace* in *The Theory of International Relations*, ed. M. G. Forsyth, H.M.A. Keens-Soper, and P. Savigear (London: George Allen and Unwin Ltd., 1970), p. 138.

25. Ernst B. Haas, "The Balance of Power as a Guide to Policy-Making," *The Journal of Politics* 15 (August 1953): 376-77; Hedley Bull, *The Anarchical Society* (London: The Macmillan Press, Ltd., 1977), p. 109.

*Moral Skepticism
and International
Relations*

rather than to their own moral, political, and religious sympathies and commitments. As balance policies required Francis I to ally himself with the Turk, and Spain to support the Huguenots against Richelieu, so democratic nations will have to favor authoritarian regimes over liberal ones when the balance requires it. Worse yet, democratic nations will have to violate their own sense of justice for they cannot take sides on the merits of any international dispute whose resolution affects the balance of power. The dispute will have to be resolved on other grounds. This applies not only to moral disputes, but to legal ones as well, and it effectively undermines the possibility of a legal world order founded on any principle other than the balance of power itself. For where the balance of power governs, the disinterested judgment, the solemn treaty, and the legal and moral rights of others must always be sacrificed to the demands of that balance if sacrificing them is required to preserve it. No doubt, many actions have been taken in the name of the balance that it did not, in fact, require. Even so, the balance has been invoked to justify (and on an appropriate view of the facts could justify) promoting civil unrest (the United States "destabilizing" Chile), opposing liberal or nationalist revolutions (the Holy Alliance), intervening in constitutional arrangements (the eighteenth-century wars of succession), preventing states and provinces from realizing their national ambitions (French and Russian policy toward the German principalities), forcing a state to unite with another against its will (Belgium with Holland), imposing neutrality on a state (Belgium), colonizing a territory (European "compensatory" colonizations of Africa), bringing states within an appropriate sphere of influence (the Yalta agreements), annexing them (Napoleon III compensating himself with Savoy and Nice), partitioning a nation and extinguishing its sovereignty (Poland), or engaging in preventive war against it (William of Orange striking at France, Austria "anticipating" Russia in the Balkans in 1914).

This is not a pleasant survey, and Morgenthau's assertion that international politics constitutes an autonomous realm in which moral considerations, if not prohibited, must be subordinated to calculations of power does nothing to quiet the objection that either a moral defense of these apparent violations of fundamental rights and interests must be provided or their unacceptability acknowledged. Many proponents of the equilibrium version of the balance doctrine undoubtedly believe that they have such a defense. They argue that arriving at an equilibrium maximizes the general welfare (by achieving stability and encouraging peace) or that it minimizes the (weighted) sum of rights which are violated (by preventing the hegemony of any state and securing the sovereignty of the parties to the balance). But neither of these justifications is acceptable from a moral point of view (and they are usually unacceptable on empirical grounds as well). Utilitarianism is an objectionable moral philosophy and especially so a version of utilitarianism that routinely permits the invasion of men's rights to achieve marginal improvements in the general welfare. (We would not be justified in depriving a minority of its fundamental political rights because this contributed marginally to the security, or markedly to the economic well-being, of the majority.)[26] Nor do we accept what Robert Nozick calls a "utilitarianism of rights," which routinely permits the violation of some rights if this will minimize the violation of rights more generally.[27] (We would not be justified in permitting a thief to steal a man's property so that the thief might subsequently join us in preventing others from stealing.) For these reasons we cannot accept a balance-of-power policy that is justified in either of these ways. It is not enough to argue, as the Abbé de Pradt did, that the extinction of Polish sovereignty contributed to the European equilibrium to show that this violation of the received rights of an ancient people could be accepted.[28] Nor is it legitimate to argue that the Prussian acquisition of Silesia in the eighteenth century or of Saxony in the nineteenth was justifiable because it improved the European balance and further secured the sovereign rights of other parties to the balance. (And it would not have been justified even if we were ignorant of the actual role played by a strengthened Germany in the history of the twentieth century.)

Even if we thought some form of traditional utilitarianism or of the "utilitarianism of rights" morally acceptable, it is doubtful whether either would provide a satisfactory foundation for the balance doctrine. This is so because achieving a balance of power is not necessarily the best way (and, indeed, it might be a disastrous way) to protect rights or to secure the general welfare. Often, for instance, it will be preferable to maneuver against, or simply to oppose, those who are actually threatening. However,

26. John Rawls, *A Theory of Justice* (Cambridge: Harvard University Press, 1971), pp. 60–61.

27. Robert Nozick, *Anarchy, State, and Utopia* (New York: Basic Books, Inc., 1974), pp. 28–29.

28. Gulick, *Europe's Classical Balance*, pp. 37n.–38n.

the balance theorist (or at least the balance theorist in his most characteristic form) asks us to focus our attention exclusively on configurations of power, and this requires us to disregard assessments of intention. Fénelon, for instance, tells us that nations should cut down to size any country that is by its nature too large, by its industry too rich, or by its inventiveness too powerful, simply on these grounds and without giving consideration to its past practice or present intentions.[29] Morgenthau invokes the authority and practice of his hero, Churchill, and tells us that if we view the world through the eyes of the political realist we will consider political consequences only, and ignore intentions (which are mainly of interest to the "legalistic-moralistic" mind).[30] But the fact is that Churchill was acutely interested in the intentions of nations and of their leaders. As Inis Claude argues, in 1936 Churchill quite properly insisted that Britain maneuver against Germany rather than France on the ground that France, although apparently the strongest power on the continent, had no aggressive intentions while Germany was possessed by a will to dominate.[31] Surely this policy served the general welfare better than a policy of maneuvering against France. This makes it clear that in certain circumstances, at least, a preponderance of power in well-intentioned hands may serve the general welfare better than a technical balance. It also shows that a balance policy is not necessarily the best way to minimize the violation of rights. If Churchill has followed Fénelon's recipe, he would not have hesitated to violate France's rights had this seemed necessary to achieve a balance. But this violation of rights, in addition to being unjust, would have been extremely imprudent (by strengthening Germany) and would almost certainly have led to a much more widespread violation of rights. In some circumstances, at least, pursuing the balance of power is not the best way to achieve the alleged objectives of the balance system.

It may be argued that there is no reason why the realist or the balance theorist is precluded from considering the intentions of statesmen and nations. He may, for instance, consider intentions if he regards them solely as evidence of future dimensions and patterns of power. It might be suggested that this is all Churchill did, but this is implausible. For an

29. Ibid., p. 50.

30. Morgenthau, *Politics Among Nations*, p. 6.

31. Inis L. Claude, Jr., *Power and International Relations* (New York: Random House, 1962), pp. 64ff.

aggressive Germany would be more dangerous than a pacific France even if France remained the greater power. After all, Churchill did not try to strengthen the enemies of the United States, as in the nineteenth century (at least after 1815) the United States did not give military support to the enemies of Great Britain. Intentions are not of interest simply as indices of power and potential power. Considering them is essential to understanding, judging, and predicting how power will be used. Great statesmanship must be realistic. But realism is not simply a matter of caution and cynicism, and it does not require that we always assume the worst. The Athenian generals who destroyed Melos exaggerated. Sometimes statesmen and nations do not intend to do "what they can."[32] Those who make this assumption cannot invoke the wisdom of a Churchill in its defense.

It is, of course, possible for the balance theorist to concede that in certain cases his preferred policy will be unfortunate for his nation and produce worse general results than a less simple-minded one. He may argue, nevertheless, that unyielding pursuit of the balance will, in general and in the long run, prove the best policy. But because this policy will often require strengthening dangerous and aggressive powers while weakening innocent and pacific ones, and since we can at least sometimes distinguish the one from the other, there is little to be said for this undiscriminating view.

This is not to deny that the relations of power among states are a matter of central and legitimate concern. They should be carefully scrutinized and intelligently managed. Nations may, as seems prudent, improve their defenses, arrange their alliances, and apportion their resources between domestic and foreign objectives in response to perceived patterns of power and their expected use. As long as these activities respect the limits set by the rights of others, they will not be open to the kind of objections we have so far brought against balance-of-power policies, although an exclusive concern for one's own, or even for the system's, security at the expense of support for one's moral friends, or for those in distress, is open to other kinds of moral objection.

Some will say that this much more benign conception of the management of power, a conception which requires that the search for a balance take place within established moral boundaries, comes very close to what

32. Thucydides, *The Peloponnesian War*, ed. John Finley, Jr. (New York: The Modern Library, 1951), p. 331.

*Moral Skepticism
and International
Relations*

some balance-of-power theorists have intended. This is, indeed, true and there is no reason to deny that some have used that disastrously ambiguous term "the balance of power" to describe an approach to international politics which acknowledges the existence and pertinence of moral considerations and limits. Brougham, for instance, would not permit intervention except where danger is extreme, and Gentz insisted on respect for acquired rights. He rejected the violations of Poland's rights as an outrage against the balance system and Brougham, who thought that something like the Prussian acquisition of Silesia necessary to stabilize the European balance, nevertheless regarded it as impermissible because it violated Austro-Hungary's ancient rights.[33] Indeed, these and other writers suggested that the balance system operated within the moral constraints of a "European" republic and that the pursuit of power within it was subject to limits well understood by those who participated in the system. This is unquestionably true and compromises any attempt to attribute the achievements of the system (the avoidance of hegemony, the survival of many small states) to a balance system in which moral concerns are always considered irrelevant or subordinate, or even to one in which the rights of peoples are routinely sacrificed to the broader requirements of the international system. For these achievements are attributable in part to the influence of the particular religious, moral, and legal restraints accepted by the parties to the system.[34]

This conclusion will seem naive to some, for it is a deeply ingrained belief among those who regard themselves as politically sophisticated that "power" politics and its "balance-of-power" considerations inevitably take precedence over ethical requirements. Here, again, we meet a confusion already encountered. For some of the actions which simple moralists condemn as immoral and realists defend as, nevertheless, politically necessary are in fact defensible on more complicated moral grounds. If, despite our commitment to the principle of national self-determination, we think that sacrificing the national aspirations of the Sudeten Germans and the Austrians at Versailles was justified, we think so because in this case the moral importance of weakening German power in order to prevent another World War was great enough to override it. To describe this as a purely "political" act is to misdescribe it, and to describe it as an attempt to achieve a balance of power is to describe it very incompletely.

33. Gulick, *Europe's Classical Balance*, pp. 48, 62–63.
34. Morgenthau, *Politics Among Nations*, pp. 194ff.

Even such a notorious act of the old "balance-of-power" politics and "secret" diplomacy as the Allies' signing of the Treaty of London (1915) can be viewed in a similar way. Had the Allies failed to accede to Italy's demands on Slav territory as the guerdon of Italy's defection from the Triple Alliance, they would have left the Central Powers free to deal with the Russians, thereby prolonging an appalling war and perhaps even risking final defeat in a contest of genuine moral significance. What some denounce as a cynical act of balance-of-power politics, and others defend as such, can also be viewed and defended as a painful, perhaps even tragic, but nevertheless morally proper, course of action. And similar remarks will need to be made about some of the occasions on which we support authoritarian regimes (perhaps Korea), engage in military interventions (possibly Lebanon in 1958), or build nuclear arsenals (of second-strike weapons) to restore the balance of power. For there will be occasions on which restoring the balance of power is a genuine matter of self-defense or where the moral rights and interests at stake are so great that they override lesser, even if very important, moral claims. In this way the complex moralist can accommodate the political realists' plausible cases, for these are cases in which a satisfactory moral argument can be given. But he will condemn the realists' theory and think that in describing even the morally justifiable cases as justified on purely political, or balance-of-power, grounds the realist has obscured (and perhaps deliberately obscured) the distinction between morally justified and morally unjustified action. Even when he agrees with the political realist on hard or controversial cases the complex moralist will do so only after having made a difficult moral judgment. And often, of course, he will reject as morally unacceptable policies and actions that realists, and if not realists then the realists' theory, recommends. It is not only simple moralists and naive liberals who condemn the partitions of Poland, the overthrow of the Spanish constitution of the Cortes, the European powers' compensatory colonizations of Africa, the United States's destabilization of chile, the Soviet intervention in Afghanistan, the superpowers' acquisition of first-strike weapons, or any of the other deplorable and even scandalous actions that have been and continue to be an all too visible feature of the international scene. For if balance-of-power policies cannot be defended by invoking the implausible thesis of the autonomy of politics, merely establishing that an action contributes to an equilibrium of power does not show that it is acceptable from a moral point of view either.

*Moral Skepticism
and International
Relations*

As we have seen, it is important to distinguish balance-of-power or equilibrium politics from pure power politics, for equilibrium politics requires that nations restrain their pursuit of the national interest when this is required to achieve a proper balance. There is, however, a strong tendency for the balance system to degenerate into a pure struggle for power. In part this is attributable to difficulties inherent in the notion of power. Even assuming that we all knew which distribution of power the balance required, there would still be grave difficulties in deciding what constitutes having power, in comparing incommensurable types of power, and in determining how much power each nation actually possesses. Do a nation's high morale and settled politics count as well as its military arsenal and industrial potential? And how, further, are we to measure and establish a nation's morale or its technical achievement? (What can the Russians actually do?) Rough estimates are, of course, possible, but the temptation is strong for nations to err on the side of safety in ambiguous or difficult situations. In doing so they will often appear threatening to others. The question of allies is crucial, too, for allies may enhance one's power. But will they, like the irredentist Italians, defect? In sheer self-defense it may seem necessary to increase one's power instead of restraining it in the interest of an indeterminate balance. There is a strong tendency, then, for the balance-of-power system to degenerate into a state of nature. And this is, surely one of the most powerful objections to it as a practical proposal. Indeed, writers from Hobbes to Raymond Aron have claimed that nations actually inhabit this state.[35] If we combine this assumption with Hobbes's contention that in a state of nature there is neither justice nor injustice, we encounter the most powerful as well as the most influential intellectual foundation for the view that the realm of international affairs cannot be judged, or governed, by moral standards. We must examine it.

HOBBES AND THE STATE OF NATURE

Hobbes's doctrines are open to many interpretations, and every major interpretation has had its influence on the theory of international relations. According to one view, Hobbes is a moral subjectivist and a moral authoritarian. In the state of nature individuals can employ moral lan-

35. Hobbes, *Leviathan*, p. 187; Raymond Aron, *Peace and War*, trans. Richard Howard and Annette Baker Fox (New York: Frederick A. Praeger, 1968), p. 580.

guage only to signify their own appetites and desires as, in the view of contemporary political realists, nations can employ language only "ideologically."[36] In Hobbes's view, as in the view of the realists, this subjective use of language only exacerbates the difficulties of endeavoring peace. The realists often suggest, therefore, that we abandon the use of moral language altogether when we speak in the international state of nature. If we confine ourselves to speaking the language of the national interest, we are more likely to achieve sensible accommodations. In Hobbes's system instituting a sovereign provides the remedy, for he can endow moral language with objectivity. Sovereigns "make the things they command just by commanding them and those which they forbid unjust by forbidding them."[37] If we accept Hobbes's account of the sovereign's commands, or his laws, as the source of justice and injustice, we shall have to concede that in the absence of an international sovereign, perhaps in the form of an effective, law-giving world government, the use of moral language in international contexts is nothing more than ideology, or in Hobbes's terms an expression of "appetites and aversions" that encourage "disputes, controversies, and at last war."[38] Hobbes's view of moral appraisal is, however, unpersuasive. If acts and omissions are just or unjust only when they are commanded or permitted by the sovereign, acts and omissions to which the sovereign's law does not speak could be neither just nor unjust. Yet we often consider harsh actions, chilly responses, and accusing words unjust although the law does not forbid them, even as we consider acts of restoration or recompense to be demanded by justice although the law does not require them. More importantly, if justice is what the sovereign commands and injustice what he forbids, it would make no sense to judge the sovereign's own acts and rules just or unjust. Yet the criticism of law and government on moral grounds is one of the central moral activities.

We cannot identify justice and injustice with the sovereign's commands and our refusal to do so suggests one of our reasons for enduring the perils of international society as we know it. We fear that a world sovereign might become an invincible international tyrant or disclose

36. J.N.W. Watkins, *Hobbes's System of Ideas* (London: Hutchinson University Library, 1973), p. 110.

37. Hobbes, *De Cive*, ed. Sterling Lamprecht (New York: Appleton-Century-Crofts, 1949), p. 129.

38. Hobbes, *Leviathan*, p. 216.

himself as our deadliest enemy invested with enhanced political legitimacy. We cannot concede that what such a sovereign deemed just would in fact be just (or that his command made it so). Nor can we acquiesce in Hobbes's view that in the absence of a sovereign our judgments about the international realm are mere expressions of appetite and aversion. Like much moral skepticism about the international realm, this view is one manifestation of a far more pervasive and unacceptable moral skepticism.

In the absence of a law-giving and law-enforcing sovereign, Hobbesian individuals inhabit a state of nature, a realm of intense competition and insurmountable insecurity in which the life of man is solitary, poor, nasty, brutish, and short. It is, in fact, a realm in which the main objective must be self-preservation and in which we enjoy what Hobbes called the right of nature, the right "by all means we can, to defend ourselves."[39] In the state of nature Hobbes thinks this requires seeking "power after power," and in this situation "to have all, and do all, is lawful to all."[40] Those who believe that the international arena is itself a state of nature often argue that states also have a right to act on what Morgenthau calls "the moral principle of self-preservation" which, in the state of nature not only permits them, but (going beyond Hobbes) may actually require them, to pursue the national interest and maximize national power (to seek "power after power") without regard to other moral considerations. As Raymond Aron says "the necessity of national egoism derives from what philosophers called the state of nature which rules among states."[41]

We may concede that in the state of nature individuals have a right to defend themselves against physical attack. Indeed, we may think they act justly when they do so, and argue that this in itself insures the notion of justice application in the state of nature. By the same token, it seems clear that (other things being equal) it would be unjust to attack others when doing so was not required for self-preservation. Even in the individual state of nature it is questionable whether this principle of self-preservation permits us to "do all."

Hobbes claims, for instance, that in the state of nature men are equal in the sense that even the weakest can kill the strongest.[42] But, in fact, young children, and those who are seriously incapacitated by injury or

39. Ibid., p. 190.
40. Hobbes, *De Cive*, p. 28.
41. Aron, *Peace and War*, p. 580.
42. Hobbes, *Leviathan*, p. 183.

disease, will often constitute no threat even in the Hobbesian state of nature. To rape or kill them would clearly be unjust.[43] Not even for all practical purposes does the right of self-defense yield a right of universal aggression. This right comes into play only in certain circumstances and incorporates principles of parsimony and proportionality.

If individuals are prohibited from attacking those who do not threaten them, so are nations. Even in the international state of nature it will not be permissible to attack the young or the unwell intentionally or, more generally, those who do not constitute a physical threat. In addition, attacks must be repelled, and offensives conducted, by appropriate means. These principles support the doctrine of civilian immunity and find expression in the laws of war. Insofar as this body of law fails to reflect such principles, it is itself open to criticism. Here law is not the source of criticism as it must be in Hobbes. Rather, it is the object of criticism.

Even in the state of nature, then, the use of violence cannot be justified on every occasion or in every degree. In particular, not every interest can be defended by an appeal to self-preservation. The implications of this fact are especially important in the international realm. For Hobbesian theorists of international relations often claim that states possess a "moral right of self-preservation" or enjoy a right to "national security." Hobbes himself called the Leviathan an "Artificial Man" and believed that like individual men it possessed a right of self-preservation. For he writes that ". . . the same elements of natural law and right . . . being transferred to whole cities and nations, may be taken for the elements of the laws and right of nations."[44] But it is far from obvious that because individual men have a natural right of self-preservation, states do so as well. Certainly we do not think that all collective entities enjoy a right to "do all" to preserve themselves. This is not true of the Mafia or the Sierra Club, of General Motors or the Ethical Culture Society, of the Comintern or the Roman Catholic Church. Or if such a right is claimed for one or another of these institutions, the right will have to be defended. This is true of the state as well. Unquestionably, there are many ways in which such a right might be defended. A right to property might be invoked, or a right of people to live together under political institutions of their own choice, or even a right to live in close association with those who share the same

43. Marcus Singer, "State of Nature Situations," in *Essays in Moral Philosophy*, ed. A. I. Melden (Seattle: University of Washington Press, 1958), p. 157.

44. Hobbes, *De Cive*, p. 158.

language and cultural aspirations. There is something to be said for (and against) each of these suggestions, but they are far from Hobbesian in spirit. For I take it that a Hobbesian defense of the state's right of self-preservation would attempt to draw its justification from the individual's natural right of self-preservation. Perhaps this is what Hobbes is suggesting in his far from lucid observation that "every Sovereign hath the same right, in procuring the safety of his people, that any particular man can have, in procuring the safety of his own body."[45]

The scope of this right is by no means clear and Arnold Wolfers, among others, has complained of a similar "ambiguity" in the concept of national security.[46] For some, the right of self-preservation permits the state to defend any of its interests including, perhaps, its ideological influence and its economic advantages. For others the right of self-preservation permits the state to defend only its legal rights. This still very expansive conception has been central to international law up to the 1930s (and has, in the questionable judgment of some, been given renewed support by the opinion of the International Court of Justice in the Corfu Channel Case). But Article X of the League of Nations Covenant and Article 2(4) of the United States Charter suggest a much narrower conception.[47] The right of self-defense (as it is now called to distinguish it from the broader conception of self-preservation) is the right to defend what for many are the essential features of the state: its territorial integrity and political independence. Some have argued that the right of self-defense permits a state to employ force solely in defense of its territorial domain. In this spirit, Article 51 of the United Nations Charter defines self-defense by reference to the concept of "armed attack."[48]

Hobbesians may claim that a defense of some, or even of all, these readings of the state's right to self-preservation can be founded on the individual's right of self-preservation. For it can be argued that the defense of all, or at least of some, of these interests is necessary if the state is to guarantee the physical security of its citizens. But this is implausible. A state's failure to defend its ideological influence, its economic advan-

---

45. Hobbes, *Leviathan*, p. 394.

46. Arnold Wolfers, "National Security as an Ambiguous Symbol," in *Discord and Collaboration*, pp. 147–67.

47. Ian Brownlie, *International Law and the Use of Force by States* (Oxford: Clarendon Press, 1963), p. 256.

48. Ibid., pp. 256, 264–68.

tages, or even many of its treaty rights, may in no way decrease its ability
to provide for the physical security of its population. The argument may
seem more persuasive when the state's territorial integrity and political
independence are at issue. But even here the argument is not compelling.
The state may actually improve its ability to guarantee the physical security of its citizens by surrendering territory (as Israel has done) or by
extinguishing its sovereignty (as the American colonies and the German
principalities did). The death of the state does not require the loss of a
single life. Indeed, it may even save some.

Hobbesians may then attempt a less ambitious argument. They may
concede that a defense of its economic advantages, or even of its territorial
integrity, is not necessarily required if a state is to protect its citizens.
They may insist, however, that the defense of these interests increases
the likelihood that the state will be able to provide that security. In view
of this fact we should concede that the state has a right to defend these
interests when it believes that doing so will enhance security. But this
line of argument is also unpersuasive.[49] We do not have a right to increase
our security by working injustices on others or by endangering their
security to an unacceptable degree. Perfect security might require, but
could not in itself justify, world domination. And incremental improvements in one nation's security do not, as a matter of course, justify the
violation of the right of others to live in communities of their choice, to
reform unfair economic arrangements, or to enjoy a reasonable measure
of security themselves. As with other goods in limited supply, individual
and national security are themselves subject to a principle of distributive
justice. The requirements of natural justice, and the political rights of
others, place strict limits on the pursuit of the "national interest" and on
the striving for "power after power" in the search for national "security."
Certainly, they do not allow those who are internationally well placed "to
do all and have all."

A weaker claim may nevertheless succeed. While the state may not
always need to defend its territory, or maintain its independence, in order
to provide for the physical security of its population, often it will. It is,
therefore, reasonable to provide a legal right to do so. Of course, legal
rights cannot always conform exactly to the contours of the moral rights
they protect, but they can nevertheless draw strong moral support from

49. Charles Beitz, *Political Theory and International Relations* (Princeton: Princeton
University Press, 1979), pp. 52ff.

them. A legal right to state self-preservation will lack moral justification
to the extent that it permits the use of force against others simply to
increase state security (as did the traditional right of "self-preservation,"
an easily penetrated disguise for a right of war). The best formulation of
the rule is an enormously difficult matter. But to be equitable and to
protect the rights of the innocent any reasonable version must (with very
few exceptions) confine the right to situations in which an attack, the
threat of an attack, or preparations for an attack can be established. A
narrowly drawn rule like the one announced in Article 51 of the United
States Charter is probably very desirable. But if the rule is understood to
forbid "preventive" attacks it may, in certain situations, conflict with the
natural right of self-defense that underlies it. Although the fact that
this rule is a rule of law itself carries moral weight (how much will depend
in part on the degree to which it is observed in international life), the
rule may have to give way in these circumstances to deeper moral considerations. Often, however, the plea of self-defense will have little plausibility. Authoritative pronouncements assure us that the plea was without
justification in such cases as the Japanese invasion of Manchuria, the
Italian invasion of Abyssinia, and the German invasion of Norway.[50] Certainly, any morally tenable account of the right of self-defense, individual
or collective, requires that a distinction between aggression and self-
defense be maintained.

Hobbesian theorists of international relations will protest that these
remarks fail to take seriously Hobbes's contention that the state of nature
is inevitably a state of war. From their point of view it is pointless to speak
of moral constraints on the pursuit of interests other than the security
interest. For the nation-state is in fact overwhelmingly and inescapably
preoccupied with the provision of security, and the logic of international
relations is the logic of individuals in the Hobbesian state of nature writ
large. As the Hobbesians see it, the "competition" for goods and resources
brings nations into direct conflict with one another and in this conflict
one nation's gain is, or will appear to be, another nation's loss. Still worse
is the effect of what Hobbes calls "diffidence." Even where nations are
content with the status quo and do not wish to threaten others, they have
no assurance of one another's present intentions, not to mention future

50. Ian Brownlie, *International Law*, pp. 242–43, 311.

ones. Out of fear nations will therefore seek "power after power" in order
to increase their security. But in doing so they inspire fear in others and
decrease, or appear to decrease, their security. In this "security" dilemma,
nations whose intentions are fundamentally pacific appear aggressive.
They will be forced to strengthen themselves in ways that alarm others
and out of fear may "anticipate" or engage in preventive attack. Thus,
even nations whose intentions are basically defensive and cooperative
will act in ways that are indistinguishable from those who are in fact
hostile and aggressive. Of course, some nations will in fact be hostile and
aggressive and this further aggravates everyone's fears. Then, too, like
Hobbesian men some nations seek "glory." If they sought glory in a
reputation for peacefulness and generosity, this would be one thing, but
nations have often understood glory to consist in the display and exercise
of military power. For them, an increase in glory must always come at
the expense of another.

   In one degree or another these features characterize many international
situations. Europe on the eve of World War I may have been one example.
But Hobbes himself observed that the state of war among nations does
not create the same degree of misery as the state of war among individuals, and it is important to notice the differences between them because
they have important moral consequences. To begin with, nations are not
as vulnerable as individuals in the state of nature and it is not true that
they and their citizens invariably live in fear of violent death. Nations in
the state of nature are better able to defend themselves than individuals
are. As Spinoza observed, states are not overcome by sleep every day,
they are not afflicted with diseases of mind and body, and they are not
prostrated by old age.[51] Even in the state of war, as Hobbes observed,
"Particular Sovereigns are able to uphold the industry of their subjects."[52]
If nations do not share the vulnerability of individuals, neither do they
share their equality. It is not true of them that the weakest can kill the
strongest. The nineteenth-century United States, because of its size, its
location, and the protection of the British navy, enjoyed a high degree of
security. Large and well-armed nations, and nations protected by oceans
and mountain ranges, are often in a similarly secure situation and do not
live in a condition of Hobbesian fear. They are in a position to show

51. Spinoza, *Tractatus Politicus* in Wernham, *The Political Works*, p. 295.
52. Hobbes, *Leviathan*, p. 188.

restraint, to calm the fears of others, and even to create the conditions of peace. Often it is their duty to do so. It is also important to note that in contrast to Hobbesian individuals, nations can often improve their security in ways that need not alarm others. Their best defense is not always an attack, and they can often give evidence of their peaceful intentions by choosing weapons and strategies that do not threaten others. They can build forts, mount fixed guns, mine harbors or, like the Russians, build wide gauge railway tracks that are useless to invaders. They can also train civilian militias, study guerilla warfare, and prepare themselves for passive resistance. To be sure, there are circumstances in which these defensive choices could be aspects of a fundamentally aggressive design, but this is not invariably the case and will not always seem to be.[53]

Individuals in the Hobbesian state of nature are anonymous and ahistorical. But nations have names and reputations, geographies and histories, principles and purposes, and these allow others to judge their intentions with considerable confidence. Sometimes these intentions will be cooperative and even friendly. For nations have allies, belong to regional blocs, engage in mutually beneficial trade, and support larger cultural enterprises. They will often have strong moral reasons to perpetuate these relationships. Hobbes's suggestion that because nations retain their sovereign independence they must be in a state of war in which every nation has a "known disposition" to attack every other and in which no "assurance" can be obtained flies in the face of the evidence and suggests the presence of a stubborn philosophical thesis that its proponents are unwilling or unable to submit to empirical test.

Some have argued that the advent of nuclear weapons brings the international realm closer to the Hobbesian state of nature than it has ever been before. As David Gauthier observes "each new effort we undertake to increase our security merely increases the insecurity of others, and this leads them to new efforts which reciprocally increase our own insecurity. This is the natural history of the arms race—a history which bids fair to conclude, later if not sooner, in mutual annihilation."[54] But some of the observations we have made about the prenuclear period are

53. Robert Jervis, "Cooperation Under the Security Dilemma," *World Politics* 30, no. 2 (January 1978): 167–214. Most of this paragraph and much else in my discussion is drawn from this article.

54. David Gauthier, *The Logic of Leviathan* (Oxford: Oxford University Press, 1969), p. 208. This quotation needs to be considered in the context of Gauthier's full discussion.

relevant to the nuclear era as well, and they show that while we may get ourselves into the situation Gauthier describes, this is by no means inevitable even in the absence of a world sovereign.

The Hobbesian situation is most closely approximated when both sides rely on vulnerable weapons that are capable of destroying weapons on the other side (highly accurate missiles in unhardened silos).[55] As in the classic Western gun duel, the obvious strategy in such circumstances is to "anticipate," to shoot and shoot first. Any nation that can mount a successful first strike without using all of its weapons is free to destroy entire enemy populations. But if the first strike does not succeed in taking out the other side's retaliatory force, both may be destroyed utterly. Nevertheless, the existence of nuclear weapons does not make a situation of this sort inevitable. By confining themselves to second-strike weapons, nuclear powers can make clear that they do not intend to initiate nuclear war. If both sides acquire invulnerable, second-strike weapons then neither side can, by shooting first, destroy the other side's deterrent, its capacity to strike back. If a nuclear nation shoots, it must be prepared to pay the penalty. In this situation there is far less reason to jump the gun, and less reason to fear that others will do so.

It is not true that in the nuclear world "each new effort we take to increase our security merely increases the insecurity of others, and (that) this leads them to new efforts which reciprocally increase our own insecurity." We can increase our second-strike capacity without increasing the insecurity of others. And to the extent that they are likely to strike out of fear of being struck, we can, as Oskar Morgenstern has suggested, increase our own security by helping our adversaries make their own second-strike forces invulnerable. Their insecurity increases our insecurity, but we can increase our security by increasing theirs. The fact that nuclear nations can destroy one another's populations unquestionably strengthens the analogy between the individual, and the international, state of nature. But the fact that nuclear nations—unlike Hobbesian men or gun duellers—can respond in kind after they have been hit undermines it. The balance created by the equality of Hobbesian men, or by the "equalizer" of the Old West, is unstable, but the nuclear balance is capable of stability if one nation cannot, by "anticipating," prevent the other from striking back.[56] In these circumstances there is no advantage

55. Jervis, "Cooperation," p. 212.

56. Thomas C. Schelling, *The Strategy of Conflict* (Oxford: Oxford University Press, 1971), p. 232.

in striking first and, if they are rational, nuclear nations will see that it is irrational to strike at all.

This stability will, of course, be lost if either side believes that the invulnerability of its retaliatory forces is endangered. There is a strong obligation, therefore, to eschew the development of a first-strike capacity if a nation can achieve reasonable assurance that the other side is not developing one. In appropriate circumstances, then, it will be morally inexcusable to reject measures (like adequate inspection schemes) that will reassure one's opponent, or even to renounce weapons whose uses are ambiguous. For these are precisely the weapons that can return us to a Hobbesian dilemma in which what one side believes, or claims to believe, are defensive, or in this case deterrent, weapons appear to the other side to be offensive, first-strike weapons. The primary obligation of the nuclear age is to abstain from the first nuclear strike and to adopt policies, especially as regards adequate conventional strength, that reduce the temptation to make such a strike. A more general obligation in situations of serious conflict is to try to see ourselves as others see us. This is always a weighty consideration for those in Hobbesian situations. But it is a supremely weighty one in the nuclear situation where the acquisition of ambiguous weapons can easily be misinterpreted by others and with disastrous effects. Moral blindness in this area may bind us all to the final wheel of fire. The Hobbesians could not be more wrong. It is precisely in what they regard as a state of nature that men and nations must acknowledge their most awesome moral responsibilities.

HUME AND THE MORALITY OF PRINCES

In Hume's view, too, there is neither justice nor injustice in the state of nature. In contrast to Hobbes, however, Hume believes that nations no longer inhabit the state of nature. The actions of states are, therefore, subject to the rules of justice.[57] In making this affirmation Hume rejects the radical skepticism concerning international morality that realists and Hobbesians profess. Hume holds, however, that the morality of nations is "more free" than the morality appropriate to individuals, and the rules of justice apply to princes with less force than they do to the conduct of private persons.[58] This moderate skepticism about international morality, though more plausible than the more radical forms we have so far con-

57. Hume, *Treatise*, p.567.   58. Ibid., p. 568.

sidered, is nevertheless unacceptable. As we shall see, Hume's analysis is unsatisfactory because he does not distinguish clearly enough between the conventions of international conduct and the requirements of international morality. (E. H. Carr, who holds a similar view, identifies individual morality with a "codification of existing practices.")[59] These conventions and practices are, however, unjust and they must be judged by the standards of morality which apply with equal force to princes and private persons, in the domestic and in the international arenas.

In Hume's view man's avidity for possessions is insatiable, perpetual, and universal. But man comes to see that in the long run his best hope of acquiring and securing possessions is to accept the restraints imposed by the rules of justice. He therefore agrees to relinquish the freedom to appropriate the goods of others that he enjoyed in the state of nature on the condition that they forgo it as well. Men therefore adopt the rules of justice and enter into mutually advantageous conventions guaranteeing the stability of possessions, their transference by consent, and the performance of promises. Because nations differ from individuals in significant ways, they regulate themselves by a new set of rules, the law of nations. Hume mentions, in this connection, the sacredness of the persons of ambassadors, the declaration of war, and the abstaining from poisoned arms. But these new rules do not abolish the fundamental rules of justice for it is as true of nations as it is of men that "Where possession has no stability, there must be perpetual war. Where property is not transferred by consent, there can be no commerce. Where promises are not observed, there can be no leagues or alliances."[60]

Hume notes, nevertheless, that "There is a maxim very current in the world, which few politicians are willing to avow, but which has been authorized by the practice of all ages, that there is a system of morals calculated for princes, much more free than that which ought to govern private persons."[61] The meaning of this maxim is, according to Hume, that though the morality of princes has the same extent, it has not the same force (or does not oblige as rigorously) as that of private persons. This freer morality of princes is to be explained by the fact that although advantageous and even sometimes necessary, the intercourse of states is neither so necessary nor so advantageous as that of individuals. Since

59. E. H. Carr, *The Twenty Years' Crisis, 1919–1939* (New York: Harper and Row, 1964), p. 146.
60. Hume, *Treatise*, p. 567.   61. Ibid., p. 567.

the mutual interest in abiding by the fundamental rules of justice is weaker, the moral obligation arising from it must partake of this weakness and we must necessarily give greater indulgence to a prince or minister who deceives another than to a private gentleman who breaks his word of honor. "However shocking such a proposition may appear to certain philosophers, 'twill be easy to defend it upon those principles, by which we have accounted for the origin of justice and equity."[62] Today there are more politicians who will openly avow the "freer" morality of princes, and many more philosophers who will support them. These views still deliver a "shock," however, and it is important to question the moral principles that make them "easy to defend."

It is useful to begin by considering Hume's reasons for thinking that in the state of nature there would be neither justice nor injustice. The first of them is that property and promising are practice-defined conceptions. In the state of nature men could possess objects and occupy land. But there could be no such thing as property in the absence of a practice that selects from the many possible rules those that will determine for a particular society when, and even whether, possession and occupancy constitute ownership. Similarly, in the absence of a rule establishing that the performance of some action, or the uttering of certain words, such as, "I promise," constitutes putting oneself under that particular kind of obligation, there could be no such thing as promising. As Hume says, "I assert that in the state of nature, or that imaginary state, which preceded society there be neither justice nor injustice, yet I assert not, that it was allowable, in such a state, to violate the property of others. I only maintain, that there was no such thing as property; and consequently could be no such thing as justice or injustice."[63]

Hume's reasons for thinking that questions of justice do not arise in the state of nature will not even begin to seem plausible unless we accept his view that issues of justice arise only in connection with the practices of property and promising. However, Hume's reasons for confining questions of justice and injustice in this way are weak. According to Hume we are possessed of three species of goods: the internal satisfaction of our minds, the external advantages of our bodies, and, as we have seen, the enjoyment of possessions we have acquired by our industry and good fortune. Hume thinks that society's chief benefit is in securing the sta-

---

62. Ibid., p. 568.   63. Ibid., p. 501.

bility of possessions because he thinks that even in the state of nature we are "perfectly secure" in the internal satisfaction of our minds and that while the external advantages of our bodies can be ravished from us, they are of no advantage to him who deprives us of them. Even if we think that Hobbes exaggerates the security problems that exist in the state of nature, these remarks will seem excessively naive. At least sometimes the fear of sudden death will rob us of the internal satisfaction of our minds. And there is little doubt that he who controls our body, or deprives us of our life, can gain sexual pleasure, economic advantage, or increased security by doing so. It is for this reason that Hobbes fixed on the problem of security as the central characteristic of the state of nature, and even if we do not accept all Hobbes has to say on this subject there can be little doubt that society benefits us at least as much in securing the internal satisfaction of our minds and the external advantages of our bodies as it does in securing our possessions.

The fact is that questions of justice arise over a much broader range of issues than Hume suggests. Rape, enslavement, and murder are all unjust and would be unjust (or morally unacceptable in some other way) even in the state of nature. Some would say that Hume could accept this amendment because he could argue that the concepts of rape, enslavement, and murder presuppose the same kind of legal and quasi-legal institutions that promising and property do. They would argue that it is only relative to some established legal system that we can say whether, for instance, when A shoots B intending to kill him, but hits C instead, A has committed murder. Consequently, Hume could be expected to reply to our line of criticism that he does not assert that in the state of nature it is permissible to rape, enslave, or murder but only that in such a state there is no such thing as rape, enslavement, or murder and, consequently, no such thing as justice or injustice. But, even if we concede (what is not obvious) that there is no rape, enslavement, or murder in the state of nature, can it be denied that coerced sex, forced labor, and unprovoked and unnecessary killing will be found there? And can it be denied that they will be unjust?

Hume's second reason for thinking that there is neither justice nor injustice in the state of nature rests on the view that justice and injustice are conventional. They are conventional in the sense that questions of justice arise exclusively in connection with social rules that have been adopted in the expectation of mutual benefit and that are observed in the

Moral Skepticism
                                and International
                                Relations

expectation of mutual conformity.[64] *Ex hypothesi*, conventions in Hume's
sense could not exist in the unsocial state of nature. Even if we waive
our previous objections to Hume, and confine our attention to the economic issues with which Hume arbitrarily associates questions of justice,
his views will not seem plausible.

It is true that in the absence of our institution of promise keeping it
would not be possible to make what is, strictly speaking, a promise. But
as Thomas Scanlon argues, even in the state of nature, in the absence
of a practice of this sort, it would be possible to get someone to do something by causing him to form an expectation of reciprocal service on some
future occasion (help harvest your corn now in the expectation that you
will help harvest his corn later).[65] The person who benefits from the first
performance is, from a moral point of view, obliged to perform when his
turn comes, for there is a natural moral prohibition against intentionally
generating expectations that one expects to disappoint or exploit. As the
obligation is independent of any linguistic convention establishing the
use of the words "I promise," so is it independent of any preexisting
"scheme of action" or Humean convention incorporating men's expectations of mutual conformity. Hume's entire project is misguided (in the
absence of this natural moral obligation it is difficult to see how the growth
of mutual expectations could by themselves yield an obligation) and his
specific account of promising is certainly unpersuasive. In any case, as
Locke says, "The Promises and Bargains for Truck, etc., between the two
Men in the Desert Island, mentioned by Garcilasso De la vega, in his
History of Peru, or between a Swiss and an Indian, in the Woods of
America, are binding to them, though they are perfectly in a State of
Nature, in reference to one another."[66] Similarly, even in the absence of
specific rules of property and an established convention of mutual restraint it would be wrong in the state of nature to deprive a man of the
land he had cultivated or the corn he had raised, for there is a natural,
though not unlimited, moral obligation of noninterference. These obligations are natural in the same sense that the obligation to refrain from

---

64. David Gauthier, "David Hume, Contractarian," *The Philosophical Review* 88, no. 464
(January 1979): 6.

65. Thomas Scanlon, "Liberty, Contract and Contribution," in *Markets and Morals*, ed.
P. Brown and G. Bermant (Washington: Hemisphere Publishing Corp., 1977), pp. 46–51.

66. Locke, *Second Treatise of Government* in *Two Treatises of Government*, ed. Peter
Laslett (Cambridge: Cambridge University Press, 1960), p. 295.

unprovoked and unnecessary assault and killing is natural. Hume's coy evasions about the concepts of property and promising cannot mask the fact that there is justice and injustice in the state of nature.

It is undoubtedly useful to develop a social institution of promising and to elaborate rules of property. Standing rules will promote efficiency, and precision will mitigate conflict and misunderstanding. It would be extremely inconvenient if we had to reinvent a law of property or some rules governing promises every time we wished to bind ourselves or buy something. But we cannot acquiesce in Hume's assumption that whatever system of rules is chosen will qualify as a system of justice. We shall have to judge the rules that inform these conventions, and ultimately the actions of those who invoke them, by the natural moral requirements Hume refuses to acknowledge. Some of these rules will be unjust, and some will be morally flawed in other ways. Thus, a convention of promising that held people to promises even when the promises were coerced would be unjust. This is why the traditional international law of treaties, which regarded peace treaties imposed by victorious powers as valid, could never carry full moral conviction. Similarly, a convention of property that made the exercise of political autonomy impossible would be morally unacceptable. This is why a system of international law that permitted the colonization of people capable of self-government, was morally offensive. These issues often come together, as when a nation agrees to the loss of its territorial integrity or its political independence as a consequence of military defeat.

It has been argued that although these sentiments are superficially attractive, they are in fact indefensible. In the international realm we must accept the validity of treaties agreed to under duress. For, if we refused to accept the validity of treaties ending wars, wars would generally be costlier to both sides and would often not be concluded until the losing side was utterly crushed. The convention conferring validity on such treaties is therefore useful, and its utility justifies it. It should be noted, however, that even traditional writers who accepted this convention were uncomfortable with it and some suggested that the validity of treaties concluded under duress was morally imperfect. Vattel wrote, for instance, that "Although natural law prescribes fidelity to promises as a means of securing the welfare and peace of nations it does not favor oppressors. All of its principles are directed to procuring the greatest good of mankind; that is the great end of all laws, written and unwritten. Shall he who violates all these principles which bind society together be allowed to invoke the aid of them? . . . when it is sought to preach a doctrine which is contrary to all the instincts of human nature, where shall hearers be found?"[67]

It can be argued that the requirements of utility and of morality are not as far apart as we have suggested them to be. For we have so far considered only the advantageous consequences of a convention upholding the validity of treaties concluded under duress. But we must recognize that a convention òf this sort constitutes a permanent inducement to aggression and to blitzkrieg tactics. This tendency must count against the convention's utility. (Besides, the obligation to obey an oppressive treaty is not likely to count very heavily with those in a position to renounce it. For this reason victors will not be able to place great confidence in an agreement of this sort in any case.) At best, then, considerations of utility suggest a compromise between these advantages and disadvantages that would endow treaties concluded under duress with a strictly limited validity. A rule of this sort might facilitate the ending of wars without adding greatly to the attraction of starting them. It is in this spirit that a utilitarian like Sidgwick approaches the problem. This can be seen in his attitude toward a treaty requiring a cession of territory, where the inhabitants formed a genuine community with the nation from which the treaty has cut them off. For he says that the treaty should be taken "to bind the vanquished to no more than a temporary suspension of hostilities, terminable at any time by the wronged state." These are, he observes, precisely the conditions under which the rebellion of "an admittedly oppressed section of a state would generally be judged legitimate, i.e., if the circumstances offer a reasonable chance of success."[68]

In circumstances of this sort Sidgwick seems to be weighing the value of putting treaties on a firm basis very lightly indeed, and it is possible to think that considerations of justice are decisive here. Certainly they will be from a non-utilitarian moral point of view that must always have reservations about a legal rule, or social arrangement, that deprives people of important moral or political rights. Contemporary international law gives unequivocal (and, perhaps, too unmodulated) expression to these moral requirements. According to Article 52 of the Vienna Convention, "A treaty is void if its conclusion has been procured by the threat or use

67. Quoted by H. Lauterpacht in *Private Law Sources and Analogies of International Law* (New York: Longmans, Green and Co., 1927), pp. 163–64.

68. Henry Sidgwick, *The Elements of Politics* (London: Macmillan and Co., 1891), pp. 265–71.

of force in violation of the principles of international law embodied in the Charter of the United Nations."[69]

Some have attempted to defend a permissive rule of the traditional sort on quite different moral grounds. They argue that in the absence of an effective centralized authority, nations must be allowed to engage in self-help and to secure for themselves the redress of grievances. Furthermore, according to a writer like Hall, since international law cannot measure what is due in a given case, or what is necessary for the protection of a state that declares itself to be in danger, international law must regard all compacts as valid, notwithstanding the use of force and intimidation. Even he, however, excepts treaties which destroy the independence of the state.[70] We may agree with Hall that at least in the pre-League days in which he wrote nations sometimes had a moral obligation to abide by peace treaties that were imposed on them. But it does not follow that this obligation arose from the fact that they had agreed to the treaty. It is more plausible to suggest that it arose, when it did arise, from the fact that the defeated nation had the obligation to make recompense or, perhaps, from the fact that it would now do far more harm than good to wage war over the issue. Any international law that tries to uphold the validity of imposed treaties simply because it has no mechanism for making an authoritative adjudication of the issues involved will be futile and unpersuasive. Certainly its moral foundations will be insecure.

We have claimed that despite their utility in bringing wars to a conclusion, treaties agreed to under duress are morally defective. But can this be correct? After all, the utility of the convention by which individual soldiers are permitted to surrender seems to justify it, despite the fact that, as Michael Walzer says, the agreement to surrender "is usually made under extreme duress," and "would have no moral consequences at all in time of peace."[71] The answer lies in the fact that the wrong to which the legal concept of duress gives expression is the illegitimacy of coercion, not the simple fact of coercion.[72]

69. Ian Brownlie, *Basic Documents in International Law* (Oxford: Clarendon Press, 1972), p. 252.

70. W. E. Hall, *A Treatise on International Law*, 7th ed. (Oxford: Clarendon Press, 1917), p. 336.

71. Michael Walzer, *Just and Unjust Wars* (New York: Basic Books, Inc., 1977), p. 46.

72. Charles Fried, *Contract as Promise* (Cambridge, MA: Harvard University Press, 1981), pp. 97–99.

*Moral Skepticism
and International
Relations*

The pressure under which a defeated, but innocent nation signs a treaty of peace has been illegitimately applied; the victim's rights have been violated. But we do not think it is illegitimate to attack a soldier in time of war. We do him no wrong when we place him in the hopeless circumstances that make surrender an attractive alternative. This is why we think that the defeated nation has been subjected to duress and also why we view the terms it has accepted as leaving it worse off. In contrast, the soldier has been made an acceptable offer (on terms which have been established in advance) that improves his position. But again, is this distinction tenable? After all, is it not the case that the terms the defeated nation accepts leave it better off? If not, why would they be accepted? The objection makes clear that we must measure better off and worse off against some baseline. But the appropriate baseline in these cases is the worst position in which the victor has a right to place the loser. If we assume that the victorious army has a right to reduce enemy soldiers to impotence, an offer of surrender improves their position and is not unfair. In the case of aggression, however, the appropriate baseline is the position of the innocent nation prior to attack. By this standard the terms it accepts make it worse off. Agreeing under pressure to terms that violate one's rights, and make one worse off, is agreeing under duress. In this sense the soldier who surrenders does not act under duress, and he has an obligation to conform to a valuable convention whose benefits he has enjoyed. But the defeated nation does agree under duress, and this agreement is defective. When the terms of the agreement deny a nation its territorial integrity and its political independence, there are few indeed who believe that it is bound by its promises. A prince who repudiates such a treaty has our admiration and our moral approval when he can do so without inviting even worse evils.

But Hume suggests that even in the absence of any moral objection to a treaty a prince could renounce it from a more trivial motive than would be required for a private individual to break a promise. Similarly, a prince could violate the territorial rights of another from a more trivial motive than it would take to justify the appropriation of private property. This is the freer morality that according to Hume princes enjoy.

But, surely, Hume cannot think it would be acceptable for a prince to repudiate his obligations under a treaty after the other side had performed, or to violate the territorial rights of others unless self-defense provided the excuse or humanitarian intervention the justification. But these are not trivial motives, and their analogues have comparable force in private life as well.

As Hume has confused the received conventions of property with rules of justice, so here he appears to have confused the actual practices of princes with a defensible system of international conduct. Given the disreputable standards of the day, this is a surprising line of thought even in so complacent a writer as Hume. In the very year Hume published the Third Book of the *Treatise*, France violated its solemn agreement to the Pragmatic Sanction (an act which, though it seemed in France's self-interest, led inevitably to its loss of empire) and Frederick launched his cynical attack on Silesia. But these acts shocked European opinion and a century later Frederick's conduct elicited from Macaulay the sublime observation: "In order that he might rob a neighbor whom he had promised to defend, black men fought on the coast of Coromondel and red men scalped each other by the Great Lakes in America."[73] The international law of war of our own day—reflecting moral opinion very accurately—presumes that treaties in force must be performed in good faith and it considers wars of aggression criminal.

If we reject Hume's view that princes enjoy a "freer" morality than private persons, we are relieved of the obligation to explain, as Hume thinks we must, why princes enjoy this dubious freedom. Nor are we likely to feel, as Hume does, that his explanation of this alleged freedom lends powerful support to his moral theory as a whole. Hume's claim is that since the rules of justice though useful, are less useful to states than to private persons, they bind states with less force. There are problems with this view, however. Even in Hume's day Rousseau's observation that "we have taken all kinds of precautions against private wars, only to kindle national wars a thousand times more terrible" was probably correct.[74] In the nuclear age it will certainly seem plausible to claim that maintaining peace among nations is more important than maintaining it among individuals. And, as the interdependence theorists have argued, nations have become far more vulnerable to one another in other ways as well. It is not clear, then, that in general nations have less interest in justice than individuals. If their conduct fails to meet private standards of justice there are many possible explanations for this, one of them being

73. Quoted by Mowat, *Public and Private Morality*, p. 59.
74. Rousseau, "Abstract," p. 132.

Moral Skepticism
                        and International
                        Relations

the widespread belief that states may violate the rules of justice for relatively trivial reasons.

Hume's theory suffers from another defect. He is far from convincing when he argues that establishing rules of justice and conforming to them is, at least in the long run, in everyone's interest. From the individual's point of view it is better still if everyone else conforms while he does not.[75] Private individuals may put themselves in this advantageous position by violating rules while escaping detection. Powerful and unscrupulous states may do the same, and if they are powerful and brazen enough it may not matter to them whether or not their injustices are known. They may openly insist that others obey rules which they themselves violate with impunity. It is even less plausible in the case of such states than it is in the case of private individuals that avidity and self-interest will provide a natural motivation for the sentiment of justice. Justice may not be, or seem to be, in the interest of the stronger, no matter how long the run. If we are to judge by their actions, many strong nations have certainly not thought it was.

We have rejected Hume's view that the morality of princes has less force than that of private persons. And we have done so because in saying that the morality of princes has less "force" Hume means that this morality may be transgressed for a more trivial motive or reason. There is, nevertheless, a strained sense in which the morality of princes may be thought to have less "force" than that of private persons. This is so because in the more Hobbesian circumstances of international politics it will be permissible to transgress the rights of property owners and promisees (to violate boundaries and breach treaties) more often and more extensively than it would be in the circumstances of domestic society. Hume himself would probably have regarded transgressions in the interests of maintaining the balance of power as legitimate. But even those who think that self-defense provides the main ground for such transgressions (and that the balance of power when it is legitimately invoked must be justified on precisely that basis) will concede that the national defense sometimes justifies wars, border crossings, and treaty violations.

We may concede, then, that in the strained sense just considered the duty of princes to respect the rules of justice, of property and promising, may have less force than the private gentleman's obligations in a domestic

75. Barry Stroud, *Hume* (London: Routledge and Kegan Paul, 1977), p. 210.

situation. This is not to concede, however, that we show greater moral "indulgence" to a prince. Self-defense may require him to do what would normally be morally and legally wrong. In this case the prince acts out of tragic necessity, not from a trivial motive. And even when others have forfeited their rights he is permitted to do nothing more than what is necessary. The prince's obligation to keep promises and respect property may be overridden more often than those of private men, but his obligation to respect the requirements of morality is no less rigorous.

Hume says that though the morality of princes does not have the same force, it has the same extent as that of private persons. He means by this that it protects property and promises. But we have seen that the most plausible account of his own position suggests that property and promises are protected to a lesser extent because in the more Hobbesian circumstances of international politics, self-defense may justify more frequent and more far-reaching invasions of property than Hume could have imagined in the domestic case. Indeed, the international law of his day acknowledged a right to war and to the acquisition of territory by conquest. Even if Hume does not go this far (he does not tell us how far he does go), he may be understood to allow that in international situations the rights of property are less extensive than they are in domestic life.

However that may be, it is clear that international legal regimes are often less extensive than well-developed municipal ones. In a municipal system we will characteristically find strict and enforceable rules governing the possession and use of arms. We will find strict central control over the ability of states and regions to issue currency, raise trade barriers, or control immigration. And we will find a system of taxation that provides at least some support for such public goods as national defense, scientific research, and environmental protection.

The international situation is often markedly different and the regime of legal agreements far less extensive. Arms races are ubiquitous, unregulated trade competitions common, and the provision of international public goods anemic or nonexistent. Hume's explanation of the freer morality of princes rests on his view that morality is less useful to princes than to private gentlemen. We have already questioned that view, and it is important to show that Hume adopts it because he infers too hastily that if self-interested nations have not entered into arrangements or established conventions, it is not in their interest to do so. But the failure to enter into mutually beneficial relationships may be explained in many other ways. For instance, the parties involved may not understand the possible benefits of the relationships, as mercantilist princes did not understand the importance of free trade. Even where ignorance, mistake, or misunderstanding are not problems, the interests of those who conduct the affairs of state may not coincide with the collective interests of those they govern. An easy appeal to arms may be in the interest of the eighteenth-century monarch (as Kant said, it may not require "the slightest sacrifice so far as his banquets, hunts, pleasure palaces and court festivals are concerned"), whereas a difficult compromise might be in the interest of his subjects.[76] Similarly, present-day leaders may fail to pursue agreements that would be in the interests of the state because their own political survival depends on taking unaccommodating "nationalistic" positions, which may not serve even the short-term interests of the state. Again, failures may be the result of the simple lack of energy or ingenuity expended in the search for solutions.

Often, however, nations find themselves in situations which, as they view them, display the familiar structure of the prisoner's dilemma. It may be argued that these situations are falsely perceived and imperfectly understood. Even if this is so, however, a consideration of the prisoner's dilemma suggests why nations often fail to enter into cooperative arrangements that would be to their mutual advantage. In prisoner's dilemma situations, agents are faced with two significant choices, a cooperative and a noncooperative one.[77] If both make the noncooperative choice, the outcome is costly to each, roughly to the same degree. If both make the cooperative choice, the outcome is very much in their mutual interest. However, if one makes the cooperative choice while the other does not, the outcome for the latter is far more advantageous than if both had been cooperative, and far worse for the former than if both had refused to cooperate. In these circumstances the rational self-interested agent will always have a "dominating" strategy, a strategy which guarantees that he will be better off no matter what the other does. Unfortunately, in the situations with a structure like that of the noniterated prisoner's dilemma, the noncooperative strategy is the dominating one and everyone is worse off than he would have been had they cooperated.

76. Kant, "Perpetual Peace," in *Kant's Political Writings*, ed. H. Reiss (Cambridge: Cambridge University Press, 1970), p. 100.

77. My discussion of the prisoner's dilemma in part follows, and in general is much indebted to, Arthur Kuflik's unpublished essay, "Prisoner's Dilemma Cases."

In these Hobbesian situations Humean conventions will not be agreed to even if they are in everyone's interest. Even though it would be in the interest of both to adopt the cooperative strategy and disarm, in the prisoner's dilemma situation the dominating strategy is the noncooperative one and both sides will remain armed. For each will reason that if the other side remains armed, remaining armed is preferable to disarming (and exposing oneself to coercion). If, however, the other side disarms, remaining armed is still the best strategy because it puts one in the controlling position.

A similar situation has often seemed to manifest itself in the trading relations of nations. Thus, it may be thought that no matter what other nations do, it will be to the advantage of a trading nation to raise its tariffs and quotas, subsidize its exports, and devalue its currency. If others impose quotas the best strategy is to impose one's own. If, on the other hand, others fail to impose quotas it is still to one's advantage. Since this reasoning is the same for everyone, everyone will raise quotas. This will adversely affect the quantity of world trade and the efficiency of world production and everyone will be worse off.[78]

The noncooperative solution also seems to dominate in many situations in which the provision of public goods is in question. (They are multi-person prisoner's dilemmas.)[79] Therefore, less of the good is provided than it would be in everyone's interest to have. This is an acute problem in an increasingly interdependent world in which many important goods are at least in part collective or public goods, that is, goods which if produced are available to all. Pollution control, scientific knowledge, international organizations, and the provision of security all possess this characteristic to some degree. But rationally self-interested nations often fail to produce these goods (or fail to produce them in optimal amounts) because they reason that not producing (or not producing more than will benefit them if others fail to contribute) is the dominating strategy. If others produce the good they can, because of the nonexclusive nature of the good, have a "free ride." On the other hand, if others do not produce the good, their own expenditures will be a waste (beyond the point at which others' contributions would be required to make them worthwhile).

78. W. J. Baumol, *Welfare Economics and the Theory of the State* (Cambridge: Harvard University Press, 1965), pp. 142–47.

79. Russell Hardin, "Collective Action as an Agreeable n-Prisoners' Dilemma," *Behavioral Science* 16 (1971): 472–81.

*Moral Skepticism
and International
Relations*

The rationality of following the noncooperative strategy in each of these cases depends on several assumptions, one of which is that the parties cannot conclude enforceable agreements that would substitute for the mutual trust they do not enjoy. If they could make such agreements it would become possible for rationally self-interested agents to follow cooperative strategies. For potential noncooperators could be deterred by threats of punishment sufficiently heavy to outweigh the benefits of double-crossing. It would then become rational for everyone to pursue a cooperative strategy. This is precisely the benefit the Hobbesian sovereign provides. Because some analogue of the Hobbesian sovereign exists in most well-ordered domestic societies they do not face internal arms races, regional trade wars, or, to anything like the degree we experience it in international society, the inadequate provision of public goods.

But even in the absence of world government it is possible to mitigate some of these problems. Consider the world situation in the postwar years. In the absence of world government, a form of authority neither side could accept, the possibility of disarming was slight. However, with the advent of nuclear weapons a new situation was created. The alternatives were now whether to pursue the noncooperative strategy of seeking a first-strike capacity or pursuing the cooperative one of developing an invulnerable second-strike force. In this new situation, however, each superpower was invested with an attribute of Hobbesian sovereignty. With its second-strike capacity it could visit a sufficient punishment on a first strike to deter it, and a troubled peace was therefore established. At the same time, however, the residual fear of escalation gave the superpowers the capacity to deter not only a first nuclear strike but anything, including conventional war, that risked precipitating one. The European political situation was frozen in a way that deprived the Czechs and the Hungarians of their fundamental freedoms and the support of their moral friends. The more reliable the "convention" of nuclear-backed, superpower spheres of domination, the more anguishing it becomes from a moral point of view. We can no more identify the conventions of superpower domination with a morally satisfactory international order than we can identify the most iniquitous command of a Hobbesian sovereign with justice. (This is not to say that it would now be prudent, or on balance morally desirable, to try altering the situation in any fundamental way.) As Nietzsche said, it was not doubt, but certainty that drove Hamlet mad. And there are circumstances in which the only thing worse than unreliabililty is reliability. The reliability of Soviet oppression in Poland is one of them. Each Humean convention must be judged on its own moral merits.

Some of them are, of course, commendable. The postwar allies were able to free themselves from the trade wars and beggar-thy-neighbor economic policies of the thirties which American leadership, especially, thought largely responsible for World War II. The wartime alliance created a new spirit of trust and cooperation that found legal expression in such institutions as the IMF and the GATT. These institutions established rules concerning monetary exchange and international trade and imposed penalties for their violation. These penalties, reinforced by memories of the world depression and the threat of Soviet domination, constituted enormous threats to noncooperators. At the same time, the promise of a more general prosperity, as well as the American willingness to accept rising Japanese imports and European trade discrimination, while continuing to hold out a security "umbrella," provided handsome inducements to cooperate. The Western powers escaped from their trade dilemma, although more recently it has become clear that Hume's tacit assumption that conventions which work out to everyone's advantage are just is very much under attack. The Europeans increasingly resent as unfair America's ability to export "negative externalities" such as high interest rates and economic recessions. The more general terms of world trade, often defended on the Humean ground that they are mutually beneficial (and leave everyone better off than he would be in the state of nature) are under much fiercer attack. *Dependencia* theorists think that the rhetoricians of interdependence fail, as Hume failed, to confront the central issue of economic justice, the fair division of mutual benefits.

The adequate provision of public goods in the absence of international institutions that have the power of taxation remains an acute problem. Often such goods are provided by the great powers in the form of scientific knowledge, support for international institutions, and the provision of security. Some will argue that great nations produce these goods only to the extent that it is in their interest to do so. I do not share this skeptical view and expect that if such goods are to be provided in the near future they will be provided by the most privileged nations as they exert their moral and political leadership.[80] As Derek Parfit has written, moral so-

80. Kenneth N. Waltz, *Theory of International Relations* (Reading, MA: Addison-Wesley Publishing Co., 1979), pp. 198ff.

lutions to prisoner's dilemmas are often the only ones possible.[81] We can, however, expect acute problems of justice to arise in connection with the provision of some public goods. Mancur Olson has pointed to what he calls the surprising tendency for the small to "exploit" the great. For, "once a smaller member has the amount of the collective good he gets free from the largest member, he has more than he would have purchased himself, and has no incentive to obtain any of the collective good at his own expense."[82] Some have felt that in providing the public good of its nuclear umbrella and military forces to NATO, the U.S. has experienced this kind of exploitation. This is not an issue to pursue here but it makes plain, again, that mutually advantageous agreements may not be fair.

We have observed that Hume attributes the freer nature of international morality to the fact that it is less important, less a matter of mutual self-interest, than interpersonal morality. We have seen, however, that there are many other explanations for the more limited reach of the international "system of justice," in particular the absence of a Hobbesian sovereign or of other mechanisms and conventions that make expectations of mutual conformity reasonable. John Mackie, who has previously made this objection to Hume's explanation of the freer morality of international relations, writes that in noting this "we do not undermine but rather strengthen [Hume's] point that the state of affairs reveals some implicit understanding of the conventional basis of morality, for it is precisely this conventional structure that is weaker in the international field."[83]

But this argument is, in turn, unacceptable. We have already argued that morality exists in the state of nature. To be sure, some obligations obtain only in the presence of conventions, which underwrite expectations of mutual reliability. But this shows, at best, that morality is relative to circumstances and that moral requirements often presuppose the existence of conventions. It is far from showing that the "basis of morality" is itself conventional in the sense Hume intends. As we have repeatedly seen, it is often necessary to judge the morality of Humean "conventions" and "rules of justice" themselves. This is an especially important consideration in the international case. For the rough equality of men that

81. Derek Parfit, "Prudence, Morality and the Prisoner's Dilemma," in *Proceedings of the British Academy for 1979* (London: Oxford University Press, 1981), p. 546.

82. Mancur Olson, Jr., *The Logic of Collective Action* (Cambridge, MA: Harvard University Press, 1965), p. 35.

83. J. L. Mackie, *Hume's Moral Theory* (London: Routledge and Kegan Paul, 1980), p. 115.

gives some plausibility to Hume's suggestion that what they agree to are "rules of justice" has no plausibility at all in the case of nations.

Indeed, one of the most conspicuous reasons for the "freer" morality of nations is that this freer morality is in the interest of the strong. Hume does not consider this possible explanation in his remarks on the morality of nations. But the idea has not escaped him altogether:

> Were there a species of creatures intermingled with men, which, though rational, were possessed of such inferior strength, both of body and mind, that they were incapable of all resistance, and could never . . . make us feel the effects of their resentments; the necessary consequence . . . is that we should be bound by the laws of humanity to give gentle usage to these creatures, but should not . . . lie under any restraint of justice with regard to them, nor could they possess any right or property, . . . the restraints of justice and property, being totally *useless*, would never have place in so unequal a confederacy.[84]

However it may be with "the laws of humanity," an adequate philosophy of justice for nations cannot be established on Humean principles. Strong princes have demonstrated this more often than great philosophers have understood it.

84. Hume, *Enquiry*, 2d ed., ed. L. A. Selby-Bigge (Oxford: Clarendon Press, 1902), p. 190.

PART II

Morality and the
Rules of War

THOMAS NAGEL   War and Massacre[1]

From the apathetic reaction to atrocities committed in Vietnam by
the United States and its allies, one may conclude that moral restrictions on the conduct of war command almost as little sympathy
among the general public as they do among those charged with the
formation of U.S. military policy. Even when restrictions on the conduct of warfare are defended, it is usually on legal grounds alone:
their moral basis is often poorly understood. I wish to argue that
certain restrictions are neither arbitrary nor merely conventional,
and that their validity does not depend simply on their usefulness.
There is, in other words, a moral basis for the rules of war, even
though the conventions now officially in force are far from giving it
perfect expression.

I

No elaborate moral theory is required to account for what is wrong
in cases like the Mylai massacre, since it did not serve, and was not
intended to serve, any strategic purpose. Moreover, if the participation of the United States in the Indo-Chinese war is entirely wrong
to begin with, then that engagement is incapable of providing a
justification for *any* measures taken in its pursuit—not only for the
measures which are atrocities in every war, however just its aims.

But this war has revealed attitudes of a more general kind, that
influenced the conduct of earlier wars as well. After it has ended, we

1. This paper grew out of discussions at the Society for Ethical and Legal
Philosophy, and I am indebted to my fellow members for their help.

shall still be faced with the problem of how warfare may be conducted, and the attitudes that have resulted in the specific conduct
of this war will not have disappeared. Moreover, similar problems
can arise in wars or rebellions fought for very different reasons, and
against very different opponents. It is not easy to keep a firm grip
on the idea of what is not permissible in warfare, because while
some military actions are obvious atrocities, other cases are more
difficult to assess, and the general principles underlying these judgments remain obscure. Such obscurity can lead to the abandonment
of sound intuitions in favor of criteria whose rationale may be more
obvious. If such a tendency is to be resisted, it will require a better
understanding of the restrictions than we now have.

I propose to discuss the most general moral problem raised by
the conduct of warfare: the problem of means and ends. In one view,
there are limits on what may be done even in the service of an end
worth pursuing—and even when adherence to the restriction may be
very costly. A person who acknowledges the force of such restrictions
can find himself in acute moral dilemmas. He may believe, for example, that by torturing a prisoner he can obtain information necessary to prevent a disaster, or that by obliterating one village with
bombs he can halt a campaign of terrorism. If he believes that the
gains from a certain measure will clearly outweigh its costs, yet
still suspects that he ought not to adopt it, then he is in a dilemma
produced by the conflict between two disparate categories of moral
reason: categories that may be called *utilitarian* and *absolutist*.

Utilitarianism gives primacy to a concern with what will *happen*.
Absolutism gives primacy to a concern with what one is *doing*. The
conflict between them arises because the alternatives we face are
rarely just choices between *total outcomes*: they are also choices between alternative pathways or measures to be taken. When one of
the choices is to do terrible things to another person, the problem
is altered fundamentally; it is no longer merely a question of which
outcome would be worse.

Few of us are completely immune to either of these types of moral
intuition, though in some people, either naturally or for doctrinal
reasons, one type will be dominant and the other suppressed or weak.
But it is perfectly possible to feel the force of both types of reason

very strongly; in that case the moral dilemma in certain situations of crisis will be acute, and it may appear that every possible course of action or inaction is unacceptable for one reason or another.

II

Although it is this dilemma that I propose to explore, most of the discussion will be devoted to its absolutist component. The utilitarian component is straightforward by comparison, and has a natural appeal to anyone who is not a complete skeptic about ethics. Utilitarianism says that one should try, either individually or through institutions, to maximize good and minimize evil (the definition of these categories need not enter into the schematic formulation of the view), and that if faced with the possibility of preventing a great evil by producing a lesser, one should choose the lesser evil. There are certainly problems about the formulation of utilitarianism, and much has been written about it, but its intent is morally transparent. Nevertheless, despite the addition of various refinements, it continues to leave large portions of ethics unaccounted for. I do not suggest that some form of absolutism can account for them all, only that an examination of absolutism will lead us to see the complexity, and perhaps the incoherence, of our moral ideas.

Utilitarianism certainly justifies *some* restrictions on the conduct of warfare. There are strong utilitarian reasons for adhering to any limitation which seems natural to most people—particularly if the limitation is widely accepted already. An exceptional measure which seems to be justified by its results in a particular conflict may create a precedent with disastrous long-term effects.[2] It may even be argued that war involves violence on such a scale that it is never justified on utilitarian grounds—the consequences of refusing to go to war will never be as bad as the war itself would be, even if atrocities were not committed. Or in a more sophisticated vein it might be claimed that a uniform policy of never resorting to military force would do less harm in the long run, if followed consistently, than a policy of deciding each case on utilitarian grounds (even though on occasion

2. Straightforward considerations of national interest often tend in the same direction: the inadvisability of using nuclear weapons seems to be overdetermined in this way.

particular applications of the pacifist policy might have worse results than a specific utilitarian decision). But I shall not consider these arguments, for my concern is with reasons of a different kind, which may remain when reasons of utility and interest fail.[3]

In the final analysis, I believe that the dilemma cannot always be resolved. While not every conflict between absolutism and utilitarianism creates an insoluble dilemma, and while it is certainly right to adhere to absolutist restrictions unless the utilitarian considerations favoring violation are overpoweringly weighty and extremely certain —nevertheless, when that special condition is met, it may become impossible to adhere to an absolutist position. What I shall offer, therefore, is a somewhat qualified defense of absolutism. I believe it underlies a valid and fundamental type of moral judgment—which cannot be reduced to or overridden by other principles. And while there may be other principles just as fundamental, it is particularly important not to lose confidence in our absolutist intuitions, for they are often the only barrier before the abyss of utilitarian apologetics for large-scale murder.

III

One absolutist position that creates no problems of interpretation is pacifism: the view that one may not kill another person under any circumstances, no matter what good would be achieved or evil averted thereby. The type of absolutist position that I am going to discuss is different. Pacifism draws the conflict with utilitarian considerations very starkly. But there are other views according to which violence may be undertaken, even on a large scale, in a clearly just cause, so long as certain absolute restrictions on the character and direction of that violence are observed. The line is drawn somewhat closer to the bone, but it exists.

The philosopher who has done most to advance contemporary philosophical discussion of such a view, and to explain it to those

3. These reasons, moreover, have special importance in that they are available even to one who denies the appropriateness of utilitarian considerations in international matters. He may acknowledge limitations on what may be done to the soldiers and civilians of other countries in pursuit of his nation's military objectives, while denying that one country should in general consider the interests of nationals of other countries in determining its policies.

unfamiliar with its extensive treatment in Roman Catholic moral theology, is G.E.M. Anscombe. In 1958 Miss Anscombe published a pamphlet entitled *Mr. Truman's Degree*,[4] on the occasion of the award by Oxford University of an honorary doctorate to Harry Truman. The pamphlet explained why she had opposed the decision to award that degree, recounted the story of her unsuccessful opposition, and offered some reflections on the history of Truman's decision to drop atom bombs on Hiroshima and Nagasaki, and on the difference between murder and allowable killing in warfare. She pointed out that the policy of deliberately killing large numbers of civilians either as a means or as an end in itself did not originate with Truman, and was common practice among all parties during World War II for some time before Hiroshima. The Allied area bombings of German cities by conventional explosives included raids which killed more civilians than did the atomic attacks; the same is true of certain fire-bomb raids on Japan.

The policy of attacking the civilian population in order to induce an enemy to surrender, or to damage his morale, seems to have been widely accepted in the civilized world, and seems to be accepted still, at least if the stakes are high enough. It gives evidence of a moral conviction that the deliberate killing of noncombatants—women, children, old people—is permissible if enough can be gained by it. This follows from the more general position that any means can in principle be justified if it leads to a sufficiently worthy end. Such an attitude is evident not only in the more spectacular current weapons systems but also in the day-to-day conduct of the nonglobal war in Indochina: the indiscriminate destructiveness of antipersonnel weapons, napalm, and aerial bombardment; cruelty to prisoners; massive relocation of civilians; destruction of crops; and so forth. An abso-

4. (Privately printed.) See also her essay "War and Murder," in *Nuclear Weapons and Christian Conscience*, ed. Walter Stein (London, 1963). The present paper is much indebted to these two essays throughout. These and related subjects are extensively treated by Paul Ramsey in *The Just War* (New York, 1968). Among recent writings that bear on the moral problem are Jonathan Bennett, "Whatever the Consequences," *Analysis* 26, no. 3 (1966): 83-102; and Philippa Foot, "The Problem of Abortion and the Doctrine of the Double Effect," *The Oxford Review* 5 (1967): 5-15. Miss Anscombe's replies are "A Note on Mr. Bennett," *Analysis* 26, no. 3 (1966): 208, and "Who is Wronged?" *The Oxford Review* 5 (1967): 16-17.

lutist position opposes to this the view that certain acts cannot be justified no matter what the consequences. Among those acts is murder—the deliberate killing of the harmless: civilians, prisoners of war, and medical personnel.

In the present war such measures are sometimes said to be regrettable, but they are generally defended by reference to military necessity and the importance of the long-term consequences of success or failure in the war. I shall pass over the inadequacy of this consequentialist defense in its own terms. (That is the dominant form of moral criticism of the war, for it is part of what people mean when they ask, "Is it worth it?") I am concerned rather to account for the inappropriateness of offering any defense of that kind for such actions.

Many people feel, without being able to say much more about it, that something has gone seriously wrong when certain measures are admitted into consideration in the first place. The fundamental mistake is made there, rather than at the point where the overall benefit of some monstrous measure is judged to outweigh its disadvantages, and it is adopted. An account of absolutism might help us to understand this. If it is not allowable to *do* certain things, such as killing unarmed prisoners or civilians, then no argument about what will happen if one doesn't do them can show that doing them would be all right.

Absolutism does not, of course, require one to ignore the consequences of one's acts. It operates as a limitation on utilitarian reasoning, not as a substitute for it. An absolutist can be expected to try to maximize good and minimize evil, so long as this does not require him to transgress an absolute prohibition like that against murder. But when such a conflict occurs, the prohibition takes complete precedence over any consideration of consequences. Some of the results of this view are clear enough. It requires us to forgo certain potentially useful military measures, such as the slaughter of hostages and prisoners or indiscriminate attempts to reduce the enemy civilian population by starvation, epidemic infectious diseases like anthrax and bubonic plague, or mass incineration. It means that we cannot deliberate on whether such measures are justified by the fact that they will avert still greater evils, for as intentional measures they cannot be justified in terms of any consequences whatever.

Someone unfamiliar with the events of this century might imagine
that utilitarian arguments, or arguments of national interest, would
suffice to deter measures of this sort. But it has become evident that
such considerations are insufficient to prevent the adoption and employment of enormous antipopulation weapons once their use is considered a serious moral possibility. The same is true of the piecemeal
wiping out of rural civilian populations in airborne antiguerrilla warfare. Once the door is opened to calculations of utility and national
interest, the usual speculations about the future of freedom, peace,
and economic prosperity can be brought to bear to ease the con-
sciences of those responsible for a certain number of charred babies.

For this reason alone it is important to decide what is wrong with
the frame of mind which allows such arguments to begin. But it is
also important to understand absolutism in the cases where it genu-
inely conflicts with utility. Despite its appeal, it is a paradoxical position, for it can require that one refrain from choosing the lesser of
two evils when that is the only choice one has. And it is additionally
paradoxical because, unlike pacifism, it permits one to do horrible
things to people in some circumstances but not in others.

IV

Before going on to say what, if anything, lies behind the position,
there remain a few relatively technical matters which are best discussed at this point.

First, it is important to specify as clearly as possible the kind of
thing to which absolutist prohibitions can apply. We must take seriously the proviso that they concern what we deliberately do to people.
There could not, for example, without incoherence, be an absolute
prohibition against *bringing about* the death of an innocent person.
For one may find oneself in a situation in which, no matter what one
does, some innocent people will die as a result. I do not mean just
that there are cases in which someone will die no matter what one
does, because one is not in a position to affect the outcome one way
or the other. That, it is to be hoped, is one's relation to the deaths of
most innocent people. I have in mind, rather, a case in which someone is bound to die, but who it is will depend on what one does.
Sometimes these situations have natural causes, as when too few resources (medicine, lifeboats) are available to rescue everyone threat-

ened with a certain catastrophe. Sometimes the situations are man-made, as when the only way to control a campaign of terrorism is to employ terrorist tactics against the community from which it has arisen. Whatever one does in cases such as these, some innocent people will die as a result. If the absolutist prohibition forbade doing what would result in the deaths of innocent people, it would have the consequence that in such cases nothing one could do would be morally permissible.

This problem is avoided, however, because what absolutism forbids is *doing* certain things to people, rather than bringing about certain *results*. Not everything that happens to others as a result of what one does is something that one has *done* to them. Catholic moral theology seeks to make this distinction precise in a doctrine known as the law of double effect, which asserts that there is a morally relevant distinction between bringing about the death of an innocent person deliberately, either as an end in itself or as a means, and bringing it about as a side effect of something else one does deliberately. In the latter case, even if the outcome is foreseen, it is not murder, and does not fall under the absolute prohibition, though of course it may still be wrong for other reasons (reasons of utility, for example). Briefly, the principle states that one is sometimes permitted knowingly to bring about as a side effect of one's actions something which it would be absolutely impermissible to bring about deliberately as an end or as a means. In application to war or revolution, the law of double effect permits a certain amount of civilian carnage as a side effect of bombing munitions plants or attacking enemy soldiers. And even this is permissible only if the cost is not too great to be justified by one's objectives.

However, despite its importance and its usefulness in accounting for certain plausible moral judgments, I do not believe that the law of double effect is a generally applicable test for the consequences of an absolutist position. Its own application is not always clear, so that it introduces uncertainty where there need not be uncertainty.

In Indochina, for example, there is a great deal of aerial bombardment, strafing, spraying of napalm, and employment of pellet- or needle-spraying antipersonnel weapons against rural villages in which guerrillas are suspected to be hiding, or from which small-arms fire has been received. The majority of those killed and wounded in these aerial attacks are reported to be women and children, even when some combatants are caught as well. However, the government regards these civilian casualties as a regrettable side effect of what is a legitimate attack against an armed enemy.

It might be thought easy to dismiss this as sophistry: if one bombs, burns, or strafes a village containing a hundred people, twenty of whom one believes to be guerrillas, so that by killing most of them one will be statistically likely to kill most of the guerrillas, then isn't one's attack on the group of one hundred a *means* of destroying the guerrillas, pure and simple? If one makes no attempt to discriminate between guerrillas and civilians, as is impossible in a aerial attack on a small village, then one cannot regard as a mere side effect the deaths of those in the group that one would not have bothered to kill if more selective means had been available.

The difficulty is that this argument depends on one particular description of the act, and the reply might be that the means used against the guerrillas is not: killing everybody in the village—but rather: obliteration bombing of the *area* in which the twenty guerrillas are known to be located. If there are civilians in the area as well, they will be killed as a side effect of such action.[5]

Because of casuistical problems like this, I prefer to stay with the original, unanalyzed distinction between what one does to people and what merely happens to them as a result of what one does. The law of double effect provides an approximation to that distinction in many cases, and perhaps it can be sharpened to the point where it does better than that. Certainly the original distinction itself needs clarification, particularly since some of the things we do to people involve things happening to them as a result of other things we do. In a case like the one discussed, however, it is clear that by bombing the village one slaughters and maims the civilians in it. Whereas by giving the only available medicine to one of two sufferers from a disease, one does not kill the other, even if he dies as a result.

The second technical point to take up concerns a possible misinterpretation of this feature of the position. The absolutist focus on actions rather than outcomes does not merely introduce a new, out-

5. This counterargument was suggested by Rogers Albritton.

standing item into the catalogue of evils. That is, it does not say that the worst thing in the world is the deliberate murder of an innocent person. For if that were all, then one could presumably justify one such murder on the ground that it would prevent several others, or ten thousand on the ground that they would prevent a hundred thousand more. That is a familiar argument. But if this is allowable, then there is no absolute prohibition against murder after all. Absolutism requires that we *avoid* murder at all costs, not that we *prevent* it at all costs.[6]

Finally, let me remark on a frequent criticism of absolutism that depends on a misunderstanding. It is sometimes suggested that such prohibitions depend on a kind of moral self-interest, a primary obligation to preserve one's own moral purity, to keep one's hands clean no matter what happens to the rest of the world. If this were the position, it might be exposed to the charge of self-indulgence. After all, what gives one man a right to put the purity of his soul or the cleanness of his hands above the lives or welfare of large numbers of other people? It might be argued that a public servant like Truman has no right to put himself first in that way; therefore if he is convinced that the alternatives would be worse, he must give the order to drop the bombs, and take the burden of those deaths on himself, as he must do other distasteful things for the general good.

But there are two confusions behind the view that moral self-interest underlies moral absolutism. First, it is a confusion to suggest that the need to preserve one's moral purity might be the *source* of an obligation. For if by committing murder one sacrifices one's moral purity or integrity, that can only be because there is *already* something wrong with murder. The general reason against committing murder cannot therefore be merely that it makes one an immoral person. Secondly, the notion that one might sacrifice one's moral integrity justifiably, in the service of a sufficiently worthy end, is an incoherent notion. For if one were justified in making such a sacrifice (or even morally required to make it), then one would not be

6. Someone might of course acknowledge the *moral relevance* of the distinction between deliberate and nondeliberate killing, without being an absolutist. That is, he might believe simply that it was *worse* to bring about a death deliberately than as a secondary effect. But that would be merely a special assignment of value, and not an absolute prohibition.

sacrificing one's moral integrity by adopting that course: one would be preserving it.

Moral absolutism is not unique among moral theories in requiring each person to do what will preserve his own moral purity in all circumstances. This is equally true of utilitarianism, or of any other theory which distinguishes between right and wrong. Any theory which defines the right course of action in various circumstances and asserts that one should adopt that course, ipso facto asserts that one should do what will preserve one's purity, simply because the right course of action *is* what will preserve one's moral purity in those circumstances. Of course utilitarianism does not assert that this is *why* one should adopt that course, but we have seen that the same is true of absolutism.

V

It is easier to dispose of false explanations of absolutism than to produce a true one. A positive account of the matter must begin with the observation that war, conflict, and aggression are relations between persons. The view that it can be wrong to consider merely the overall effect of one's actions on the general welfare comes into prominence when those actions involve relations with others. A man's acts usually affect more people than he deals with directly, and those effects must naturally be considered in his decisions. But if there are special principles governing the manner in which he should *treat* people, that will require special attention to the particular persons toward whom the act is directed, rather than just to its total effect.

Absolutist restrictions in warfare appear to be of two types: restrictions on the class of persons at whom aggression or violence may be directed and restrictions on the manner of attack, given that the object falls within that class. These can be combined, however, under the principle that hostile treatment of any person must be justified in terms of something *about that person* which makes the treatment appropriate. Hostility is a personal relation, and it must be suited to its target. One consequence of this condition will be that certain persons may not be subjected to hostile treatment in war at all, since nothing about them justifies such treatment. Others will be proper objects of hostility only in certain circumstances, or when they are engaged in certain pursuits. And the appropriate manner and extent of hostile treatment will depend on what is justified by the particular case.

A coherent view of this type will hold that extremely hostile behavior toward another is compatible with treating him as a person—even perhaps as an end in himself. This is possible only if one has not automatically stopped treating him as a person as soon as one starts to fight with him. If hostile, aggressive, or combative treatment of others always violated the condition that they be treated as human beings, it would be difficult to make further distinctions on that score *within* the class of hostile actions. That point of view, on the level of international relations, leads to the position that if complete pacifism is not accepted, no holds need be barred at all, and we may slaughter and massacre to our hearts' content, if it seems advisable. Such a position is often expressed in discussions of war crimes.

But the fact is that ordinary people do not believe this about conflicts, physical or otherwise, between individuals, and there is no more reason why it should be true of conflicts between nations. There seems to be a perfectly natural conception of the distinction between fighting clean and fighting dirty. To fight dirty is to direct one's hostility or aggression not at its proper object, but at a peripheral target which may be more vulnerable, and through which the proper object can be attacked indirectly. This applies in a fist fight, an election campaign, a duel, or a philosophical argument. If the concept is general enough to apply to all these matters, it should apply to war—both to the conduct of individual soldiers and to the conduct of nations.

Suppose that you are a candidate for public office, convinced that the election of your opponent would be a disaster, that he is an unscrupulous demagogue who will serve a narrow range of interests and seriously infringe the rights of those who disagree with him; and suppose you are convinced that you cannot defeat him by conventional means. Now imagine that various unconventional means present themselves as possibilities: you possess information about his sex life which would scandalize the electorate if made public; or you learn that his wife is an alcoholic or that in his youth he was associated for a brief period with a proscribed political party, and you believe that this information could be used to blackmail him into withdrawing his candidacy; or you can have a team of your supporters flatten the tires of a crucial subset of his supporters on election day; or you are in a position to stuff the ballot boxes; or, more simply, you can have him assassinated. What is wrong with these methods, given that they will achieve an overwhelmingly desirable result?

There are, of course, many things wrong with them: some are against the law; some infringe the procedures of an electoral process to which you are presumably committed by taking part in it; very importantly, some may backfire, and it is in the interest of all political candidates to adhere to an unspoken agreement not to allow certain personal matters to intrude into a campaign. But that is not all. We have in addition the feeling that these measures, these methods of attack are *irrelevant* to the issue between you and your opponent, that in taking them up you would not be directing yourself to that which makes him an object of your opposition. You would be directing your attack not at the true target of your hostility, but at peripheral targets that happen to be vulnerable.

The same is true of a fight or argument outside the framework of any system of regulations or law. In an altercation with a taxi driver over an excessive fare, it is inappropriate to taunt him about his accent, flatten one of his tires, or smear chewing gum on his windshield; and it remains inappropriate even if he casts aspersions on your race, politics, or religion, or dumps the contents of your suitcase into the street.[7]

The importance of such restrictions may vary with the seriousness of the case; and what is unjustifiable in one case may be justified in a more extreme one. But they all derive from a single principle: that hostility or aggression should be directed at its true object. This means both that it should be directed at the person or persons who provoke it and that it should aim more specifically at what is provocative about them. The second condition will determine what form the hostility may appropriately take.

7. Why, on the other hand, does it seem appropriate, rather than irrelevant, to punch someone in the mouth if he insults you? The answer is that in our culture it is an insult to punch someone in the mouth, and not just an injury. This reveals, by the way, a perfectly unobjectionable sense in which convention may play a part in determining exactly what falls under an absolutist restriction and what does not. I am indebted to Robert Fogelin for this point.

It is evident that some idea of the relation in which one should stand to other people underlies this principle, but the idea is difficult to state. I believe it is roughly this: whatever one does to another person intentionally must be aimed at him as a subject, with the intention that he receive it as a subject. It should manifest an attitude to *him* rather than just to the situation, and he should be able to recognize it and identify himself as its object. The procedures by which such an attitude is manifested need not be addressed to the person directly. Surgery, for example, is not a form of personal confrontation but part of a medical treatment that can be offered to a patient face to face and received by him as a response to his needs and the natural outcome of an attitude toward *him*.

Hostile treatment, unlike surgery, is already addressed *to* a person, and does not take its interpersonal meaning from a wider context. But hostile acts can serve as the expression or implementation of only a limited range of attitudes to the person who is attacked. Those attitudes in turn have as objects certain real or presumed characteristics or activities of the person which are thought to justify them. When this background is absent, hostile or aggressive behavior can no longer be intended for the reception of the victim as a subject. Instead it takes on the character of a purely bureaucratic operation. This occurs when one attacks someone who is not the true object of one's hostility—the true object may be someone else, who can be attacked through the victim; or one may not be manifesting a hostile attitude toward anyone, but merely using the easiest available path to some desired goal. One finds oneself not facing or addressing the victim at all, but operating on him—without the larger context of personal interaction that surrounds a surgical operation.

If absolutism is to defend its claim to priority over considerations of utility, it must hold that the maintenance of a direct interpersonal response to the people one deals with is a requirement which no advantages can justify one in abandoning. The requirement is absolute only if it rules out any calculation of what would justify its violation. I have said earlier that there may be circumstances so extreme that they render an absolutist position untenable. One may find then that one has no choice but to do something terrible. Nevertheless, even in such cases absolutism retains its force in that one cannot claim *justification* for the violation. It does not become *all right*.

As a tentative effort to explain this, let me try to connect absolutist limitations with the possibility of justifying *to the victim* what is being done to him. If one abandons a person in the course of rescuing several others from a fire or a sinking ship, one *could* say to him, "You understand, I have to leave you to save the others." Similarly, if one subjects an unwilling child to a painful surgical procedure, one can say to him, "If you could understand, you would realize that I am doing this to help you." One could *even* say, as one bayonets an enemy soldier, "It's either you or me." But one cannot really say while torturing a prisoner, "You understand, I have to pull out your fingernails because it is absolutely essential that we have the names of your confederates"; nor can one say to the victims of Hiroshima, "You understand, we have to incinerate you to provide the Japanese government with an incentive to surrender."

This does not take us very far, of course, since a utilitarian would presumably be willing to offer justifications of the latter sort to his victims, in cases where he thought they were sufficient. They are really justifications to the world at large, which the victim, as a reasonable man, would be expected to appreciate. However, there seems to me something wrong with this view, for it ignores the possibility that to treat someone else horribly puts you in a special relation to him, which may have to be defended in terms of other features of your relation to him. The suggestion needs much more development; but it may help us to understand how there may be requirements which are absolute in the sense that there can be no justification for violating them. If the justification for what one did to another person had to be such that it could be offered to him specifically, rather than just to the world at large, that would be a significant source of restraint.

If the account is to be deepened, I would hope for some results along the following lines. Absolutism is associated with a view of oneself as a small being interacting with others in a large world. The justifications it requires are primarily interpersonal. Utilitarianism is associated with a view of oneself as a benevolent bureaucrat distributing such benefits as one can control to countless other beings, with whom one may have various relations or none. The justifications it requires are primarily administrative. The argument between the two moral attitudes may depend on the relative priority of these two conceptions.[8]

VI

Some of the restrictions on methods of warfare which have been adhered to from time to time are to be explained by the mutual interests of the involved parties: restrictions on weaponry, treatment of prisoners, etc. But that is not all there is to it. The conditions of directness and relevance which I have argued apply to relations of conflict and aggression apply to war as well. I have said that there are two types of absolutist restrictions on the conduct of war: those that limit the legitimate targets of hostility and those that limit its character, even when the target is acceptable. I shall say something about each of these. As will become clear, the principle I have sketched does not yield an unambiguous answer in every case.

First let us see how it implies that attacks on some people are allowed, but not attacks on others. It may seem paradoxical to assert that to fire a machine gun at someone who is throwing hand grenades at your emplacement is to treat him as a human being. Yet the relation with him is direct and straightforward.[9] The attack is aimed specifically against the threat presented by a dangerous adversary, and not against a peripheral target through which he happens to be vulnerable but which has nothing to do with that threat. For example, you might stop him by machine-gunning his wife and children, who are standing nearby, thus distracting him from his aim of blowing you up and enabling you to capture him. But if his wife and children are not threatening your life, that would be to treat them as means with a vengeance.

8. Finally, I should mention a different possibility, suggested by Robert Nozick: that there is a strong general presumption against benefiting from the calamity of another, whether or not it has been deliberately inflicted for that or any other reason. This broader principle may well lend its force to the absolutist position.

9. It has been remarked that according to my view, shooting at someone establishes an I-thou relationship.

This, however, is just Hiroshima on a smaller scale. One objection to weapons of mass annihilation—nuclear, thermonuclear, biological, or chemical—is that their indiscriminateness disqualifies them as direct instruments for the expression of hostile relations. In attacking the civilian population, one treats neither the military enemy nor the civilians with that minimal respect which is owed to them as human beings. This is clearly true of the direct attack on people who present no threat at all. But it is also true of the character of the attack on those who *are* threatening you, viz., the government and military forces of the enemy. Your aggression is directed against an area of vulnerability quite distinct from any threat presented by them which you may be justified in meeting. You are taking aim at them through the mundane life and survival of their countrymen, instead of aiming at the destruction of their military capacity. And of course it does not require hydrogen bombs to commit such crimes.

This way of looking at the matter also helps us to understand the importance of the distinction between combatants and noncombatants, and the irrelevance of much of the criticism offered against its intelligibility and moral significance. According to an absolutist position, deliberate killing of the innocent is murder, and in warfare the role of the innocent is filled by noncombatants. This has been thought to raise two sorts of problems: first, the widely imagined difficulty of making a division, in modern warfare, between combatants and noncombatants; second, problems deriving from the connotation of the word "innocence."

Let me take up the latter question first.[10] In the absolutist position, the operative notion of innocence is not moral innocence, and it is not opposed to moral guilt. If it were, then we would be justified in killing a wicked but noncombatant hairdresser in an enemy city who supported the evil policies of his government, and unjustified in killing a morally pure conscript who was driving a tank toward us with the profoundest regrets and nothing but love in his heart. But moral innocence has very little to do with it, for in the definition of murder "innocent" means "currently harmless," and it is opposed not to "guilty" but to "doing harm." It should be noted that such an analysis has the consequence that in war we may often be justified in kill-

10. What I say on this subject derives from Anscombe.

ing people who do not deserve to die, and unjustified in killing people who do deserve to die, if anyone does.

So we must distinguish combatants from noncombatants on the basis of their immediate threat or harmfulness. I do not claim that the line is a sharp one, but it is not so difficult as is often supposed to place individuals on one side of it or the other. Children are not combatants even though they may join the armed forces if they are allowed to grow up. Women are not combatants just because they bear children or offer comfort to the soldiers. More problematic are the supporting personnel, whether in or out of uniform, from drivers of munitions trucks and army cooks to civilian munitions workers and farmers. I believe they can be plausibly classified by applying the condition that the prosecution of conflict must direct itself to the cause of danger, and not to what is peripheral. The threat presented by an army and its members does not consist merely in the fact that they are men, but in the fact that they are armed and are using their arms in the pursuit of certain objectives. Contributions to their arms and logistics are contributions to this threat; contributions to their mere existence as men are not. It is therefore wrong to direct an attack against those who merely serve the combatants' needs as human beings, such as farmers and food suppliers, even though survival as a human being is a necessary condition of efficient functioning as a soldier.

This brings us to the second group of restrictions: those that limit what may be done even to combatants. These limits are harder to explain clearly. Some of them may be arbitrary or conventional, and some may have to be derived from other sources; but I believe that the condition of directness and relevance in hostile relations accounts for them to a considerable extent.

Consider first a case which involves both a protected class of noncombatants and a restriction on the measures that may be used against combatants. One provision of the rules of war which is universally recognized, though it seems to be turning into a dead letter in Vietnam, is the special status of medical personnel and the wounded in warfare. It might be more efficient to shoot medical officers on sight and to let the enemy wounded die rather than be patched up to fight another day. But someone with medical insignia is supposed to be left alone and permitted to tend and retrieve the wounded. I believe this is because medical attention is a species of attention to completely general human needs, not specifically the needs of a combat soldier, and our conflict with the soldier is not with his existence as a human being.

By extending the application of this idea, one can justify prohibitions against certain particularly cruel weapons: starvation, poisoning, infectious diseases (supposing they could be inflicted on combatants only), weapons designed to maim or disfigure or torture the opponent rather than merely to stop him. It is not, I think, mere casuistry to claim that such weapons attack the men, not the soldiers. The effect of dum-dum bullets, for example, is much more extended than necessary to cope with the combat situation in which they are used. They abandon any attempt to discriminate in their effects between the combatant and the human being. For this reason the use of flamethrowers and napalm is an atrocity in all circumstances that I can imagine, whoever the target may be. Burns are both extremely painful and extremely disfiguring—far more than any other category of wound. That this well-known fact plays no (inhibiting) part in the determination of U.S. weapons policy suggests that moral sensitivity among public officials has not increased markedly since the Spanish Inquisition.[11]

11. Beyond this I feel uncertain. Ordinary bullets, after all, can cause death, and nothing is more permanent than that. I am not at all sure why we are justified in trying to kill those who are trying to kill us (rather than merely in trying to stop them with force which may also result in their deaths). It is often argued that incapacitating gases are a relatively humane weapon (when not used, as in Vietnam, merely to make people easier to shoot). Perhaps the legitimacy of restrictions against them must depend on the dangers of escalation, and the great utility of maintaining *any* conventional category of restriction so long as nations are willing to adhere to it.

Let me make clear that I do not regard my argument as a defense of the moral immutability of the Hague and Geneva Conventions. Rather, I believe that they rest partly on a moral foundation, and that modifications of them should also be assessed on moral grounds.

But even this connection with the actual laws of war is not essential to my claims about what is permissible and what is not. Since completing this paper I have read an essay by Richard Wasserstrom entitled "The Laws of War" (forthcoming in *The Monist*), which argues that the existing laws and conventions do not even attempt to embody a decent moral position: that their provisions have been determined by other interests, that they are in fact immoral

Finally, the same condition of appropriateness to the true object of hostility should limit the scope of attacks on an enemy country: its economy, agriculture, transportation system, and so forth. Even if the parties to a military conflict are considered to be not armies or governments but entire nations (which is usually a grave error), that does not justify one nation in warring against every aspect or element of another nation. That is not justified in a conflict between individuals, and nations are even more complex than individuals, so the same reasons apply. Like a human being, a nation is engaged in countless other pursuits while waging war, and it is not in those respects that it is an enemy.

The burden of the argument has been that absolutism about murder has a foundation in principles governing all one's relations to other persons, whether aggressive or amiable, and that these principles, and that absolutism, apply to warfare as well, with the result that certain measures are impermissible no matter what the consequences.[12] I do not mean to romanticize war. It is sufficiently utopian to suggest that when nations conflict they might rise to the level of limited barbarity that typically characterizes violent conflict between individuals, rather than wallowing in the moral pit where they appear to have settled, surrounded by enormous arsenals.

VII

Having described the elements of the absolutist position, we must now return to the conflict between it and utilitarianism. Even if certain types of dirty tactics become acceptable when the stakes are high enough, the most serious of the prohibited acts, like murder and torture, are not just supposed to require unusually strong justifica-

---

in substance, and that it is a grave mistake to refer to them as standards in forming moral judgments about warfare. This possibility deserves serious consideration, and I am not sure what to say about it, but it does not affect my view of the moral issues.

12. It is possible to draw a more radical conclusion, which I shall not pursue here. Perhaps the technology and organization of modern war are such as to make it impossible to wage as an acceptable form of interpersonal or even international hostility. Perhaps it is too impersonal and large-scale for that. If so, then absolutism would in practice imply pacifism, given the present state of things. On the other hand, I am skeptical about the unstated assumption that a technology dictates its own use.

tion. They are supposed *never* to be done, because no quantity of resulting benefit is thought capable of *justifying* such treatment of a person.

The fact remains that when an absolutist knows or believes that the utilitarian cost of refusing to adopt a prohibited course will be very high, he may hold to his refusal to adopt it, but he will find it difficult to feel that a moral dilemma has been satisfactorily resolved. The same may be true of someone who rejects an absolutist requirement and adopts instead the course yielding the most acceptable consequences. In either case, it is possible to feel that one has acted for reasons insufficient to justify violation of the opposing principle. In situations of deadly conflict, particularly where a weaker party is threatened with annihilation or enslavement by a stronger one, the argument for resorting to atrocities can be powerful, and the dilemma acute.

There may exist principles, not yet codified, which would enable us to resolve such dilemmas. But then again there may not. We must face the pessimistic alternative that these two forms of moral intuition are not capable of being brought together into a single, coherent moral system, and that the world can present us with situations in which there is no honorable or moral course for a man to take, no course free of guilt and responsibility for evil.

The idea of a moral blind alley is a perfectly intelligible one. It is possible to get into such a situation by one's own fault, and people do it all the time. If, for example, one makes two incompatible promises or commitments—becomes engaged to two people, for example—then there is no course one can take which is not wrong, for one must break one's promise to at least one of them. Making a clean breast of the whole thing will not be enough to remove one's reprehensibility. The existence of such cases is not morally disturbing, however, because we feel that the situation was not unavoidable: one had to do something wrong in the first place to get into it. But what if the world itself, or someone else's actions, could face a previously innocent person with a choice between morally abominable courses of action, and leave him no way to escape with his honor? Our intuitions rebel at the idea, for we feel that the constructibility of such a case must show a contradiction in our moral views. But it is not in itself a contradiction to say that someone can do X or not do X, and that for him to take either course would be wrong. It merely contradicts the supposition that *ought* implies *can*—since presumably one ought to refrain from what is wrong, and in such a case it is impossible to do so.[13] Given the limitations on human action, it is naïve to suppose that there is a solution to every moral problem with which the world can face us. We have always known that the world is a bad place. It appears that it may be an evil place as well.

13. This was first pointed out to me by Christopher Boorse.

GEORGE I. MAVRODES   Conventions and the
                         Morality of War

The point of this paper is to introduce a distinction into our thinking
about warfare, and to explore the moral implications of this distinction.
I shall make two major assumptions. First, I shall assume without discussion that under some circumstances and for some ends warfare is
morally justified. These conditions I shall lump together under such
terms as "justice" and "just cause," and say no more about them. I
shall also assume that in warfare some means, including some killing,
are morally justified. I sometimes call such means "proportionate," and
in general I say rather little about them. These assumptions, inciden-
tally, are common to all of the philosophers whom I criticize here.

The distinction which I introduce can be thought of either as dividing wars into two classes, or else as distinguishing wars from certain
other international combats. I have no great preference for one of
these ways of speaking over the other, but I shall generally adopt the
latter alternative. I am particularly interested in the moral significance
of this distinction, and I shall explore in some detail its bearing on one
moral question associated with warfare, that of the intentional killing
of noncombatants.

My paper has two main parts. In the first I examine three closely
related treatments of this moral question: the arguments of Elizabeth
Anscombe, John C. Ford, and Paul Ramsey. These treatments seem
to ignore the distinction which I will propose. I argue that on their own
terms, and without reference to that distinction, they must be counted
as unsatisfactory.

In the second part of the paper I propose and explain my distinction.

I then explore what I take to be some of its moral implications, especially with reference to the alleged immunity of noncombatants, and I argue that it supplies what was missing or defective in the treatments previously criticized.

I. The Immunity Theorists

A number of philosophers have held that a large portion of the population of warring nations have a special moral status. This is the *noncombatant* segment of the population, and they have a moral immunity from being intentionally killed. This view seems to have been especially congenial to philosophers who have tried to apply Christian ethics to the problems of warfare. Among the philosophers who have held this view are Elizabeth Anscombe, John C. Ford, and Paul Ramsey. I shall refer to this trio of thinkers as the *immunity theorists*.

Perhaps we should indicate a little more in detail just what the immunity theorists appear to hold, specifying just what segment of the population is being discussed and just what their immunity consists in. The immunity theorists commonly admit that there is some difficulty in specifying exactly who are the noncombatants.[1] Roughly, they are those people who are not engaged in military operations and whose activity is not immediately and directly related to the war effort. Perhaps we could say that if a person is engaged only in the sort of activities which would be carried on even if the nation were not at war (or preparing for war) then that person is a noncombatant. So generally farmers, teachers, nurses, firemen, sales people, housewives, poets, children, etc. are noncombatants.[2] There are, of course, difficult cases, ranging from the high civilian official of the government to the truck driver (either military or civilian) who hauls vegetables toward the front lines. But despite the hard cases it is held that warring nations contain large numbers of readily identifiable people who are clearly noncombatants.

1. Elizabeth Anscombe, "War and Murder," *War and Morality* ed. Richard A. Wasserstrom (Belmont, Calif., 1970), p. 52; John C. Ford, "The Morality of Obliteration Bombing," ibid., pp. 19–23; Paul Ramsey, *The Just War* (New York, 1968), pp. 157, 158.

2. Ford gives a list of over 100 occupations whose practitioners he considers to be "almost without exception" noncombatants.

What of their immunity? The writers whom I consider here make use of the "principle of double-effect."[3] This involves dividing the consequences of an act (at least the foreseeable consequences) into two classes. Into the first class go those consequences which constitute the goal or purpose of the act, what the act is done for, and also those consequences which are means to those ends. Into the other class go those consequences which are neither the sought-after ends nor the means to those ends. So, for example, the bombing of a rail yard may have among its many consequences the following: the flow of supplies toward the front is disrupted, several locomotives are damaged, and a lot of smoke, dust, etc. is discharged into the air. The disruption of transport may well be the end sought by this action, and perhaps the damage to locomotives is sought as a means of disrupting transport. If so, these consequences belong in the first class, a class which I shall generally mark by using the words "intentional" or "intended." The smoke, on the other hand, though as surely foreseeable as the other effects, may be neither means nor end in this situation. It is a side-effect, and belongs in the second class (which I shall sometimes call "unintentional" or "unintended").

Now, the moral immunity of noncombatants consists, according to these writers, in the fact that their death can never, morally, be made the intended consequence of a military operation. Or to put it another way, any military operation which seeks the death of noncombatants either as an end or a means is immoral, regardless of the total good which it might accomplish.

The *unintended* death of noncombatants, on the other hand, is not absolutely forbidden. A military operation which will foreseeably result in such deaths, neither as means nor ends but as side effects, may be morally acceptable according to these writers. It will be morally acceptable if the good end which it may be expected to attain is of sufficient weight to overbalance the evil of these noncombatant deaths (as well as any other evils involved in it). This principle, sometimes called the principle of proportionality, apparently applies to foreseen but unintended noncombatant deaths in just the same way as it applies to the intended death of combatants, the destruction of resources, and so on. In all of these cases it is held to be immoral to cause many deaths,

3. Anscombe, pp. 46, 50, 51; Ford, pp. 26–28; Ramsey, pp. 347–358.

much pain, etc., in order to achieve minor goals. Here combatant and noncombatant stand on the same moral ground, and their deaths are weighed in the same balances. But when the slaying of noncombatants is envisioned as an end or, more commonly, as a means—perhaps in order to reduce the production of foodstuffs or to damage the morale of troops—then there is an unqualified judgment that the projected operation is flatly immoral. The intentional slaying of combatants, on the other hand, faces no such prohibition. This, then, is the place where the moral status of combatant and noncombatant differ sharply.

Now, if a scheme such as this is not to appear simply arbitrary it looks as though we must find some morally relevant basis for the distinction. It is perhaps worthwhile to notice that in this context the immunity of noncombatants cannot be supported by reference to the sanctity or value of human life, nor by reference to a duty not to kill our brothers, etc. For these authors recognize the moral permissibility, even perhaps the duty, of killing under certain circumstances. What must be sought is the ground of a distinction, and not merely a consideration against killing.

Such a ground, however, seems very hard to find, perhaps unexpectedly so. The crucial argument proposed by the immunity theorists turns on the notions of guilt and innocence. Anscombe, for example, says:

> Now, it is one of the most vehement and repeated teachings of the Judaeo-Christian tradition that the shedding of innocent blood is forbidden by the divine law. No man may be punished except for his own crime, and those "whose feet are swift to shed innocent blood" are always represented as God's enemies.[4]

Earlier on she says, "The principal wickedness which is a temptation to those engaged in warfare is the killing of the innocent,"[5] and she has titled one of the sections of her paper, "Innocence and the Right to Kill Intentionally." Clearly enough the notion of innocence plays a large role in her thinking on this topic. Just what that role is, or should be, will be considered shortly. Ford, in the article cited earlier, repeatedly

4. Anscombe, p. 49.
5. Ibid., p. 44.

couples the word "innocent" with "civilian" and "noncombatant." His
clearest statement, however, is in another essay. There he says:

> Catholic teaching has been unanimous for long centuries in declar-
> ing that it is never permitted to kill directly noncombatants in war-
> time. Why? Because they are innocent. That is, they are innocent
> of the violent and destructive action of war, or of any close partici-
> pation in the violent and destructive action of war. It is such par-
> ticipation *alone* that would make them legitimate targets of violent
> repression themselves.[6]

Here we have explicitly a promising candidate for the basis of the
moral distinction between combatants and noncombatants. It is promising because innocence itself seems to be a moral property. Hence,
if we could see that noncombatants were innocent while combatants
were not it would be plausible to suppose that this fact made it morally
proper to treat them in different ways.

If we are to succeed along this line of thought, then we must meet
at least two conditions. First, we must find some one sense of "innocence" such that all noncombatants are innocent and all combatants
are guilty. Second, this sense must be morally relevant, a point of the
greatest importance. We are seeking to ground a moral distinction,
and the facts to which we refer must therefore be morally relevant.
The use of a morally tinged word, such as "innocent," does not of itself
guarantee such relevance.

Well, is there a suitable sense for "innocent"? Ford said that noncombatants "are innocent of the violent and destructive action of war."
Anscombe, writing of the people who can properly be attacked with
deadly force, says, "What is required, for the people attacked to be
noninnocent in the relevant sense, is that they themselves be engaged
in an objectively unjust proceeding which the attacker has the right
to make his concern; or—the commonest case—should be unjustly attacking him." On the other hand, she speaks of "people whose mere
existence and activity supporting existence by growing crops, making
clothes, etc.," might contribute to the war effort, and she says, "such

6. John C. Ford, "The Hydrogen Bombing of Cities," *Morality and Modern
Warfare* ed. William J. Nagle (Baltimore: Helicon Press, 1960), p. 98.

people are innocent and it is murderous to attack them, or make them a target for an attack which he judges will help him towards victory."[7] These passages contain, I think, the best clues we have as to the sense of "innocent" in these authors.

It is probably evident enough that this sense of "innocent" is vague in a way parallel to the vagueness of "noncombatant." It will leave us with troublesome borderline cases. In itself, that does not seem to me a crucial defect. But perhaps it is a clue to an important failing. For I suspect that there is this parallel vagueness because "innocent" here is just a synonym for "noncombatant."

What can Ford mean by saying that some people are "innocent of the violent and destructive action of war" except that those people are not engaged in the violence of war? Must not Anscombe mean essentially the same thing when she says that the noninnocent are those who are themselves "engaged in an objectively unjust proceeding"? But we need not rely wholly on these rhetorical questions. Ramsey makes this point explicitly. He first distinguishes between close and remote cooperation in military operations, and then he alludes to the distinction between the "guilty" and the "innocent." Of this distinction he says, "These are very misleading terms, since their meaning is exhaustively stated under the first contrast, and is reducible to degrees of actual participation in hostile force."[8] In this judgment Ramsey certainly seems to me to be right.

Now, we should notice carefully that a person may be an enthusiastic supporter of the unjust war and its unjust aims, he may give to it his voice and his vote, he may have done everything in his power to procure it when it was yet but a prospect, now that it is in progress he may contribute to it both his savings and the work which he knows best how to do, and he may avidly hope to share in the unjust gains which will follow if the war is successful. But such a person may clearly be a noncombatant, and (in the sense of the immunity theorists) unquestionably "innocent" of the war. On the other hand, a young man of limited mental ability and almost no education may be drafted, put into uniform, trained for a few weeks, and sent to the front as a replacement in a low-grade unit. He may have no under-

7. Anscombe, p. 45.   8. Ramsey, p. 153.

standing of what the war is about, and no heart for it. He might want nothing more than to go back to his town and the life he led before. But he is "engaged," carrying ammunition, perhaps, or stringing telephone wire or even banging away ineffectually with his rifle. He is without doubt a combatant, and "guilty," a fit subject for intentional slaughter. Is it not clear that "innocence," as used here, leaves out entirely all of the relevant moral considerations—that it has no moral content at all? Anscombe suggests that intentional killing during warfare should be construed on the model of punishing people for their crimes, and we must see to it, if we are to be moral, that we punish someone only for his own crime and not for someone else's. But if we construe the criminality involved in an unjust war in any reasonable moral sense then it must either be the case that many noncombatants are guilty of that criminality or else many combatants are innocent. In fact, it will probably be the case that *both* of these things are true. Only if we were to divest "crime" of its moral bearings could we make it fit the combatant/noncombatant distinction in modern wars.

The fact that both Anscombe and Ramsey[9] use the analogy of the criminal in discussing this topic suggests that there is an important fact about warfare which is easily overlooked. And that is that warfare, unlike ordinary criminal activity, is not an activity in which individuals engage qua individuals or as members of voluntary associations. They enter into war as members of nations. It is more proper to say that the nation is at war than that its soldiers are at war. This does not, of course, entail that individuals have no moral responsibility for their acts in war. But it does suggest that moral responsibility may not be distributed between combatant and noncombatant in the same way as between a criminal and his children. Many of the men who are soldiers, perhaps most of them, would not be engaged in military operations at all if they did not happen to be citizens of a warring nation. But noncombatants are citizens of warring nations in exactly the same sense as are soldiers. However these facts are to be analyzed they should warn us not to rely too heavily on the analogy with ordinary criminality.

We seem, then, to be caught in a dilemma. We can perhaps find

9. Ibid., p. 144.

some sense for notions such as *innocence* and *criminality* which will make them fit the distinction in which we are interested. But the price of doing so seems to be that of divesting these notions of the moral significance which they require if they are to justify the moral import of the distinction itself. In the ordinary senses, on the other hand, these notions do have the required moral bearings. But in their ordinary senses they do not fit the desired distinction. In neither way, therefore, can the argument from innocence be made to work, and the alleged moral immunity of noncombatants seems to be left as an arbitrary claim.

II. CONVENTION-DEPENDENT MORALITY

Despite the failure of these arguments I have recently come to think that there may be something of importance in this distinction after all, and even that it may have an important moral bearing. How might this be?

Imagine a statesman reflecting on the costliness of war, its cost in human life and human suffering. He observes that these costs are normally very high, sometimes staggering. Furthermore, he accepts the principle of proportionality. A consequence of this is that he sometimes envisions a just war for a just cause, but nevertheless decides not to prosecute that war even though he believes it could be won. For the cost of winning would be so high as to outweigh the good which would be attained. So he must sometimes let oppression flourish and injustice hold sway. And even in those wars which can be prosecuted the costs eat very seriously into the benefits.

Then he has an idea. Suppose—just suppose—that one could replace warfare with a less costly substitute. Suppose, for example, that one could introduce a convention—and actually get it accepted and followed by the nations—a convention which replaced warfare with single combat. Under this convention, when two nations arrived at an impasse which would otherwise have resulted in war they would instead choose, each of them, a single champion (doubtless a volunteer). These two men would then meet in mortal combat, and whoever won, killing his opponent or driving him from the field, would win for his nation. To that nation would then be ceded whatever territory, influence, or other prize would have been sought in the war, and the nation whose champion was defeated would lose correspondingly.

Suppose, too, that the statesman believes that if such a convention were to come into force his own nation could expect to win and lose such combats in about the same proportion as it could now expect to win and lose ordinary wars. The same types of questions would be settled by such combats as would otherwise be settled by war (though perhaps more questions would be submitted to combat than would be submitted to war), and approximately the same resolutions would be arrived at. The costs, however—human death and suffering—would be reduced by several orders of magnitude. Would that not be an attractive prospect? I think it would.

While the prospect may seem attractive it may also strike us as hopelessly utopian, hardly to be given a serious thought. There seems to be some evidence, however, that exactly this substitution was actually attempted in ancient times. Ancient literature contains at least two references to such attempts. One is in the Bible, I Samuel 17, the combat between David and Goliath. The other is in the *Iliad*, book 3, where it is proposed to settle the seige of Troy in the very beginning by single combat between Menelaus and Paris. It may be significant that neither of these attempts appears to have been successful. The single combats were followed by bloodier and more general fighting. Perhaps this substitute for warfare is too cheap; it cannot be made practical, and nations just will not consent in the end to abide by this convention. But consider, on the one hand, warfare which is limited only by the moral requirements that the ends sought should be just and that the means used should be proportionate, and, on the other hand, the convention of single combat as a substitute for warfare. Between these extremes there lie a vast number of other possible conventions which might be canvassed in the search for a less costly substitute for war. I suggest that the long struggle, in the western world at least, to limit military operations to "counter-forces" strategies, thus sparing civilian populations, is just such an attempt.

If I am right about this, then the moral aspects of the matter must be approached in a way rather different from that of the immunity theorists. Some, but not all, of their conclusions can be accepted, and somewhat different grounds must be given for them. These thinkers have construed the immunity of noncombatants as though it were a moral fact which was independent of any actual or envisioned convention or practice. And they have consequently sought to support this immunity by argument which makes no reference to convention. I have already argued that their attempts were failures. What I suggest now is that all such attempts *must* be failures, for they mistake the sort of moral requirement which is under consideration. Let me try to make this clearer.

I find it plausible to suppose that I have a moral obligation to refrain from wantonly murdering my neighbors. And it also seems plausible to discuss this, perhaps in utilitarian terms, or in terms of the will of God, or of natural law, or in terms of a rock-bottom deontological requirement, but in any case without essential reference to the laws and customs of our nation. We might, indeed, easily imagine our laws and customs to be other than they are with respect to murder. But we would then judge the moral adequacy and value of such alternative laws and customs by reference to the moral obligation I have mentioned and not vice versa. On the other hand, I may also have a moral obligation to pay a property tax or to drive on the right side of the street. It does not seem plausible to suppose, however, that one can discuss these duties without immediately referring to our laws and customs. And it seems likely that different laws would have generated different moral duties, e.g. driving on the left. These latter are examples of "convention-dependent" moral obligations. More formally, I will say that a given moral obligation is convention-dependent if and only if (1) given that a certain convention, law, custom, etc., is actually in force one really does have an obligation to act in conformity with that convention, and (2) there is an alternative law, custom, etc. (or lack thereof) such that if that had been in force one would not have had the former obligation.

At this point, before developing the way in which it may apply to warfare, let me forestall some possible misunderstandings by a series of brief comments on this notion. I am not claiming, nor do I believe, that all laws, customs, etc., generate corresponding moral obligations. But some do. I am not denying that one may seek, and perhaps find, some more general moral law, perhaps independent of convention, which explains why this convention generates the more specific obligation. I claim only that one cannot account for the specific obligation apart from the convention. Finally, I am not denying that one might have an obligation, perhaps independent of convention, to try to change a convention of this sort. For I think it possible that one might simultaneously have a moral obligation to conform to a certain convention and also a moral obligation to replace that convention, and thus to eliminate the first obligation.

Now, the core of my suggestion with respect to the immunity of noncombatants is this. The immunity of noncombatants is best thought of as a convention-dependent obligation related to a convention which substitutes for warfare a certain form of limited combat. How does this bear on some of the questions which we have been discussing?

To begin with, we might observe that the convention itself is presumably to be justified by its expectable results. (Perhaps we can refer to some moral rule to the effect that we should minimize social costs such as death and injury.) It seems plausible to suppose that the counter-forces convention, if followed, will reduce the pain and death involved in combat—will reduce it, that is, compared to unlimited warfare. There are surely other possible conventions which, if followed, would reduce those costs still more, e.g. the substitution of single combat. Single combat, however, is probably not a live contender because there is almost no chance that such a convention would actually be followed. It is possible, however, that there is some practical convention which is preferable to the present counter-forces convention. If so, the fact that it is preferable is a strong reason in favor of supposing that there is a moral obligation to promote its adoption.

It does not follow, however, that we now have a duty to act in conformity with this other possible convention. For the results of acting in conformity with a preferable convention which is not widely observed may be much worse than the results of acting in conformity with a less desirable convention which is widely observed. We might, for example, discover that a "left-hand" pattern of traffic flow would be preferable to the present system of "right-hand" rules, in that it would result in fewer accidents, etc. The difference might be so significant that we really would be morally derelict if we did not try to institute a change in our laws. We would be acquiescing in a very costly procedure when a more economical one was at hand. But it would be a disaster, and, I suspect, positively immoral, for a few of us to begin driving on the left before the convention was changed. In cases of convention-dependent obligations the question of what convention is actually in force is one of considerable moral import. That one is reminded to take this question seriously is one of the important differences between this approach and that of the immunity theorists.

Perhaps the counter-forces convention is not really operative now in a substantial way. I do not know. Doubtless, it suffered a severe blow in World War II, not least from British and American bombing strategies. Traffic rules are embedded in a broad, massive, comparatively stable social structure which makes their status comparatively resistant to erosion by infraction. Not so, however, for a convention of warfare. It has little status except in its actual observance, and depends greatly on the mutual trust of the belligerents; hence it is especially vulnerable to abrogation by a few contrary acts. Here arises a related difference with the immunity theorists. Taking the obligation to be convention-independent they reject argument based on the fact that "the enemy did it first," etc.[10] If the obligation were independent they would be correct in this. But for convention-dependent obligations, what one's opponent does, what "everyone is doing," etc., are facts of great moral importance. Such facts help to determine within what convention, if any, one is operating, and thus they help one to discover what his moral duties are.

If we were to decide that the counter-forces convention was dead at present, or, indeed, that no convention at all with respect to warfare was operative now, it would not follow that warfare was immoral. Nor, on the other hand, would it follow that warfare was beyond all moral rules, an area in which "anything goes." Instead, we would simply go back to warfare per se, limited only by independent moral requirements, such as those of justice and proportionality. That would, on the whole, probably be a more costly way of handling such problems. But if we live in a time when the preferable substitutes are not available, then we must either forgo the goods or bear the higher costs. If we had no traffic laws or customs, traffic would be even more dangerous and

10. For example, Ford, "The Morality of Obliteration Bombing," pp. 20, 33.

Conventions and the Morality of War

costly than it is now. Traveling, however, might still be justified, if the reason for traveling were sufficiently important.

In such a case, of course, there would be no obligation to drive on the right, or in any regular manner, nor would there be any benefit in it. Probably the best thing would be to drive in a completely ad hoc way, seeking the best maneuver in each situation as it arose. More generally, and ignoring for the moment a final consideration which will be discussed below, there is no obligation and no benefit associated with the unilateral observance of a convention. If one's cause is unjust then one ought not to kill noncombatants. But that is because of the independent moral prohibition against prosecuting such a war at all, and has nothing to do with any special immunity of noncombatants. If one's cause is just, but the slaying of noncombatants will not advance it to any marked degree, then one ought not to slay them. But this is just the requirement of proportionality, and applies equally and in the same way to combatants. If one's cause is just and the slaying of noncombatants would advance it—if, in other words, one is not prevented by considerations of justice and proportionality—this is the crucial case. If one refrains unilaterally in this situation then he seems to choose the greater of two evils (or the lesser of two goods). By hypothesis, the good achieved, i.e. the lives spared, is not as weighty as the evil which he allows in damage to the prospects for justice or in the even more costly alternative measures, e.g. the slaying of a larger number of combatants, which he must undertake. Now, if the relevant convention were operative, then his refraining from counter-population strategies here would be related to his enemy's similar restraint, and indeed it would be related to the strategies which would be used in future wars. These larger considerations might well tip the balance in the other direction. But by hypothesis we are considering the case in which there is no such convention, and so these larger considerations do not arise. One acts unilaterally. In such a situation it certainly appears that one would have chosen the worse of the two alternatives. It is hard to suppose that one is morally obligated to do so.

I said above that we were ignoring for the moment one relevant consideration. It should not be ignored forever. I have already called attention to the fact that conventions of warfare are not, like traffic rules, embedded in a more massive social structure. This makes them especially precarious, as we have noted. But it also bears on the way in which they may be adopted. One such way, perhaps a rather important way, is for one party to the hostilities to signal his willingness to abide by such a convention by undertaking some unilateral restraint on his own part. If the opponent does not reciprocate, then the offer has failed and it goes no further. If the opponent does reciprocate, however, then the area of restraint may be broadened, and a kind of mutual respect and confidence may grow up between the belligerents. Each comes to rely on the other to keep the (perhaps unspoken) agreement, and therefore each is willing to forgo the immediate advantage which might accrue to him from breaking it. If this happens, then a new convention has begun its precarious life. This may be an event well worth seeking.

Not only may it be worth seeking, it may be worth paying something for it. For a significant increase in the likelihood that a worthwhile convention will be adopted it may be worth accepting an increased risk or a higher immediate cost in lives and suffering. So there may be some justification in unilateral restraint after all, even in the absence of a convention. But this justification is prospective and finite. It envisions the possibility that such a convention may arise in the future as a result of this restraint. Consequently, the justification should be proportioned to some judgment as to the likelihood of that event, and it should be reevaluated as future events unfold.

III. CONVENTION VS. MORALITY

I began by examining some attempts to defend a certain alleged moral rule of war, the immunity of noncombatants. These defenses have in common the fact that they construe this moral rule as independent of any human law, custom, etc. I then argued that these defenses fail because they leave a certain distinction without moral support, and yet the distinction is essential to the rule. Turning then to the task of construction rather than criticism, I suggested that the immunity of noncombatants is not an independent moral rule but rather a part of a convention which sets up a morally desirable alternative to war. I argued then that some conventions, including this one, generate special moral obligations which cannot be satisfactorily explained and defended without reference to the convention. And in the final pages I explored some of the special features of the obligation at hand and of the arguments which are relevant to it.

The distinction I have drawn is that between warfare per se on the one hand, and, on the other hand, international combats which are limited by convention and custom. But the point of the distinction is to clarify our thinking about the *morality* of such wars and combats. That is where its value must be tested.

ROBERT K. FULLINWIDER   War and Innocence

I

In a war, is it morally permissible intentionally to kill noncombatants?
Elizabeth Anscombe and Paul Ramsey argue that noncombatants may
not be intentionally killed.[1] We are obligated to refrain from such
killing because it is murder; and it is murder because noncombatants
are innocent.

George Mavrodes questions the grounds for asserting that in war
noncombatants are "innocent" and combatants are "guilty." If immunity of noncombatants from killing is to be established this way,
he says, then we must find a "sense of 'innocence' such that all noncombatants are innocent and all combatants are guilty," and "this
sense must be morally relevant." Mavrodes fears, however, that immunity theorists such as Anscombe and Ramsey are actually using
"innocent" and "noncombatant" synonymously. He believes that the
sense of "innocence" used in their arguments has no moral content.[2]

Mavrodes' main argument is this. There are noncombatants who
may enthusiastically endorse and support the war their nation is
waging, while there are combatants who may be under arms unhappily and unwillingly, who may not support the war but are unable to

[1]. Elizabeth Anscombe, "War and Murder," in *War and Morality*, ed. Richard
Wasserstrom (Belmont, Ca., 1970); Paul Ramsey, *The Last War* (New York,
1968). See also John C. Ford, "The Morality of Obliteration Bombing," in *War
and Morality*.

[2]. George I. Mavrodes, "Conventions and the Morality of War," *Philosophy &
Public Affairs* 4, no. 2 (Winter 1975): 121, 123.

resist conscription. It is odd to claim that the enthusiastically supportive noncombatant is innocent and the reluctant conscript guilty.
"Is it not clear," Mavrodes asks, "that 'innocence,' as used here, leaves
out entirely all morally relevant considerations . . . ?"[3]

Anscombe and Ramsey both invite this sort of counterargument by
the way they defend their immunity thesis. Anscombe implies that the
thesis is rooted in the Principle of Punishment: no man is to be punished except for his own crime.[4] Ramsey, too, employs the model of
the criminal in defending the thesis.[5] But, from the point of view of
punishment, it is odd, if not perverse, to view the enthusiastically
supportive noncombatant as innocent and the reluctant combatant as
guilty. Mavrodes, in my judgment, is right in believing this defense
fails to establish the immunity of noncombatants from intentional
killing.

Mavrodes believes that the obligation not to kill noncombatants
intentionally can rest only on a convention among nations. Such an
obligation, if it exists, is at best contingent, conditioned as it is on the
existence of such a convention in force. Anscombe and Ramsey believe
the obligation to refrain from intentionally killing noncombatants is
noncontingent. It is not convention-dependent.[6]

In this paper I shall briefly sketch an argument for the immunity
of noncombatants which avoids Mavrodes' criticisms. It will establish
that in warfare there is a morally relevant distinction between noncombatants and combatants which prohibits the intentional killing of
the former at the same time as it justifies the intentional killing of the
latter. My argument will appeal to a nonconventional principle, and
thus the obligation deriving from the principle will not be convention-
dependent (or anyway not wholly so). I will then go on to show that
even if certain considerations undercut drawing the line of immunity
between combatants and noncombatants, a weaker version of the
immunity thesis is still viable.

3. Mavrodes, pp. 122–123.
4. Anscombe, p. 49; Mavrodes, pp. 120, 123.
5. Ramsey, p. 144; Mavrodes, p. 123.
6. For Mavrodes' definition of convention-dependent obligation, see p. 126 of
his article.

II

To set the scene, first consider an example. Jones is walking down a street. Smith steps from behind the corner of a nearby building and begins to fire a gun at Jones, with the appearance of deliberate intent to kill Jones. Surrounded by buildings, Jones is afforded no means of escape. Jones, who is carrying a gun himself, shoots at Smith and kills him.

Jones is morally justified in killing Smith by the Principle of Self-Defense. Smith's actions put Jones' life directly and immediately in mortal jeopardy, and Jones' killing Smith was necessary to end that threat. From the point of view of self-defense, these facts about Smith's actions are the *only* relevant ones. The moral justification of the killing rests on them alone given the legitimacy of self-defense.

But let me now sketch in some possible background circumstances to Smith's assault on Jones. Suppose Smith's wife, spurned by Jones when she made advances toward him, tells Smith she has been raped by Jones. Furious, and egged on by his wife, Smith seeks out Jones and begins firing. Or, suppose Smith, through heavy gambling losses, is in debt to the mob for $100,000. The mobsters propose to Smith that if he will kill Jones (a crusading district attorney, say), they will forgive his debt. Unable to pay the debt, and knowing what will happen to him if he fails to pay it, Smith seeks out Jones and begins firing. Or, suppose the mobsters kidnap Smith's children and threaten to kill them unless he kills Jones. Driven by the threat, Smith seeks out Jones and begins firing.

None of this background information alters the situation from the point of view of self-defense. Whatever prompted Smith to fire at Jones, the justification for Jones' killing Smith lies solely in the fact that Smith was the direct and immediate agent of a threat against Jones' life. From the point of view of self-defense, this fact justifies Jones in killing Smith—and *only* Smith.

Again, suppose that Smith's wife was standing across the street egging Smith on as he fired at Jones. Jones, though he justifiably shot Smith in self-defense, could not justifiably turn his gun on the wife in self-defense. Or suppose the mobsters were parked across the street to observe Smith. After killing Smith, Jones could not turn his gun on them (assuming they were unarmed). No matter how causally implicated the wife or the mobsters were in Smith's assault on Jones, in the situation it was only Smith who was the agent of immediate threat to Jones; the wife and the mobsters were not posing a direct and immediate danger. From the point of view of justifiably killing in self-defense, they are not justifiably liable to be killed by Jones; they are immune.

There is a point of view from which these background features I have drawn in become morally relevant, namely the point of view of retribution or punishment. Smith's wife and the mobsters would be viewed as morally culpable for their contribution to Smith's assault on Jones' life. They ought to be punished. Perhaps Jones might be justified in taking his own retribution, and killing the wife or mobsters in revenge; but even if he is justified in killing them in retribution, he still cannot justify killing them on the grounds of self-defense.

In these cases of killing and attempted killing there are two points of view: the point of view of self-defense and the point of view of punishment. Some considerations that become morally relevant from the second point of view in justifying killing are not relevant from the first point of view. We use the notions of guilt and innocence almost always in connection with the second point of view, the perspective of punishment. From that point of view, Smith's wife and the mobsters are as guilty as Smith. In the instance where the mobsters cause Smith to act under duress, perhaps they are more guilty.

If we were to speak of innocence and guilt as categories applying in cases of self-defense, then for the purpose of justifiably killing in self-defense and from that point of view we would say that Smith alone was guilty (justifiably liable to killing) and his wife and the mobsters were innocent (not justifiably liable to killing), though all are guilty from the point of view of punishment.

It should be obvious now how my argument for the immunity thesis is going to run. The moral relevance of the distinction in war between combatants and noncombatants will be derived from the Principle of Self-Defense. Because we most commonly speak of innocence in connection with crime and punishment and because we also speak of innocent victims of war, Anscombe and Ramsey have been led to defend the innocents in war by appeal to the wrong model. For these same reasons, Mavrodes has failed to see an alternative to his conventionalism.

III

I shall now sketch an argument for the moral immunity of noncombatants from intentional killing.

The question at hand is the killing in war and its justifiability. Why is any killing at all justified? I claim that a nation may justifiably kill in self-defense. From the point of view of self-defense, only those are justifiably liable to be killed who pose the immediate and direct jeopardy. In the case of war, it is nations' armed forces which are the agents of the jeopardy. In a war, the armed forces of nation A stand to opponent nation B as Smith stood to Jones.[7] It is against them that B may defend itself by the use of force. The active combatants, their arms, ammunition, war machines and facilities, are the legitimate targets of intentional destruction.

Though A's civilian population may support its war against B and contribute to it in various ways, they stand to B as Smith's wife or the mobsters stood to Jones. For the purpose of justifiably killing in self-defense and from that point of view, the civilian population is morally immune—it is "innocent." To intentionally kill noncombatants is to kill beyond the scope of self-defense. It is to kill unjustifiably from the point of view of self-defense.

This, in brief, is my argument. It provides for drawing a line between combatants and noncombatants, and prohibits intentionally killing the latter. This is just where the immunity theorists want to draw the line of prohibition. Furthermore, they see the prohibition as "natural," not convention-dependent. My argument supports them in this. The distinction between combatants and noncombatants derives from the operation of the Principle of Self-Defense. Our obligation not to kill noncombatants stems from our obligation not to kill without justification; and the Principle of Self-Defense justifies killing only combatants. Since both the obligation to not kill without justifica-

7. In a war each side is likely to view the other as the aggressor and itself as the defender; thus each side will claim to be acting in self-defense. I ignore the question of how we determine who is correct in making such a claim. My argument has to do with how *much* one may claim if one claims to act in self-defense.

tion and the Principle of Self-Defense are "natural" rather than conventional, the moral immunity of noncombatants does not rest (solely) upon the existence of appropriate conventions among nations.[8]

IV

From the point of view of killing in self-defense in war, Mavrodes' reluctant conscript is "guilty" (justifiably liable to killing), and his noncombatant partisan is "innocent" (not justifiably liable to killing). To say that the reluctant conscript is guilty and the noncombatant partisan is innocent is to stand the matter on its head, claims Mavrodes. So it is—from the point of view of punishment. This, I have urged, is not the fundamentally governing point of view when it comes to justifying killing in war. The innocence of the noncombatant seems inexplicable to Mavrodes because he takes up the wrong point of view for evaluating killing in war. He is, of course, encouraged to take up this view by Anscombe's and Ramsey's own arguments in defense of the innocence of noncombatants. Viewing killing in war from this evaluative standpoint, and finding it incapable of explaining the prohibition against killing combatants, Mavrodes turns to conventionalism.

Might it not be contended against my defense of the immunity thesis that the point of view of self-defense is not the sole governing point of view when it comes to killing in war? Nations, it might be argued, exist in a state of nature, and thus possess the right to exact their own punishments on transgressors. Thus, in war, justifying deliberate killing may be done by appeal to both the Principle of Self-Defense *and* the Principle of Punishment. Finally, to the extent that retribution justifies some of the killing in war, it will justify killing some noncombatants.[9]

I have two answers to this challenge. The first answer preserves

8. In his argument against Anscombe and Ramsey, Mavrodes does not claim that conventionalism is true because the Principle of Punishment, to which they appeal, is itself conventional. Mavrodes does not dispute their assumption that the Principle of Punishment is a nonconventional source of obligation. Nor does Mavrodes support his conventionalism by arguing that *all* moral obligation is convention-dependent. Thus, I take it that the Principle of Self-Defense and the obligation not to kill without justification are nonconventional sources of obligation, since they are at least as nonconventional as the Principle of Punishment.

9. Some Allied air raids against German cities in World War II seem to have been clearly punitive in intent.

the strong immunity thesis, but it requires an assumption of fact which may, theoretically, not obtain. The second answer, dropping the assumption, requires me to weaken the immunity thesis.

For purposes of argument, I will concede that nations have the right to exact their own punishment in war. Even so, the Principle of Punishment justifies punishing *only* the *morally guilty* (culpable from the point of view of punishment), not the *morally innocent* (innocent from the point of view of punishment). Techniques of warfare—combat, bombing, shelling, burning—are too indiscriminate in their destruction to serve as legitimate instruments of punishment. They cannot be used discriminatingly between the morally guilty and the morally innocent. It is not justified by the Principle of Punishment intentionally to kill the morally innocent. If a nation claims punitive rights in war, it must adopt mechanisms of punishment which will discriminate between those who deserve punishment and those who do not. Bombing, shelling, and other such techniques kill guilty and innocent alike. Consequently, if we wish to justify killing during war by the means of war, the only applicable perspective is self-defense.[10]

If, however, contrary to the facts, there were some perfectly discriminating techniques of warfare, then, since I have conceded the right of nations to exact their own punishment, I see no argument against a nation legitimately taking up both points of view in its prosecution of a war. Some of the justified killing will be justified by self-defense, some by merited punishment. This would require a weakening of the immunity thesis, since the Principle of Punishment would justify some intentional killing of noncombatants, namely those that were morally guilty. Nevertheless, a version of the immunity thesis can be preserved: some line prohibiting intentional killing would still be mandated. The Principle of Self-Defense will

10. The Principle of Self-Defense also requires discrimination—between combatants and noncombatants. Since usually combatants are in uniform, with weapons, on battlefields, instruments of war can be used in a way which (roughly) avoids the death of noncombatants. However, instruments which cannot be used in a discriminating way, and whose use entails extensive noncombatant casualties (e.g. hydrogen bombs), are ruled out for use even in self-defense. See Richard Wasserstrom, "On the Morality of War: A Preliminary Inquiry," in *War and Morality*, pp. 100–101. (See also pp. 89 ff. where Wasserstrom discusses the justification of self-defense; and pp. 94–96, where he discusses the meaning of innocence in war.)

justify intentionally killing combatants, even the morally innocent among them. The Principle of Punishment will justify killing (if this is proportional to the crime) the morally guilty noncombatant. But neither principle will sanction or permit the intentional killing of the morally innocent noncombatant, many of whom will be found in any nation at war.[11] There will thus be a line of immunity required to be drawn around a certain class in war, the class of morally innocent noncombatants. We shall be morally obliged to refrain from intentionally killing members of this class, and this moral obligation will not disappear in the absence of any particular convention among nations.

Because of the indiscriminate nature of modern techniques of destruction, I see two reasons why the line of immunity is to be maintained between combatants and noncombatants. First, if nations recognize the Principle of Punishment, they may nevertheless be required to refrain from attempting to use it as a justification for killing because they shall not be able to meet the discrimination requirement. Second, nations may find it collectively beneficial to agree to forgo the exercise of their punishment rights during war (the exercise of which is morally ruled out anyway). They might thus, as Mavrodes suggests, adopt conventions confirming the line of immunity during warfare between combatant and noncombatant. To this extent, Mavrodes' conventionalism has support. The obligation not to kill noncombatants may be partly conventional; but if my arguments have been correct, it is not wholly so.[12]

11. Consider merely what percentage of a nation's population is made up of children under the age of ten.

12. In order to present a clean line of argument I have omitted discussion of various questions and qualifications that must be dealt with in any thorough defense of killing in war. Sometimes self-defense will not sufficiently justify killing. The Principle of Punishment may not justify any killing—I only assume that it does in order to consider a strong objection to the immunity thesis. I omit important questions such as whether persons have a moral right to a hearing before they may be punished, and so on. I believe that none of these issues, when resolved, will justify *more* killing.

LAWRENCE A. ALEXANDER   Self-Defense and the Killing
of Noncombatants: A Reply
to Fullinwider

In a recent article[1] Robert Fullinwider argued that the distinction
between combatants and noncombatants is morally relevant (in a
sense unrelated to the existence of a specific convention among
nations)[2] to the question of who among the enemy may be intentionally killed by a nation acting in self-defense. He concedes that the
distinction is not based on the relative moral guilt or innocence of the
two groups in connection with the prosecution of the war, recognizing that many combatants might be morally innocent (for example,
reluctant conscripts) and many noncombatants morally guilty (for
example, the governmental officials who launched the war). Moreover, he admits that guilt or innocence is relevant to the question
of who should be punished by the defending nation. However, says
Fullinwider, punishment of the guilty is not the only justification for
intentional killing in war. Under the Principle of Self-Defense, innocent combatants, but not innocent noncombatants, may also justifiably be killed.

I do not intend to deny the widely held view that morally innocent
persons may be intentionally killed in self-defense (although I believe
a case can be made against it).[3] Rather, I intend to show that the

1. Robert K. Fullinwider, "War and Innocence," *Philosophy & Public Affairs* 5,
no. 1 (Fall 1975): 90.

2. See George I. Mavrodes, "Conventions and the Morality of War," *Philosophy
& Public Affairs* 4, no. 2 (Winter 1975): 121, 126.

3. The formulation I shall give of the principle that allows the killing of innocent persons in self-defense can, for example, logically be extended to cover acts
of terrorism, atomic bombings of cities, etc. See text and notes at fnn. 6 and 7
below.

permissibility of killing innocents in self-defense does not, as Fullinwider maintains, justify the moral distinction between combatants
and noncombatants.

The heart of Fullinwider's argument is the following passage:

> . . . Suppose Smith, through heavy gambling losses, is in debt to
> the mob for $100,000. The mobsters propose to Smith that if he
> will kill Jones (a crusading district attorney, say), they will forgive
> his debt. Unable to pay the debt, and knowing what will happen to
> him if he fails to pay it, Smith seeks out Jones and begins firing.
> Or, suppose the mobsters kidnap Smith's children and threaten to
> kill them unless he kills Jones. Driven by the threat, Smith seeks
> out Jones and begins firing.
>
> None of this background information alters the situation from
> the point of view of self-defense. Whatever prompted Smith to fire
> at Jones, the justification for Jones' killing Smith lies solely in the
> fact that Smith was the direct and immediate agent of a threat
> against Jones' life. From the point of view of self-defense, this fact
> justifies Jones in killing Smith—and *only* Smith.
>
> Again . . . suppose the mobsters were parked across the street to
> observe Smith. After killing Smith, Jones could not turn his gun
> on them (assuming they were unarmed). No matter how causally
> implicated . . . the mobsters were in Smith's assault on Jones, in the
> situation it was only Smith who was the agent of immediate threat
> to Jones; . . . the mobsters were not posing a direct and immediate
> danger. From the point of view of justifiably killing in self-defense,
> they are not justifiably liable to be killed by Jones; they are
> immune.[4]

Fullinwider is correct that *after* killing Smith, Jones may not invoke
the Principle of Self-Defense to then turn and kill the mobsters. *The
threat to his life has been removed.* At most the mobsters may be
punished for their guilt in instigating the attempted murder.

However, Fullinwider's hypothetical is inapposite when we are discussing whether noncombatants along with combatants may be killed
in an on-going war. Surely no one has contended that after surrender,
the point analogous to the killing of Smith by Jones, innocent non-

4. Fullinwider, "War and Innocence," pp. 92–93.

combatants may still be killed in self-defense. (Indeed, no one has contended as much for innocent combatants either.) Fullinwider has constructed a straw man.

Let us amend Fullinwider's hypothetical to make it relevant to the issue he is addressing. Suppose the situation is the same except that Jones has not yet killed Smith. May Jones invoke the Principle of Self-Defense to kill the mobsters instead of Smith if by doing so he will cause Smith to relent? Of course he may. If the mobsters had a gun trained on Smith and had ordered him to kill Jones, and he were about to comply, Jones not only could, but should, kill the mobsters rather than Smith if killing them would be no riskier than killing Smith and would remove the threat to Jones by removing Smith's motive for killing him. Jones should kill the mobsters in such a situation even if the mobsters could not kill Jones directly (say, because the range of their guns was sufficient to reach Smith but not Jones, who carried a longer-range gun). From the standpoint of the Principle of Self-Defense, both the mobsters and Smith are necessary causes of the danger to Jones because killing either the mobsters or Smith removes the danger. Jones should, therefore, kill the ones who are morally guilty, not the one who is morally innocent. Such an interpretation of the Principle of Self-Defense is consistent with its application in the law,[5] and any interpretation that permitted only the killing of Smith would be morally perverse.

Indeed, it would be morally perverse to limit Jones' right of self-defense to the killing of Smith, even where the mobsters have not threatened Smith's life. Suppose the chief mobster has merely offered Smith money. The mobster, unarmed, is across the street from Smith and Jones, so that if Jones kills the mobster, Smith will realize that he will not get paid for killing Jones. Jones should be able to kill the mobster instead of Smith if the mobster is morally as guilty or guiltier than Smith (who might have been driven to the wall financially).

5. Although I have found no cases directly on point, the interpretation follows logically from a combination of the two legal principles of self-defense and defense of others. Because Smith is otherwise justifiably subject to being killed by Jones in self-defense if the mobsters are not killed first (thus removing Smith's motive for threatening Jones), Jones' killing the mobsters is a defense of Smith's life and hence legally justifiable (assuming the requirements in the text at fnn. 6 and 7 below are otherwise met).

What I propose as the correct formulation of the Principle of Self-Defense is that X (a person or persons) may be killed in self-defense, regardless of X's moral innocence, if the defender perceives (reasonably) that: (1) there exists the requisite threshold level of danger or greater; (2) killing X will reduce that danger;[6] (3) more desirable courses of action,[7] such as killing fewer or guiltier persons, or not

6. It should be noted that condition (2) of the formulation does not specify how killing X will reduce the danger. Suppose A is threatened by B and so kills C, an innocent party, in order to frighten B or cause C to fall on B and remove B's threat. A libertarian, who believes it wrong generally for one to appropriate other persons' bodies or products in order to make himself better off than he would be had the other persons not existed, would object to such a use of the Principle of Self-Defense. However, an egalitarian, who would not object to appropriating other persons' bodies or products, would have difficulty in distinguishing this use of the Principle of Self-Defense from other uses involving the killing of innocent persons.

7. "More desirable courses of action" is often construed to mean those courses of action not involving major sacrifices of the defender's rights. For example:

> . . . The majority of American jurisdictions holds that the defender (who was not the original aggressor) need not retreat, even though he can do so safely, before using deadly force upon an assailant whom [sic] he reasonably believes will kill him or do him serious bodily harm. A strong minority, however, taking what might be regarded as a more civilized view, holds that he must retreat ("retreat to the wall," it is sometimes said), before using deadly force, if he can do so in safety. But even in those jurisdictions which require retreat, the defender need not retreat unless he knows he can do so in complete safety; and he need not retreat from his home or place of business, except perhaps when the assailant is a co-occupant of those premises. [La Fave & Scott, *Criminal Law* (1972), pp. 395–396]

However, one might reasonably ask why there should not be an absolute duty of retreat when X (the one to be killed in self-defense) is morally innocent. Indeed, why should our rights not be constrained generally so that we might avoid having to take one innocent life in order to save another?

It should be noted also that if an innocent person, A, attempts to exercise his right to kill another innocent person, B, in self-defense, A's action presumably gives rise to a right in B to kill A in self-defense. Cf. Robert Nozick, *Anarchy, State, and Utopia* (1974), pp. 34–35. Moreover, third parties apparently may intervene on behalf of either. Would not a cogent moral position attempt to eliminate the possibility of such situations, perhaps by positing rigorous duties to avoid sacrificing innocent lives and, where that fails, by considering such factors as the relative worth of the persons, or their ages, or their value to others? On the problem of the innocent aggressor and the related problem of proportionality between threat (innocent and non-innocent) and defensive response, see Fletcher, "Proportionality and the Psychotic Aggressor: A Vignette in

killing at all, will not eliminate condition (1); and (4) more desirable courses of action will not reduce the danger as much as killing X.

In war, many noncombatants, guilty and innocent, are threats to the defending nation. Many of them are greater threats than many combatants. A combatant at a camp miles behind the lines is often less a threat than a noncombatant delivering arms and ammunition to combatants at the front. Indeed, the combatants at the front individually will quite likely be less of a threat than the noncombatant supplier. In such a case the Principle of Self-Defense would demand that the noncombatant be killed in preference to the combatants, especially if he is no less guilty than they. Consider, also, two alternative courses of action in fighting a hypothetical unjust aggressor: (1) killing millions of enemy soldiers, most of whom are morally innocent (indeed, many are children); or (2) killing a handful of noncombatant enemy leaders, all of whom are morally innocent because of insanity. If either course would end the war, the latter would have to be preferred. Similarly, if one madman is about to deliver bombs to a thousand other madmen, who in turn will throw them, the Principle of Self-Defense demands that we end the danger by killing the former if we are going to be forced to kill in self-defense in any event.

Fullinwider's error could have resulted from assuming that one whose activity or existence is a remote cause (in terms of space, time, or intervening mechanisms or acts) of a threat to another's life is immune from being killed in self-defense, even though he is a necessary or sufficient cause of that threat. In the domestic context, causal remoteness will usually mean that the threat is insufficient to permit killing in self-defense. For in the domestic context, the more remote the cause of the threat, the more likely it is that factors such as the intervention of the police will prevent the harm from occurring, thus obviating the need to kill the cause of the threat. In the context of international warfare, remoteness, although relevant to the degree of

---

Comparative Criminal Theory," *Israel Law Review* 8 (1973): 367. See also English, "Abortion and the Concept of a Person," *Canadian Journal of Philosophy* 5, no. 2 (October 1975): 233, 237–239.

In any event, these problems do not affect my disagreement with Fullinwider (who obviously believes that defenders may stand and fight innocent aggressor combatants) nor my general formulation of the Principle of Self-Defense.

the threat, is less significant, for there is less reason to assume that other factors short of killing will intervene and prevent the threat's materializing.

Although causal remoteness is relevant to the questions of whether a threat exists and whether a person is a necessary or sufficient cause of it, it is irrelevant to the right of self-defense once the threat, the necessary or sufficient causal relation, and the lack of superior alternatives to remove the threat are posited. Moreover, even if causal remoteness were the source of immunity from being killed in self-defense, it would not be the source of an immunity for noncombatants vis-à-vis combatants. As the example of the noncombatant front-line supplier and the rear guard combatants illustrates, some combatants are at any time more remote threats than some noncombatants. Fullinwider could, of course, respond that killing rear guard combatants is not consistent with the Principle of Self-Defense, or, what amounts to the same thing, that only front-line combatants are truly combatants. I do not take him to be making such a claim, which would be an indictment of widely accepted norms of warfare.

There is one other possible source of Fullinwider's error. He may hold the view that one is immune from being killed in self-defense if any further choice of a human agent is necessary for the harm to materialize.[8] This view, he might believe, leads to the conclusion that only those who are sufficiently likely themselves to pull triggers (the infantry, but not the top generals, the ordnance personnel) or release bombs (the bombardiers, but not the pilots or navigators) may be killed. Although this view would not necessarily result in a distinction between combatants and noncombatants, because the likelihood of being killed in the future by one who is presently a noncombatant may exceed both the threshold required for self-defense and also the likelihood of being killed by particular combatants, it deserves a short comment. One cannot hold the view forbidding intervention before the last choice necessary for the harm as an absolute and at the same time accept the Principle of Self-Defense. Most acts sanctioned by the

8. The view appears to be closely akin to the principle, held by many, that it is wrong to prevent acts, harmless in themselves, merely because they make it more likely in the future that someone will choose to do, and succeed in doing, something immoral or illegal. See, for example, Nozick, *Anarchy, State, and Utopia*, pp. 126–130.

Principle of Self-Defense occur at a point when at least one choice still remains before someone is actually harmed—that is, they occur when the aggressor can still choose to cease his aggression. The fact that further choices are necessary to bring about the harm affects the likelihood of that harm's materializing; and the greater the number of choices required, the less likely it is that the harm will result. Under the Principle of Self-Defense, however, only the likelihood of harm, not the number of choices required to bring it about, is directly relevant.

In some of the hypotheticals I have used, only one choice is required for the harm to result. The mobsters, if they are out of range of Smith's hearing, cannot through any choice affect, in the short run, the likelihood of Smith's killing Jones. Only Smith can.

In other hypotheticals, more than once choice is required. Either the noncombatant munitions supplier or the combatants could through their choices reduce or eliminate the danger. Both must choose to aid the war effort to create the danger.

Whether one or more choices is required, however, is morally irrelevant (so long as the threshold probability of danger has been reached) and in any event is irrelevant to the combatant-noncombatant distinction. Suppose the noncombatant supplier is driving a truck full of munitions under the watchful eyes of his armed countrymen. If he attempts to turn the truck around, he will be stopped, and someone else will drive it. At that point only the choices of those whose hands are on the triggers, not the choice of the supplier, can be considered necessary or sufficient to bring about the harm to the defending nation. The supplier is in a situation analogous to that of a pilot of a bomber which also carries a bombardier. Once the bomber is over the target, no further choice *by the pilot* (at least no choice which would not lead to his death anyway) is necessary or sufficient to cause the bombing to commence. No one who accepts the Principle of Self-Defense could argue that the plane may not be shot down because the bombardier still has a choice to make and might decide not to release the bombs. And I cannot imagine that anyone would argue that the Principle of Self-Defense permits killing *only* the bombardier, not the pilot, where the most effective means of preventing the bombing is shooting down the plane (which, let us suppose, presents a far greater risk of death to the pilot than to the bombardier). But if the pilot, normally thought of as a combatant, may be killed in self-defense, so may the supplier, a noncombatant, perhaps by bombing the truck in order to blow up the munitions.

Finally, if noncombatants (say, children) were involuntarily harnessed with bombs and pushed down a slippery slope towards the troops of the defending nation, the bombs to be released automatically once the children were halfway down the slope, *no* further choice would be necessary to bring about the threatened harm. If the bombs could not be safely shot and detonated once they were released, self-defense would permit shooting the bombs before they were released and blowing up them and their noncombatant carriers, just as it would permit such an act if the carriers were morally innocent conscripted soldiers.

It is apparent, therefore, that neither the number of choices required to bring about the harm nor combatant-noncombatant status is morally relevant to the right to kill in self-defense.

In summary, punishment requires guilt, but guilt, even relative guilt, does not mark the distinction between combatants and noncombatants. On the other hand, the right to kill in self-defense requires only that the person killed be a necessary or sufficient cause of a danger, not that he be morally guilty. Again, however, being a cause of danger does not mark the distinction between combatants and noncombatants. Moreover, noncombatants are not necessarily more remote causes of danger than are combatants; nor is the danger noncombatants pose necessarily more dependent upon further choices than is the danger posed by combatants. Finally, neither causal remoteness nor the necessity of further choices is per se relevant to the Principle of Self-Defense. I conclude, therefore, that the intentional killing of innocent noncombatants is not necessarily immoral if one accepts the Principle of Self-Defense.[9]

9. For an excellent treatment of some of the issues discussed in this article, see Richard Wasserstrom, "On the Morality of War: A Preliminary Inquiry," in Richard Wasserstrom, ed., *War and Morality* (Belmont, Calif., 1970).

PART III

Deterrence Ethics

DOUGLAS P. LACKEY Missiles and Morals:
A Utilitarian Look at
Nuclear Deterrence

Though American foreign policy since 1945 has oscillated between conciliation and confrontation, American military policy at the strategic level has remained firmly tied to the notion of nuclear deterrence. After Hiroshima and Nagasaki, it was apparent that the effects of nuclear weapons were so terrible that their future use could never be condoned. But the threat to use nuclear weapons need not require their use, and such threats, in themselves, might prevent great evils. For those worried about Soviet expansion, a credible threat to use nuclear weapons might hold Soviet power in check. For those worried about future nuclear wars, the threat to use the bomb in retaliation might prevent nuclear wars from beginning. For an American public eager for demobilization, nuclear threats provided an appealing substitute for foot soldiering on foreign soil.[1] The stance of deterrence, of threat

1. In the sequence of these things, the idea of nuclear threats as a deterrent to nuclear war seems, oddly, to have come first. As early as 1946, Bernard Brodie wrote:

The first and most vital step in any American security program for the age of atomic bombs is to take measures to guarantee to ourselves in case of attack the possibility of retaliation in kind. The writer in making this statement is not for the moment concerned about who will win the next war in which atomic bombs have been used. Thus far the chief purpose of our military establishment has been to win wars. From now on its chief purpose must be to avert them. It can have almost no other useful purpose (Bernard Brodie, ed., *The Absolute Weapon* [New York: Harcourt Brace, 1946], p. 76).

But the idea of nuclear retaliation as a deterrent to nonnuclear aggression followed soon after, and to this date the United States has persistently and repeatedly refused to announce a policy of "no first use."

without use, appeared to both liberals and conservatives to command an overwhelming moral and prudential case. Small wonder, then, that after several abortive, perhaps deliberately abortive,[2] attempts at the internationalization of atomic weapons, the United States opted for unilateral development of nuclear weapons and delivery systems. Whatever residual qualms policy makers felt about the possession of nuclear arms were effectively silenced by the explosion of the first Soviet bomb in 1949. That the Soviets should possess nuclear weapons when the United States did not was politically unthinkable. Thirty-two years and ten thousand American nuclear weapons later, it still is.

Nevertheless it was arguable almost from the first that the case for deterrence was weaker than it seemed. The effectiveness of nuclear threats as a deterrent to Soviet aggression or Communist expansion was and remains barely credible. If the threat to use nuclear weapons did not prevent the subversion of Czechoslovakia, the blockade of Berlin, the collapse of Chiang Kai-shek, the fall of Dienbienphu, or the invasion of Hungary, all of which occurred before the Soviet Union could effectively deter an American nuclear strike with nuclear weapons and missiles of its own, how much less effective must nuclear threats have been towards deterring the Soviet invasion of Czechoslovakia in 1968 and the invasion of Afghanistan in 1979, and how little effect could such threats have as a deterrent to the much discussed but little expected invasion of West Germany by forces of the Warsaw pact?[3]

2. The case that the 1946 Baruch Plan for the internationalization of atomic weapons was deliberately designed to be nonnegotiable is persuasively made by Gregg Herken, *The Winning Weapon: The Atomic Bomb in the Cold War* (New York: Knopf, 1980). According to Herken the earlier Acheson-Lilienthal plan might have been negotiable.

3. Nigel Calder in *Nuclear Nightmares: An Investigation into Possible Wars* (New York: Viking, 1980), p. 42 notes that the NATO concept of deterring a Warsaw pact invasion of West Germany with NATO nuclear retaliation assumes that NATO will not be deterred from this nuclear first strike by the thought of a massive Soviet second strike in return. Calder correctly observes that this is odd thinking, since the possibility of an American second strike is supposed to be the threat which deters a Soviet first strike. Apparently the tacticians believe that the thought of destruction of Russian cities will deter the Soviets in a way that the thought of the destruction of American cities will not deter NATO. Since this belief is very probably false, we have a paradox: either nuclear deterrence will deter nonnuclear aggression but not nuclear aggression, or it will

Since there have been no uses of nuclear weapons in war since 1945, the case for nuclear threats as a deterrent to first uses of nuclear weapons seems a bit stronger. Nevertheless the role that nuclear deterrence has played in keeping the world free of nuclear war is a matter for debate. In the case of wars in progress, nuclear weapons have not been introduced in many cases because they cannot be effectively deployed relative to overall military objectives. The Israelis cannot use nuclear weapons on the Golan for fear of polluting the Kennerit; the Iraqis could not use them against Jerusalem without destroying the mosques they seek to liberate. The United States could not use nuclear weapons in South Vietnam without contaminating the countryside of our own allies; the Soviets could not use them against Prague and Budapest without destroying the industries they seek to exploit. As for the prevention through deterrence of large-scale nuclear war, it can be argued that every decrease in the chance of a nuclear first strike that results from fear of a retaliatory second strike is matched by an increase in the chance of a nuclear first strike that results from accident or mistake, human or mechanical failure; that every decrease in the chance that innocent millions will die from an undeterred first strike is matched by an increase in the chance that innocent millions will die from a nuclear second strike that cannot be stopped after initial deterrence has failed. To these dangers we should add the consideration that the American argument, "the United States must have the bomb if the Soviet Union has one," is replicable by every nation state, producing pressure for proliferation which in turn increases the chance of war, and the consideration that no degree of threat can deter a nuclear terrorist who prefers to be dead rather than blue, or red, or green, and who has built his bomb with the help of weapons technology developed by states that are sworn "to deterrence only." There is little, at least in a preliminary survey of the evidence, that supports the idea that the construction of nuclear weapons for the purpose of issuing nuclear threats has contributed to the prevention of nuclear wars since 1945, or will contribute towards preventing them in the future. Whatever the game theorists say, the common sense view that you cannot prevent wars by building bombs still has some weight.

---

deter nuclear aggression but not nonnuclear aggression. Thus deterrence in the European theater cannot simultaneously do the two jobs for which it was originally designed: deterring Soviet aggression, and deterring nuclear war.

The argument that nuclear deterrence can replace the war of soldiers on the ground with a war of threats in the air has also seen hard sledding since 1945. The need for retaining conventional forces has been apparent since the Berlin blockade, and the effect that reliance on nuclear deterrence has had on the quality of conventional forces is by now well known. It is no accident that the last successful American military operation (Inchon) precedes the development of ICBMs, and the increasing ineptitude of American conventional forces exhibited in the successively botched Son Tay, Mayaguez, and Iranian rescue attempts is too obvious to bear comment. There is no necessary connection between nuclear strength and conventional weakness, but in a world of limited resources the development of strategic forces has twisted military budgets in favor of high technology, and the result has been complicated guns that won't shoot and complicated planes that can't fly.[4] The idea that the nation's "first line" of defense consists of radar towers and missiles rather than men on the battlefield must inevitably weaken the morale of the Army and the Marines. However plausible it may have seemed to John Foster Dulles, there is little support now for the view that nuclear threats can substitute in any way for the painful sacrifices of conventional war.

The moral and prudential case for deterrence seems overcome by events. But there is a rejoinder to these criticisms that many find decisive: deterrence is bad, but disarmament is worse. Elected officials remember well that the only Presidential candidate since 1945 with a kind word for nuclear disarmament was humiliated in 1972 and voted out of the Senate in 1980. Fortunately moral philosophers do not stand for election and are free to examine all the options regardless of practical constraints. This is what I propose to do, with the important limitation that the moral systems I shall bring to bear upon the subject are all utilitarian systems. In normal circumstances one may have one's doubts about utilitarianism, but if nuclear war is among the results of policies under consideration, the gravity of the consequences carries all else before.

---

4. The gun is the M-16 and the plane is the F-111. For the tragic history of the M-16 see James Fallows, *National Defense* (New York: Random House, 1981), chap. 4.

I. Four Decision Rules

The agreeable utilitarian idea that the moral worth of acts and policies is to be measured in the value of their consequences has been troubled from the beginning by the problem that the consequences of policies are often uncertain. Suppose that Policy 1 will produce either A or B, that Policy 2 will produce either C or D, and that by some accepted standard of value A is better than C but B is worse than D. The rule that the best policy is the one with the best consequences will not tell us which policy to choose, and there is no consensus among utilitarian theorists as to how the general rule should be modified in order to generate the morally right choice. Nevertheless there are many ingenious suggestions about how to deal with choice under uncertainty, and in this essay we will deploy four different principles of choice: Minimax, Dominance, Disaster Avoidance, and Expected Value Maximization. Each principle will be used twice over, first, for the utilitarian calculation, which we will call the moral calculation; second, for a prudential calculation, which will indicate, from the standpoint of the United States, what the prudential course of action might be.

Each prudential and moral calculation requires a standard of value, and in the essay the usual standard of value will be the satisfaction of preferences. In the utilitarian calculation, we will consider outcome A to be better than outcome B if the vast majority of persons in this and in several future generations would prefer A to B. In the prudential calculation, we will consider outcome A to be better than outcome B if the vast majority of Americans in this and in several future generations would prefer A to B. Given the subject matter of nuclear war, for many problems value can be equated with human lives, and outcome A can be considered better than outcome B if fewer people are killed by war in A than are killed by war in B. But considering that at least some Americans are on record as preferring being dead to being red, and since many Americans (I think) would prefer a small chance of nuclear attack to a very large chance of Soviet world domination, the equation of value with human lives cannot always be relied upon, especially in the prudential calculation.

In all four models of choice we confine our inquiry to just two nations—the United States and the Soviet Union. These are the primary protagonists in the nuclear drama, and we will argue in a later section that conclusions reached about the bilateral case can also be applied straightforwardly to the multilateral case. Furthermore, we will apply our four models of choice to just three strategies, *Superiority, Equivalence*, and *Nuclear Disarmament*. Though there are many strategies for nuclear armament, these three have been at the center of the strategic debate at least since the late 1950s:

S: Maintain second strike capacity; seek first strike capacity; threaten first and second strikes ("Superiority").

E: Maintain second strike capacity; do not seek first strike capacity; threaten second strikes only ("Equivalence").

ND: Do not seek to maintain second strike capacity ("Nuclear Disarmament").

In the statement of these strategies the terminology is standard: Nation A is presumed to have *first-strike capacity* against B if A can launch a nuclear attack on B without fear of suffering unacceptable damage from B's subsequent counterstrike; nation A is said to have *second-strike capacity* against B if A is capable of inflicting unacceptable damage on B after having suffered a nuclear first strike by B.

Strategy S has been the favored strategy of hard-line anticommunists ever since the early 1950s. In its original form, as we find it in John Foster Dulles, the Superiority Strategy called for threats of American first strikes against Russian cities in retaliation for what American policy defined as Soviet acts of aggression. In its present form, as it is developed by Paul Nitze, Colin Gray, and others, the Superiority Strategy calls for threats, or implied threats, of American first strikes against Soviet military forces, combined with large-scale increases in American strategic arms.[5]

5. On "massive retaliation" see John Foster Dulles, Dept. of State Bulletin 30, 791, 25 Jan. 1954. For Superiority policy in the 1960s see, for example, Barry Goldwater, *Why Not Victory?* (New York: McGraw-Hill, 1962), p. 162:

We must stop lying to ourselves and our friends about disarmament. We must stop advancing the cause of the Soviet Union by playing along with Communist inspired deception.

"Disarmament," for Goldwater, includes arms control, since he warns against the danger of "disarmament, or arms control, as the 87th Congress cutely puts

The Superiority Strategy, however, is not the exclusive property of doctrinaire anticommunists or hard-line "forward" strategists. Since aiming one's missiles at enemy missiles implies a desire to destroy those missiles before they are launched, that is, a desire to launch a first strike, all retargeting of American missiles from Soviet cities to Soviet missiles, up to and including President Carter's Directive 59 in the summer of 1980, imply partial endorsement of Strategy S.[6] Such "counterforce" as opposed to "countervalue" targetings are entailed by Strategy S even if they do not in fact bring first strike capacity; Strategy S as defined implies that the United States will *seek* first strike capacity, not that it will in fact obtain it. Strategy S advocates steps which will produce first strike capacity unless new countermeasures are developed by the Soviet Union to cancel them out.

Strategy E, the "equivalence" strategy, enshrines Robert McNamara's doctrine of Assured Destruction, and includes both massive retaliations against massive strikes and flexible responses against lesser strikes.[7] The possibility and permanence of Strategy E seemed assured by SALT I in 1972, since negotiated restrictions on the deployment of antiballistic missiles seemed to guarantee permanent second-strike capacity to both sides. Unfortunately, SALT I did not limit the development and deployment of MIRVs (multiple independently targeted reentry vehicles), and the deployment of MIRVs through the 1970s has led to cries on both sides that mutual second-strike capacity is dissolving and mutual first-strike capacity is emerging.[8]

---

it" (p. 99). For a recent interpretation of Superiority see Colin Gray and Keith Payne, "Victory Is Possible," *Foreign Policy* 39 (Summer 1980): 14–27, and Colin Gray, "Nuclear Strategy: The Case for a Theory of Victory," *International Security* 4 (Summer 1979): 54–87.

6. The uproar caused by the announcement of Directive 59 on 25 July 1980 prompted administration defenders to make the discomfiting revelation that counterforce retargetings are regarded by the Defense Department as matters of course. See for example, Walter Slocombe, "The Countervailing Strategy," *International Security* 5, no. 4 (Spring 1981).

7. Robert McNamara. *The Essence of Security* (London: Hodder and Stoughton, 1968).

8. The much discussed Soviet threat to American land-based missiles does *not* imply Soviet progress towards a first strike, given the invulnerability of

Notice that although Strategy E permits bilateral arms control, it actually prohibits substantial reductions in nuclear arms. The delicate balance of mutual second-strike capacity becomes increasingly unstable as arms levels are lowered, and sooner or later, mutual disarmament brings a loss of second-strike capacity on one side and the emergence of first-strike capacity on the other, contrary to E.

Strategy ND calls for a unilateral halt in the development of American nuclear weapons and delivery systems, even if such a halt eventuates in Soviet first strike capacity. Strategy ND is a policy of *nuclear* disarmament; it does *not* call for the abandonment of conventional weapons and should not be equated with pacifism or confused with general and complete disarmament. In fact, increases in conventional weapons levels are compatible with Strategy ND.

II. Minimax

Considering the hundreds of billions of dollars the United States has spent on strategic weapons since 1945, it is remarkable how little anyone knows about what would happen should these weapons be used. In an unsettling account of the present state of national defense James Fallows writes:

> There has never been a nuclear war, and nobody knows what a nuclear war would mean. . . . No one knows how these weapons would perform if they were fired; whether they would hit the targets at which they are aimed; whether human society would be set back for decades, centuries as a result. . . . Most strategic arguments (are) disputes of faith rather than fact.[9]

Fallows's gloomy judgment is confirmed by a report presented to Congress in 1979 by the Office of Technology Assessment:

American nuclear submarines. But the development of the American MIRV, combined with the vulnerability of Soviet missile submarines, most of which remain in port and all of which, apparently, can be tracked by American antisubmarine forces, *does* imply the development of *American* first-strike capacity. Under current conditions my estimate is that the United States can pursue strategy E only by abandoning some fraction of its antisubmarine surveillance. For a recent study of vulnerability of land-based missiles see Eliot Marshall, "A Question of Accuracy," *Science*, 11 September 1981, pp. 1230–31.

9. Fallows, *National Defense*, pp. 139–40.

The effects of nuclear war that cannot be calculated are at least as important as those for which calculations are attempted. Moreover even these very limited calculations are subject to large uncertainties . . . This is particularly true for indirect effects such as deaths resulting from injuries and the unavailability of medical care, or for economic damage resulting from disruptions and disorganization rather than direct disruption.[10]

Fallows and the OTA do not exaggerate. To date no Minuteman missile has been test-fired from an operational silo; no American ICBM has been properly tested on a North-South trajectory, and missile accuracy reports are a guessing game subject to vagaries of wind, gravitational anomaly, and fratricidal interference from other "friendly" missiles. On top of all this, the entire defense communications network and all electronic guidance systems may be disrupted by the electromagnetic pulses that emanate from thermonuclear blasts.[11]

Anyone who accepts such estimates of the depth of our ignorance about nuclear war will be encouraged to use a principle of choice that does not require knowledge of the probabilities that a given nuclear policy will produce a given result. Of such principles, perhaps the most widely used in both prudential and moral calculation is the Minimax Principle:

Choose any policy the worst outcome of which is at least as good as the worst outcome of any other policy.

Let us do the Minimax moral calculation first. The worst outcome of both the Superiority Strategy and the Equivalence Strategy is a large scale thermonuclear exchange in which both sides launch as many of their missiles as possible. The worst outcome of the Nuclear Disarmament Strategy is a unilateral nuclear strike on the United States by the Soviet Union followed by whatever increases in Soviet power such a strike might bring. (I list a unilateral Soviet nuclear attack as an outcome of ND not because ND makes such attacks likely but be-

10. "The Effects of Nuclear War," U.S. Congress, Office of Technology Assessment, 1979, p. 3.
11. On the electromagnetic pulse or EMP, see Janet Raloff, "EMP: A Sleeping Dragon," *Science News*, 9 May 1981, pp. 300–302, and 16 May 1981, pp. 314–15.

cause they are physically possible given ND. Minimax pays no heed to probabilities.) Since the vast majority of persons (especially Russian persons) in this and several future generations would prefer a one-sided attack on the United States to all-out nuclear war between the United States and the Soviet Union, the utilitarian Minimax Principle declares that the morally right policy is Nuclear Disarmament.

The prudential calculation is not so straightforward. Americans as a group will agree with people at large as to the worst outcome associated with each policy. But it is not so clear that Americans will agree that an outcome in which the Soviet Union attacks an unresponding United States is preferable to an outcome in which the Soviet Union attacks and the United States responds. A reasonable survey of prevailing American sentiments would probably report (a) that a substantial number of Americans would prefer one-sided destruction to two-sided destruction, even if the destroyed side happens to be the American side, on grounds that more lives are saved if only one side is destroyed, and (b) that a substantial number of Americans would prefer two-sided destruction to one-sided destruction, on the grounds that if the Soviet Union attacks the United States, the Soviet Union deserves to be punished. If these are the genuine American preferences, the Minimax Principle yields no verdict in the prudential case. For the record, we might also note that Minimax reasoning fails to distinguish, either morally or prudentially, between the Equivalence Strategy and the Superiority Strategy, since the same disaster is the worst outcome in either case.

III. DOMINANCE

Like Minimax, Dominance is a principle of choice under uncertainty which makes no reference to probabilities of outcomes:

> Choose a policy (if any) yielding results which cannot be improved, no matter what the opposition or nature may choose to do.

Obviously such policies are rarely found, but many writers feel that such a dominant strategy is available in the arena of nuclear choice. For simplicity, let us consider only the Equivalence Strategy and the Nuclear Disarmament Strategy, and let us assume that the only variable in the environment is the Soviet choice between E and ND. Since each side has two options, there are four outcomes:

1. The United States arms; the Soviet Union disarms;
2. The United States and the Soviet Union both disarm;
3. The United States and the Soviet Union both arm; and
4. The United States disarms; the Soviet Union arms.

If we suppose (as most students of strategy do) that the vast majority of American people prefer these outcomes in the order in which they are presented, then prudentially the United States should remain armed, no matter what the Soviet Union does.[12] By the Dominance Principle, then, the United States should stick with Equivalence.

Since these ratings are made from the national point of view, the conclusion thus far is strictly prudential. The moral argument yields surprisingly different results. Presumably a large majority of people in the world prefer 2 to 1, that is, they prefer neither side having nuclear arms to one side having them. This suffices to show that Equivalence does not dominate from the moral point of view. Furthermore, if we assume that a large majority of people in the world, fearful of all-out nuclear war, prefer that the United States practice ND even if the Soviet Union does not, it is Nuclear Disarmament that dominates from the moral point of view.

We have the consistent but disagreeable result that, if we follow Dominance, prudence dictates one policy while morality dictates another. We could challenge this conclusion by making different assessments of preferences. But there are other grounds which might lead

12. Technically, it might be possible to develop a prudential case for nuclear disarmament as follows: (a) take all alleged preferences for two-sided destruction, (b) subtract from these all preferences based on the idea that a second strike against Russia is needed to deter their first strike; this idea is illicit since the preference poll in all cases assumes that the first strike has already occurred, and (c) subtract all preferences based on considerations of retributive justice on the grounds that these are political preferences rather than personal evaluations of the utility present in the situations judged. (For the distinction between political preferences and personal preferences see Ronald Dworkin, "What is Equality? Part 1: Equality of Welfare," *Philosophy & Public Affairs* 10, no. 3 [Summer 1981]: 197–98.) The residue of support for nuclear retaliation might be small enough for us to judge that the American people prudentially prefer disarmament.

us to conclude that the real problem here is not the assessment of preferences but the Dominance Principle itself.

IV. CONCEPTUAL PROBLEMS

Both the Minimax and the Dominance Principles are examples of game-theoretical strategic principles that treat each outcome as the result of equally permissible and equally possible moves in a gamelike situation. Rapoport, Green, and others in the past have criticized certain aspects of the game-theoretical approach;[13] its tendency, for example, to treat situations of nuclear strategy as zero sum games in which cooperation is impossible, rather than as constant sum games in which it can be prudent to cooperate. But the game-theoretical approach is inadequate in a way that cannot be remedied by shifting to broader principles and a wider range of games. In the standard logic of games each alternative is taken as given, and there is no room for calculating how the threat to make one move will influence the chance that another move is made, a consideration which is at the heart of the argument for deterrence. Consider the following argument, which proceeds on the basis of fixed alternatives: "The logical possibilities are that either the Soviets will attack or they will not attack. If they attack, there is no point in threatening to counterattack, since the whole point of the threat was to prevent the attack. If they do not attack, there is no point in threatening to counterattack, since there is no initial attack for the threat to deter: we conclude, therefore, nuclear threats are futile, or they are otiose." The notion that threats might diminish the chance of attack goes by the board. Perhaps we should dispense with deterrence, but the argument for dispensing with it cannot be this easy!

Even worse difficulties can be generated by combining information about outcomes with the dominance principle. Suppose that Americans prefer outcomes 1 through 4 as stated in the previous Section, and suppose that it is given information that (a) whenever the United States arms, the Soviet Union will arm, and that (b) whenever the

13. For criticisms of the zero-sum approach to nuclear strategy see Anatol Rapoport, *Strategy and Conscience* (New York: Harper & Row, 1964); and Philip Green, *Deadly Logic* (Columbus, OH: Ohio State University Press, 1966).

United States disarms, the Soviet Union will disarm. Since Americans prefer mutual disarmament to mutual armament, the preferred strategy in the light of the given information is for the United States to disarm. But game-theoretical reasoning still insists that the preferred strategy is to remain armed. Even if the Soviets will disarm when the United States disarms, it remains true that they will either arm or disarm. If they arm, it is better for the United States to arm. If they disarm, it is better for the United States to arm. Therefore the United States should arm in any event. The result will be mutual armament, a situation worse than that which could confidently be achieved by the choice of disarmament. It is not possible here to review all the systems devised in recent years by game theorists attempting to cope with this problem. Suffice it to say that there is a consensus that something must be done but no consensus about what to do, and the state of the field is sufficiently unsettled to warrant serious investigation of more information-sensitive decision principles.[14]

14. For approaches which attempt to break out of the static analyses which have prevailed since von Neumann and Morgenstern see Nigel Howard, *Paradoxes of Rationality* (Cambridge, MA: The M.I.T. Press, 1971); Michael Taylor, *Anarchism and Cooperation* (New York: John Wiley & Sons, 1976); and Steven Brams and Donald Wittman, "Nonmyopic Equilibria in a 2×2 Games" (forthcoming). Howard, Taylor, and Brams and Wittman all note that the prudential argument for armament presented here for the United States will lead Soviet strategists to the same result, and thus individual prudence produces a collective result (mutual armament), which is less liked by each side than mutual disarmament. In sum, all these authors assume that nuclear arms races are Prisoners' Dilemmas. Howard's theory of metagames, Taylor's theory of supergames, and the Brams/Wittman theory of moves all try to show that a proper theory of games will establish that the mutually preferred solution is an equilibrium from which prudent players will not depart. I find it impossible to connect Howard's metagame equilibria with the psychology of the players; see, *contra* Howard, John Harsanyi, "Communication," *American Political Science Review* 68 (1974): 729–31; 1692–95. Taylor's supergame equilibria require repeated plays of the game, and for obvious reasons repeated plays of games involving nuclear war have little relation to reality. Furthermore, Taylor's equilibria require low discount rates, and in most thought about nuclear war, long run payoffs are highly discounted in favor of such short run results as political intimidation or war prevention. Brams's theory of moves is not affected by discount rates, but it provides no clue as to how to move to the cooperative solution when history has trapped players in a noncooperative equilibrium. A far better approach to escaping the Prisoners' Dilemma is to never enter into it, and I have suggested ("Ethics and Nuclear Deterrence," in *Moral Problems* 2d ed., ed. James Ra-

V. DISASTER AVOIDANCE

Let us suppose that one type of information that we *do* have about nuclear war is information pertaining to the ordering of the probabilities of the various outcomes. For example, most people would agree that the chance of nuclear war on the Superiority Strategy is greater than the chance of war on the Equivalence Strategy, though what quantitative probabilities are, in either case, is difficult to say. If this type of information is all the information we have, and if there are outcomes all parties identify as disastrous, the rational course of action, Gregory Kavka suggests, is dictated by what he calls the Disaster Avoidance Principle:

> When choosing between potential disasters under two dimensional uncertainty, it is rational to select the alternative that minimizes the probability of disaster occurrence.[15]

Kavka does not advance the Avoidance Principle as a solution for all problems of two dimensional uncertainty, but he recommends its use in situations in which nine special conditions are satisfied. Use of the Avoidance Principle is rational if and only if: (i) quantitative probabilities and utilities are unknown; (ii) conditional probabilities are known; (iii) all disastrous outcomes are extremely unacceptable; (iv) all disastrous outcomes are roughly the same order of magnitude; (v) the chooser regards the difference in utility between nondisastrous outcomes to be small compared to the difference between disastrous outcomes and nondisastrous outcomes; (vi) the choice is unique, that is, not one of a series of choices; (vii) the probabilities of the disasters are not thought to be insignificant; (viii) the probability of the greater disaster is not thought to be very large; and (ix) the probabilities of the disasters are not thought to be very close to equal.

Kavka argues that all nine of these conditions are satisfied by the problem of nuclear choice, and proceeds to apply the Disaster Avoidance Principle to the choice between Equivalence and Nuclear Dis-

chels [New York: Harper & Row, 1975], pp. 332–45) that nuclear arms races in particular are not Prisoners' Dilemmas if the payoffs are properly evaluated.

15. Gregory Kavka, "Deterrence, Utility, and Rational Choice," *Theory and Decision* 12 (1980): 50.

armament. (He does not consider the Superiority Strategy.) Arguing that:

> We can be confident that the likelihood of Soviet domination if the U.S. disarms is greater than the likelihood of war if the U.S. practices deterrence,[16]

he concludes that the rational choice is the Equivalence Strategy. Since there is no place in the calculations for differences between the preferences of Americans and the preferences of all people, it follows from Kavka's reasoning that the Equivalence Strategy is the morally preferred choice—at least for utilitarians.

This is not the place for full theoretical analysis of Kavka's Avoidance Principle, which supplies a principle of rational choice to problems beset by what Daniel Ellsberg called "ambiguity," as opposed to "risk."[17] For our purposes, let us agree that the principle *does* represent a principle of rational choice *if* all nine of Kavka's qualifying conditions are satisfied. What is more at issue is whether the conditions are in fact satisfied in the case of nuclear choice and whether the principle has been properly applied to this particular problem.

Kavka's fourth condition is that "disastrous outcomes must be roughly of the same order of magnitude." Obviously if one outcome is hundreds of times more disastrous than the other, and the probabilities of the disasters are not known, minimax reasoning should prevail. Kavka argues that the disaster which might be produced by the Equivalence Strategy is nuclear war, and the disaster which might be produced by nuclear disarmament is Soviet domination. For Kavka these are disasters "roughly equal in magnitude," which shows that, for Kavka, "roughly equal" is very rough indeed. But it would be useless to belabor the comparison of nuclear war with Soviet domination, since in fact the comparison is irrelevant. The main catastrophe of the Equivalence Strategy is *all-out* nuclear war; the main catastrophe of Nuclear Disarmament is a *one-sided* nuclear war. Are *these* disasters roughly equal in magnitude?

Clearly a two-sided nuclear war would be rated by everyone as a

16. Ibid., p. 51.
17. Daniel Ellsberg, "Risk, Ambiguity, and the Savage Axioms," *Quarterly Journal of Economics* 75 (1961): 643–69.

"great disaster" and a one-sided nuclear war would be rated by everyone as a "great disaster." This might tempt us to conclude that these are disasters roughly equal in magnitude. Indeed, most people are not capable of discriminating finely between nuclear wars, a psychological fact that advocates of limited nuclear war are given to deplore. But let us suppose that 20,000,000 Americans will die in a one-sided nuclear war and that 60,000,000 Americans and 60,000,000 Russians will die in a two-sided nuclear war, figures which are not unreasonable and which reflect the fact that a Soviet first strike would be relatively smaller against an America practicing nuclear disarmament. If we shake the Strangelovian dizziness out of our heads, we can make a serious attempt to compare the magnitude of 20,000,000 deaths and 120,000,000 deaths. If we take the comparison to be *six to one*, we might agree with Kavka that the two disasters are "roughly equal in magnitude." But this is obviously not the proper way to make the comparison. We must ask whether X and Y should be rated roughly equal in magnitude given that X and Y are quite the same *except* that in Y there are 100,000,000 more deaths than in X. Certainly 100,000,000 dead as opposed to no dead at all is a matter of very great magnitude, and thus Kavka's assumption that there is no difference between the magnitude of the disaster produced by deterrence and the magnitude of the disaster produced by disarmament is false—even if it makes the disaster produced by disarmament much *greater* than he assumes it to be.

Even more disturbing than Kavka's claim that his nine conditions are satisfied is his final deduction of the result that disarmament is irrational. The major premise of this argument is the Avoidance Principle; the minor premise—a crucial step in the deduction—is the claim that the likelihood of disaster under disarmament is greater than the likelihood of disaster under deterrence. This empirical claim is presented as a proposition of which "we can be confident," but I feel no confidence whatsoever about it, and it is asserted without argument or evidence.[18] Not a single author who has discussed nuclear deterrence

18. Kavka, "Deterrence," p. 45, writes, "This appears to be the way things stand with respect to expert opinion, as seen from the point of view of the United States. (See, e.g., Levine 1963, Herzog 1965, and Van Cleave 1973)." Unpaginated footnotes are a curse, and I cannot find passages in the books

feels that the risk of nuclear war resulting from the practice of deterrence is negligible, and there are many—the whole staff of the *Bulletin of Atomic Scientists*, for example—who consider it to be substantial. In discussion of nuclear disarmament, there are many who feel that the Soviet Union might *attempt* nuclear blackmail if it gained first-strike capacity, but there are not many who are sure that such attempts at blackmail would succeed. The sole evidence which history provides on this subject is the sobering fact that the period of nuclear supremacy for the United States was precisely the period of greatest communist expansion in the world (1945–49). One can only speculate that Kavka, like many authors who dismiss nuclear disarmament as unwise and impractical, has blurred together the effects of *nuclear* disarmament and the effects of *general and complete* disarmament.[19] As a result, he has illicitly upgraded the chance of Soviet domination resulting from the strategy of *nuclear* disarmament and begs the question in favor of Equivalence.

VI. EXPECTED VALUE

Perhaps the most natural of all responses to the problem of uncertainty is to discount the weight of consequences by whatever chance there is that they will not occur. To compute the "expected value" of a policy, then, we should consider each possible outcome of the policy, multiply the utility of that outcome by the probability that it will occur, and take the sum of all these products. In the area of nuclear strategy we cannot supply precise numbers for the probabilities of the outcomes, nor can we attempt to supply precise figures for the corresponding utilities. Nevertheless, we *do* have much more information about these

---

cited that defend Kavka's case. Levine and Herzog, throughout, seem to be leaning to the opposite view. Van Cleave is summarizing and takes no stand of his own. See Arthur Herzog, *The War-Peace Establishment* (New York: Harper & Row, 1965); Arthur Levine, *The Arms Debate* (Cambridge, MA: Harvard University Press, 1963); and Van Cleave's chapter in *American Defense Policy*, 3rd ed., ed. Richard Head and Ervin Bakke (Baltimore, MD: Johns Hopkins University Press, 1973).

19. The speculation that Kavka has confused nuclear with general and complete disarmament is not idle. On page 44 he writes of "unilateral nuclear disarmament," but on pages 45 and 51, in the thick of the argument, he speaks only of "unilateral disarmament."

subjects than the orderings of probabilities to which we were restricted in the Disaster Avoidance model, and what imprecision there is in our information can be respected by stating the information in the form of approximations. For example, we can classify the probability of outcomes as "negligible," "small but substantial," "fifty-fifty," "very likely," and "almost certain," and we can classify outcomes as "extremely bad," "bad," "neutral," and so forth. In considering the products of utilities and outcomes, we can neglect all outcomes of negligible probability, and all outcomes of small but substantial probability *except* those classified as extremely good or extremely bad. In many cases, use of such estimates will yield surprisingly definite results.

Now, what are the "outcomes" the probabilities of which we ought to consider? Given the traditionally assumed goals of deterrence, we should certainly consider the effects of each policy on the probability of nuclear war, the probability of Soviet nonnuclear aggression, and the probability of Soviet nuclear blackmail. As we have noted, in considering the probability of nuclear war, it is essential to distinguish the probability of a one-sided nuclear strike from the probability of all-out nuclear war. Among other outcomes, we will consider only the effects of nuclear strategies on military spending, since the impact of policies on spending can be determined with little controversy. Since we have four outcomes and three policies to consider, the probabilities can be represented on a three-by-four grid (see table 1). Each probability assessment will be defended in turn.

TABLE 1

	One-sided Strike*	All-out Nuclear War	Soviet Aggression	Very High Military Spending
Superiority	Fifty-fifty [a]	Fifty-fifty [b]	Small [c]	Certain [d]
Equivalence	Small [e]	Small [f]	Small [g]	Fifty-fifty [h]
Nuclear Disarmament	Small [i]	Zero [j]	Small [k]	Small [l]

* A "one-sided strike" is a first strike that may or may not be answered by a second strike. A comparison of the probability of one-sided strikes and two-sided strikes in a given row indicates that a first strike will lead to an all-out nuclear war.

Value of the Superiority Strategy

[a] Strategists disagree about the probability of Soviet or American first strike under the Superiority Strategy. All students of the subject rate it as having at least a small but substantial probability. I believe that it is more reasonable to rate the probability as fifty-fifty within a time frame of about fifty years, since (1) every real or presumed step towards first strike capacity by either side raises the chance of a preemptive first strike by the side falling behind; (2) the concentration on technological development prompted by the Superiority Strategy raises that chance of a technological breakthrough that might destabilize the balance of power; (3) the increasing technological complexity of weapons required by the Superiority Strategy raises the chance of a first strike as a result of accident or mistake; (4) the constant changes of weaponry required by the Superiority Strategy creates pressure for proliferation, either because obsolete weapons are constantly disposed of on the international arms market or because wealthy developing countries, dazzled by new weapons, make buys to keep up with appearances.

[b] Under Superiority, the chance of an American second strike—given a Soviet first strike—is practically the same as the chance of a Soviet first strike. Though it is always possible that the President or his survivor will not respond to a Soviet first strike, the military and technological systems installed under the Superiority Strategy are geared for belligerence. Accordingly the chance of an American failure to respond is negligible.

[c] Even in the face of the Superiority Strategy, the chance of Soviet nonnuclear aggression (an invasion of West Germany or Iran, for example) must be rated as small but not negligible. The prospect of an American first strike in response to a Soviet conventional attack may not be taken seriously by the Soviets, especially if Soviet military personnel think that they can deter any American first strike with the prospect of a massive Soviet second strike.

[d] The sums of money required to sustain the Superiority Strategy are staggering. The Reagan administration's rejection of SALT and its apparent acceptance of the Superiority Strategy will produce an increase in the fraction of the American gross national product devoted

to defense from five to six and one-half percent: an increase of over $150 billion per year over the Carter projections, which were largely keyed to the Equivalence Strategy.

Value of the Equivalence Strategy

[e] Most students of strategy agree that the chance of an American or Soviet first strike under the Equivalence Strategy is small but substantial. The peculiar pressures for a first strike listed under the Superiority Strategy are absent, but there is still the chance of a first strike through accident, mistake, human folly, or a suicidal leadership.

[f] Since the chance of a first strike is less under Equivalence than under Superiority, there is less chance of an all-out nuclear war under Equivalence than under Superiority. The chance of a first strike under Equivalence is small, and the chance of all-out war following a first strike is smaller still. Since the primary aim of the Equivalence Strategy is not to "defeat" the Soviet Union or to develop a first-strike capacity, but to deter a Soviet first strike, it may be obvious to the President or his survivor that once a Soviet first strike is actually launched, there is no point whatsoever in proceeding with an American second strike. If the chance that the President will fail to respond is substantial, the chance of an all-out war under Equivalence is considerably less than the chance of a first strike under Equivalence.[20] On the other hand,

20. The thought that an American President may lack the nerve to destroy civilization depresses the military mind. In stating the requirements of deterrence, General Maxwell Taylor writes, "So understood, deterrence depends essentially on an assured destruction capability, a strong communications net, and a strong President unlikely to flinch from his responsibility. . . . Such reflections emphasize the importance of the character and will of the President as a factor adding to the deterrent effect of our weapons. Since the attitude of the President will be strongly influenced by that of the people whom he represents, national character also participates in the effectiveness and stability of deterrence. . . . In addition to the moral [*sic*] qualities of the President and the nation there are a number of other factors which may stabilize or undermine deterrence" (Maxwell Taylor, *Precarious Security* [New York: W.W. Norton, 1976], pp. 68–69). On the other hand, some military figures, at least in their public statements, are entirely confident that the President will respond and launch the second strike. General George Seignious, former director of the joint staff of the Joint Chiefs of Staff, testified in 1979, "I find such a surrender scenario irresponsible—for it sends the wrong message to the Soviets. We have not built and maintained our strategic forces—at the cost of billions—in order to

the credibility of the American deterrent to a first strike depends on the perception by Soviet planners that an American second strike is inevitable once a Soviet first strike is launched, and the President and his defense strategists may decide that the only convincing way to create this perception is to make the American second strike a *semiautomatic* response. Thus it might be difficult to stop an American second strike even if the President wished to forgo it. On balance, it seems reasonable to rate the chance of the second strike as greater than one-half the chance that the Soviet first strike will be launched. This would make the chance small but still substantial.

[g] Over the years two arguments have been proposed to show that Superiority provides a more effective deterrent against Soviet aggression than does Equivalence.

(1) The Superiority Strategy requires constant technological innovation, and technological innovation is an area in which the United States possesses a relative advantage. If the United States presses forward with strategic weapons development, the Soviet Union will be so exhausted from the strain of keeping up with the United States that it will have little money or energy left over for nonnuclear aggression In the end, the strain such competition will exert on the Soviet economy might produce food riots like those in Poland in 1970, and might even bring down the Soviet socioeconomic system.

But since "the strain of keeping up" did not stop the Soviets from invading Hungary, Czechoslovakia, and Afghanistan, the level of expenditure needed to produce truly effective strain is unknown. Furthermore, the assumption of *relative* economic stress is undemonstrated: at least one economist who has seriously studied the subject has argued on various grounds that a unit of military spending by the United States disrupts the American economy far more than the equivalent military spending by the Soviet Union.[21]

(2) It is occasionally argued that the Soviets will take the possibility of an American second strike more seriously under the Superi-

---

weaken their deterrent impact by telling the Russians and the world that we would back down—when, in fact, we would not" (quoted in Herbert Scoville, *MX: Prescription for Disaster* [Cambridge, MA: The M.I.T. Press, 1981], p. 82).

21. See Seymour Melman, *Our Depleted Society* (New York: Holt, Rinehart & Winston, 1965), and *Pentagon Capitalism* (New York: McGraw-Hill, 1970).

ority Strategy than under the Equivalence Strategy, since the Superiority Strategy gives the United States something closer to first-strike capacity and therefore something less to fear from a Soviet second strike.

But in the game of nuclear strategy one cannot "almost" have first strike capacity; one either has it or one doesn't. There is no reason to think that the Superiority Strategy will ever yield first-strike capacity, since the Soviet Union will feel forced to match the United States step for step. The Soviets know that the President will never by confident enough in American striking capacity to risk the survival of the United States on a nuclear response to Soviet nonnuclear aggression. Consequently, there is no reason to think that Superiority provides a better deterrent against Soviet aggression than does Equivalence. The chance of serious nonnuclear Soviet aggression under Equivalence is small.

[h] In the presence of serious efforts at arms control, expenditures for strategic weapons will be much less under Equivalence than under Superiority. If efforts at arms control fail, then expenditures will remain very high. The chance of very high expenditures under Equivalence would best be put at about fifty-fifty.

Value of the Nuclear Disarmament Strategy

[i] Most strategists are agreed that the chance of a Soviet first strike under the Equivalence Strategy is small. I believe that the chance of a Soviet first strike is small even under the strategy of Nuclear Disarmament.

(1) Since under Nuclear Disarmament at most one side retains nuclear arms, the chance of nuclear war occurring by accident is reduced at least by one half, relative to the Equivalence Strategy. Since only half the technology is deployed, there is only half the chance of a mechanical malfunction leading to war.

(2) Since at most one side remains armed, there is considerably less chance under Nuclear Disarmament that a nuclear war will occur by mistake. The principal mistake that might cause a nuclear war is the mistake of erroneously thinking that the other side is about to launch a nuclear attack. Such mistakes create enormous pressure for the launching of preemptive strikes, in order to get one's weapons in the air before they are destroyed on the ground. There is no chance that this mistake can occur under Nuclear Disarmament. The side that remains armed (if any) need not fear that the other side will launch a nuclear attack. The side that chooses to disarm cannot be tempted to launch a preemptive strike no matter what it believes the other side is doing, since it has no weapons with which to launch the strike.

(3) Even the opponents of Nuclear Disarmament describe the main peril of nuclear disarmament as nuclear blackmail by the Soviet Union. Opponents of disarmament apparently feel that after nuclear disarmament, nuclear threats are far more probable than nuclear disasters.

(4) Though nuclear weapons are not inherently more destructive than other sorts of weapons, conceived or actual (the napalm raids on Tokyo in March 1945 caused more deaths than Hiroshima or Nagasaki), nuclear weapons are universally *perceived* as different in kind from nonnuclear weapons. The diplomatic losses a nation would incur upon using even tactical nuclear weapons would be immense.

(5) A large scale nuclear attack by the Soviet Union against the United States might contaminate the American and Canadian Great Plains, a major source of Soviet grain imports. The Soviets could still turn to Argentina, but the price of grain after the attack would skyrocket, and no combination of Argentinean, Australian, or other grain sources could possibly compensate for American or Canadian losses.

(6) The Soviets will find it difficult to find actual military situations in which it will be practical to use atomic weapons against the United States, or against anyone else. Nuclear weapons proved superfluous in the Soviet invasions of Hungary and Czechoslovakia, and they do not seem to be practicable in Afghanistan, where the human costs of the Soviet attempt to regain control are high. If the Soviets did not use nuclear weapons against China between 1960 and 1964 in order to prevent the development of Chinese nuclear capacity, it is hardly likely that they could use them against a nonnuclear United States. Of course it is always *possible* that the Soviet Union might launch a nuclear attack against a nonnuclear United States, perhaps as an escalatory step in a conventional conflict, but it is also *possible* that the Soviet Union will launch a nuclear attack on the United States *right now*, despite the present situation of Equivalence. The point is that

there is no such thing as a guarantee against nuclear attack, but the probability of an actual attack is small under either strategy.

[j] The chance of all-out nuclear war under the Equivalence Strategy is slight, but the chance of all-out nuclear war under Nuclear Disarmament is zero. There cannot be a two-sided nuclear war if only one side possesses nuclear arms.

[k] In considering the threat of Soviet nonnuclear aggression under Nuclear Disarmament, we must consider Soviet nuclear threats—usually called "nuclear blackmail"—as well as possible uses of conventional arms by the Soviets.

(1) Suppose that the United States unilaterally gives up second-strike-capacity. What are the odds that the Soviet Union would attempt to influence American behavior through nuclear threats? Obviously, one's views about the chances for successful nuclear blackmail depends on one's views about the chances of a Soviet first strike against a nonnuclear United States. If the chances of a Soviet first strike are slight, then the chances of successful blackmail will also be slight. We have already argued on a variety of grounds that chances of a Soviet first strike under ND are small. I would suggest that the ability of the Soviet Union to manipulate a nonnuclear United States would be the same as the ability of the United States to manipulate the Soviet Union from 1945 to 1949, when strategic conditions were reversed. Anyone who reflects on events from 1945 to 1949 will conclude that nuclear threats have little effect on nations capable of acting with resolve.

There is always the chance that the Soviet Union will carry out its nuclear threats, but there is always the chance that the Soviet Union will carry out its threats even if the United States retains nuclear weapons. There is no device that provides a guarantee against nuclear blackmail. Consequently it cannot be argued that Equivalence provides a guarantee against blackmail that Nuclear Disarmament does not.

The foregoing dismissal of nuclear blackmail violates conventional strategic wisdom, which is concerned with nuclear blackmail almost to obsession. Numerous authors, for example, cite the swift fall of Japan after Hiroshima as evidence of the strategic usefulness of nuclear weapons and nuclear threats. The case of Japan is worth considering. Contrary to the canonical view certified by Secretary Stimson in his famous (and self-serving) *Harper's* article in 1947,[22] I believe that the bombings of Hiroshima and Nagasaki had almost no effect on events leading to the surrender of Japan. If so, the force of the Japanese precedent, which still influences strategic thought, is greatly attenuated.

Obviously the bombings of Hiroshima and Nagasaki had no effect on the popular desire for peace in Japan, since the Japanese public did not know of the atomic bombings until the war was over. What is more surprising is that the bombings do not seem to have influenced either the Emperor or the military command in making the decision to sue for peace. The Emperor, as is now well known, had decided for peace as early as January 1945, and if he was set on peace in January, he did not need the bombings of August to make up his mind. The military, on the other hand, do not seem to have desired peace even after the bombs were dropped; the record shows that the military (a) correctly surmised that the United States had a small supply of these bombs, (b) debated improved antiaircraft measures to prevent any further bombs from being delivered, and (c) correctly inferred that bombs of this type could not be used to support a ground invasion, which they felt they could repulse with sufficient success to secure a conditional surrender. What tipped the political scales so that the Emperor could find his way to peace was not the bombing of Nagasaki on 9 August, but the Russian declaration of war on 8 August. Unaware of Stalin's commitment at Yalta to enter the war against Japan, the Japanese had hoped through the spring and summer of 1945 that the Soviets would mediate a negotiated settlement between the United States and Japan rather than send the Red Army into a new theater of war. When the Russians invaded Manchuria on 9 August, Premier Suzuki, according to reports, cried, "The game is over," and when the Emperor demanded surrender from the Council of Elders on 10 August, he never mentioned atomic bombs as the occasion of his demand

22. Stimson's "The Decision to Use the Atomic Bomb" appeared in the February 1947 *Harper's Magazine*, pp. 97–107. Typical of Stimson's *post hoc ergo propter hoc* is:

We believed that our attacks struck cities which must certainly be important to the Japanese military leaders, both Army and Navy, and we waited for a result. We waited one day.

for peace.[23] Little can be inferred from such evidence about the effectiveness of nuclear threats.

(2) The strategy of Nuclear Disarmament does not forbid uses of conventional arms in response to acts of aggression. Since there is no reason to believe that adoption of the strategy of Nuclear Disarmament by the United States will make acts of Soviet aggression any more palatable than they are at present, in all probability the American government under ND will appropriate funds for conventional arms sufficient to provide a deterrent to Soviet aggression roughly comparable to the deterrent provided by nuclear arms under S and E. This argument assumes that the deterrent effects of the American strategic nuclear arsenal (whatever they are) can be obtained with a developed arsenal of modern conventional weapons. A review of the difficulties involved in the use of strategic nuclear weapons in concrete situations may convince the reader that conventional weapons can match the deterrent effect of nuclear weapons. Indeed, the whole development of "flexible response" systems during the McNamara era testifies to the widespread recognition that strategic nuclear weapons provide little leverage to nations who would seek to control the flow of world events.

[1] Since it is impossible to predict how much money must be spent on conventional forces in order to supply a deterrent equal to the present (nuclear) deterrent against Soviet nonnuclear aggression, it is possible that levels of military spending under ND will be greater than levels under E. But it is also possible that the levels of spending will be much less. The technical equipment needed to maintain E is fantastically expensive, but the labor costs of training and improving conven-

23. For the Emperor's active attempts to obtain peace see Herbert Feis, *The Atomic Bomb and the End of World War II* (Princeton: Princeton University Press, 1966), p. 66. For the military response to the atomic bombings see Hanson Baldwin, *Great Mistakes of the War* (New York: Collins-Knowlton-Wing, 1950), pp. 87–107. For Suzuki's remark that "The game is over" see W. Craig, *The Fall of Japan* (New York: Dial, 1967), p. 107. One interesting suggestion about the special effectiveness of the atomic bomb against Japan is found in a remark made by General Marshall to David Lilienthal in 1947, "We didn't realize its value to give the Japanese such a shock that they could surrender without loss of face" (quoted in Feis, *The Atomic Bomb*, p. 6). Marshall's remark is prima facie reasonable, but I can find nothing in the documents on the Japanese side that supports it.

tional forces can also be staggering. All things considered, it is still likely that spending will be less under ND than under E, especially if the draft is revived.

Comparison of Superiority and Equivalence

The chance of a Soviet first strike is greater under Superiority than under Equivalence, and the chance of all-out nuclear war is greater under Superiority than under Equivalence. The ability of Equivalence to deter Soviet nonnuclear aggression is equal to the ability of Superiority to deter such aggression, and the Equivalence strategy costs less. Thus Equivalence is preferable to Superiority from both the prudential and the moral point of view.

Comparison of Equivalence and Nuclear Disarmament

We have argued that Nuclear Disarmament and Equivalence are equal in their ability to deter Soviet nonnuclear aggression. In the category of military spending Nuclear Disarmament is preferable to Equivalence. In the category of "all-out war" ND is clearly superior to E, and in the category of "first strikes," ND seems to be about equal to E. Thus we have what seems to be a decisive prudential and moral argument in favor of Nuclear Disarmament: in every category, ND is either equal to or superior to E.

VII. FURTHER COMPARISON OF EQUIVALENCE AND NUCLEAR DISARMAMENT

Despite the preceding argument, the vast majority of authors who consider these subjects prefer E to ND. Since the case for ND in the categories of all-out war and military spending is decisive, and since the equality of ND and E in the area of nonnuclear aggression is established in section [k], the only category in which a counterargument against ND can be mounted is the category of first strikes. Many authors will argue that although the chance of a first strike under ND is small, it is nevertheless *much larger* than the chance of a Soviet first strike under E, and they seem to believe that this substantially larger chance of a first strike under ND outweighs the inferiority of E in the categories of all-out war and military spending. To resolve the question we must attempt a more precise determination of the probabilities and the utilities involved in the outcomes. We assume a universal overriding preference for continued life, and introduce, as a unit of disutility, the notion of an "expected death," which is the death of a single person multiplied by the chance that it will occur. To further simplify matters, we will ignore the category of military spending and concentrate solely on the categories of first strike and all-out war. The problem of comparing ND and E *morally* then reduces to this: if we consider first strikes and their aftermaths, does ND yield a greater number of expected deaths than E? The problem of comparing ND and E *prudentially* becomes: considering first strikes and their aftermaths, does ND yield a greater number of expected *American* deaths than E?

Probability of First Strikes under E

The most likely origins of first strikes under E are accidents and mistakes.

(1) *War by Accident.*

Nuclear war by accident can result from either human or mechanical failure. A scenario for human failure was popularized in the movie *Dr. Strangelove*; a scenario for mechanical failure was popularized in the movie *Fail Safe*. Defense Department officials have assured the public dozens of times since that there is almost no chance that either type of failure could start a nuclear war. The chances of war by accident are indeed small, but I see little reason to agree with Defense Department officials that the chances are negligible. In 1979 and 1980 alone, there were at least three serious instances of computer failure leading to the conclusion that the United States was being attacked by Soviet missiles.[24] In each case the error was discovered in time, but

24. Since the great nuclear scares of the early 1960s, reports of accidents that might lead to nuclear war have been rare in the public press. But, in late 1979, new reports of mishaps began to appear, and these reports multiplied alarmingly through 1980. On 16 November 1979 the Defense Department announced that a "mechanical error" had led to a false nuclear war alert seven days before, and that ten American jet interceptors had been scrambled in response (*Facts on File*, 16 November 1979). On 7 June 1980 the Defense Department announced that a malfunction in a 60¢ silicon chip had produced on June 3 and June 5 computer indications that land-based and submarine-based Russian missiles

this is no guarantee that all future errors will be discovered in sufficient time to prevent irreversible action. The sanguine analysis presented by the Defense Department of the 1979–80 incidents neglected to consider that the American alerts triggered by these incidents might have prompted a Soviet response, which in turn could have prompted an American counterresponse ultimately leading to war. Furthermore, those who disparage the idea that nuclear war might begin by accident usually ignore the possibility that the accident might occur on the Russian side, prompting an American second strike. The multiple failsafe devices so proudly displayed in Minuteman missile silos and elsewhere might not be present in their Soviet counterparts.

(2) *War by Mistake.*

In the situation of Equivalence, neither side can in fact gain anything by starting a nuclear war. Nevertheless, it is possible that leaders may mistakenly come to believe that it is to their advantage to launch a first strike. Such an error may arise from sheer human folly, or perhaps for some of the following reasons:

(a) American leaders might mistakenly come to believe that they have achieved first-strike capacity against the Soviet Union, and launch a first strike in order to solidify this advantage; or

(b) Soviet leaders might mistakenly come to believe that they have obtained first-strike capacity against the United States, and act to solidify this presumed advantage; or

---

were launched towards the United States. In each case the error was detected "within three minutes." On 17 June 1980 Assistant Secretary of Defense Gerald P. Dineen summarized the incidents of June 3 and June 5 and commented, "In a real sense, the total system worked in that even though the mechanical electronic part produced false information, the human part correctly evaluated it and prevented any irrevocable reaction" (*Facts on File*, 20 June 1980). Dineen did not comment on the fact that, since Soviet submarine-launched missiles will reach the United States in about nine minutes, "the human component" had used 33 percent of the discretionary time available (three of nine minutes) before detecting the error, leaving the world six minutes short of all-out nuclear war. On 15 June 1980 the Chicago *Tribune* reported that United States forces went "on alert" about 50 times a year, usually in response to spy satellite warnings of missile launches that turn out, on evaluation, to be Russian ballistic missile tests. To round out the year, a report to the Senate Armed Services Committee stated that the nation's missile-monitoring system produced about 147 false indications of Russian missile attacks in the preceding year (*Facts on File*, 31 December 1980).

(c) American leaders might feel that they are losing second-strike capacity, and decide to launch a strike before things get worse; or

(d) Soviet leaders might feel that they are losing second-strike capacity, and strike to prevent themselves from losing the nuclear race; or

(e) American leaders might mistakenly believe that they are under Soviet attack, and launch American missiles in order to prevent their presumed destruction on the ground. This mistaken belief might arise from mistaken interpretations of a terrorist nuclear attack, catastrophes in an American nuclear reactor, etc.; or

(f) Soviet leaders might make the same mistake and take the same action.

Thus, the chance of war by mistake is probably larger than the advocates of Equivalence are willing to admit. History generally confirms this pessimism. One need not produce Richardson process models or recite the litany of the seven elementary catastrophes in order to realize that the majority of acts of aggression and onsets of wars in this century have been prompted by mistaken beliefs about prevailing intentions—not just by mistaken beliefs about the probability of ultimate success. The difficulties involved in assessing the intentions of one's opponents on the international scene were ruefully summarized by Viscount Grey ten years after he led Britain into World War I:

> The distinction between preparations made with the intention of going to war and precautions against attack is a true distinction, clear and definite in the minds of those who build up armaments. But it is a distinction that is not obvious or certain to others. . . . Each government, therefore, while resenting any suggestion that its own measures are anything more than precautions for defense, regards similar measures of another government as preparation for attack. . . . The increase of armaments that is intended in each nation to produce consciousness of strength, and a sense of security, does not produce these effects. On the contrary, it produces consciousness of the strength of other nations and a sense of fear. . . . The enormous growth of armaments in Europe, the sense of insecurity and the fears caused by them—it was these that made war

inevitable. . . . This is the real and final account of the origin of the
Great War.[25]

(3) *Relative Probability of American First Strike under E*

Obviously it is difficult to quantify the probability of a first strike
even after running through all the elements of accident and mistake.
For the moment, let us simply keep all these factors in mind and desig-
nate the chance of a first strike under E as:

PE = Probability of first strike under E

Notice that PE is the sum of probability that the Soviet Union will attack the United States *and* the probability that the United States will
attack the Soviet Union.[26] (One important but little noticed difference
between the calculation of first strikes under E and the calculation of
first strikes under ND is that under E there are two first strikes to consider, while under ND there is at most one.)

The chance of an American first strike clearly must be considered in
making the moral calculation of expected deaths. It is interesting that
the chance of an American first strike also enters the prudential calculation, since an American first strike, though initially killing only Russians, may well lead to an all-out war in which many Americans will
die.

What are the chances of an *American* first strike, in terms of PE?
Many Americans are convinced that their nation's intentions are peace-
able and that the Defense Department exists only for defense. On the
other hand, (a) American troops have actually invaded the Soviet
Union with the intention of overthrowing the government; Soviet
troops have never set foot in the United States; (b) the United States
has used nuclear bombs before; the Soviet Union has never used them;
(c) the United States has never publicly announced that it will not, in
fact, launch a first strike; (d) many conservative Americans desire
that the government of the Soviet Union be overthrown, and this is not
likely to happen unless that government loses a war or is destroyed by

25. Viscount Grey of Fallodon, *Twenty Five Years* (London: Hoddard and
Stoughton, 1925), 1: 91–92. Grey was the British Secretary of State for Foreign
Affairs, 1905–1916. It is a pity that Grey did not hold these views in 1914.

26. Since all probabilities are low, we will systematically ignore subtractions
for joint occurrence.

one, but (e) communist ideology maintains that the American system will fall of itself, without the need of force from without. With these points in mind, it seems only fair to infer that the chance of a Soviet first strike is roughly equal to the chance of an American first strike. Thus the chance of an American first strike is PE/2.

Intensity of First Strikes under E

In the great debate of the late 1970s concerning the ability of land-based American ICBMs to survive Soviet attack, Defense Department officials initially alleged that the Soviet Union could destroy most American ICBMs by precision attacks that would leave only 800,000 American dead. In this event, it was argued, the United States might fail to launch a second strike, in order to spare the 96 percent of its surviving citizens the devastating effects of a Soviet counter-counter strike. These claims led to comprehensive studies of the effects of Soviet attacks on land ICBMs—by far the most probable form of a Soviet first strike—and in the end many experts came to agree that the number of casualties from such an attack would probably be not 800,000 but 20,000,000 American dead,[27] a figure that left students of strategy much relieved. Likewise an American first strike against Soviet weapons might be expected to leave 20,000,000 Soviet dead in the long run. In the moral calculation, then, the number of expected deaths from a first strike is (PE × 20,000,000). In the prudential calculation, the number of expected American dead is ($\frac{PE}{2}$ × 20,000,000).

Probability of First Strikes under ND

As already indicated, the chance of a first strike by accident or mistake is less under ND than under E. Furthermore, since there is the possibility of *two* first strikes under E and *at most*[28] the possibility of one first strike under ND, there is considerable reason to conclude that the

27. The figure of 800,000 was given by Secretary of Defense James Schlesinger in testimony before the Senate Foreign Relations Committee 11 September 1974. The figure of 20,000,000 is from the Office of Technology Assessment report of 1979.

28. We say "at most" because ND requires unilateral disarmament but does not exclude mutual disarmament.

probability of a first strike under ND is less than the probability of a first strike under E.

On the other hand, the chance that the Soviet Union will start a nuclear war through calculation of presumed advantage is greater under ND than under E. Certainly the fact that the Soviet Union could use nuclear weapons against the United States without fear of American nuclear reprisal might tempt them to use these weapons, especially if the United States and the Soviet Union were involved in a large-scale war using conventional weapons.[29] After all, that was the way nuclear weapons came to be used the first time around. But such a strike would have difficulties and costs, which we have already enumerated, and in general the Soviet Union might be disinclined to use nuclear weapons against a nation it does not perceive as a source of nuclear threats. Though aggression studies have been among the most lavishly funded of recent psychological projects, we still do not have anything like a set of rules which tell us whether aggression is more or less likely between two parties who fear each other than it is between two parties, one of whom has nothing to fear from the other.

Considering the military awkwardness and diplomatic costs of using nuclear weapons, I find it quite incredible that the majority of official statements on this subject consider the chance of a calculated Soviet attack on a nonnuclear United States as greater than the chance under Equivalence of a Soviet attack by accident *or* a Soviet attack by mistake *or* an American attack by accident *or* an American attack by mistake. Perhaps the most reasonable compromise among competing arguments is to rate the chance of a Soviet attack under ND as greater than the chance of a Soviet attack under E, and the chance of an American *or* Soviet attack under E as greater than the chance of a Soviet attack under ND. Call the probability of a first strike under ND:

PD = Probability of first strike under ND

29. The chance of war between the Soviet Union and the United States is small, even if the United States gives up its nuclear weapons. The sorts of acts that would provoke the Soviet Union to declare war against the United States under ND are precisely those acts which the United States dare not do now, even with nuclear weapons. For example, if the United States will not stop a Soviet invasion of Poland now, it is hardly likely to provoke the Soviets by attempting to stop such an invasion under ND.

We are thus assuming that:

$$PE > PD > \frac{PE}{2}$$

Intensity of First Strikes under ND

The usual accounts of a Soviet first strike envisage a large counterforce strike designed to emasculate, as far as possible, any American nuclear counterstrike. If the United States possessed no nuclear weapons with which to counterattack, the most probable Soviet first strike would be quite different. The most likely first use of nuclear weapons by the Soviets would be on a battlefield outside United States territory; the most likely first strike against U.S. territory would be a punitive or threatening strike against a military installation. There is no scenario of more than negligible probability in which a Soviet first strike under ND would equal the severity of a Soviet first strike under E, if for no other reason than that there is probably no military objective, short of the independence of the United States, that the United States would not concede (and rightly so) in order to save the lives of tens of millions of Americans. Since the Soviet Union has never made the conquest of the United States or a change in its form of government an announced policy goal, and since there is no scenario short of fantasy in which it could become a Soviet policy goal, it is safe to estimate the number of American dead from a Soviet first strike under ND as no more than 10,000,000. In the moral calculation, the number of expected American deaths in a first strike under ND is (PD × 10,000,000).

Preliminary Comparison of E and ND

If we compare E and ND as regards first strikes alone, we have:

(1) PE × 20,000,000 > PD × 10,000,000

This is obvious since PE > PD. Thus, considering first strikes *alone*, ND is morally preferable to E. People who do not accept this conclusion should consider that this result will hold unless the probability of *either* a Soviet or American first strike under E is half as great as the probability of a Soviet first strike under ND. Also:

(2) $\frac{PE}{2}$ × 20,000,000 > PD × 10,000,000

This follows, once again, since PE > PD. Thus, considering first strikes *alone*, ND is prudentially preferable to E. But the prudential case is not as decisive as the moral case, and ND will cease to be prudentially preferable to E if PE = PD, that is, if the chance of a Soviet first strike under ND is twice as great as the chance of a Soviet first strike under E.

Probability and Intensity of All-Out War under E

For purposes of simplicity we will consider an all-out nuclear war as a four step process consisting of (a) a first strike, (b) a counterstrike, or second strike, (c) a counter-counter strike, and (d) a counter-counter-counter strike. In the most probable scenarios, the first strike is a counterforce strike, directed principally at enemy missiles; the second strike is a massive counterforce and countervalue strike, directed at enemy weapons, industry, and cities, using the residue of missiles and planes left over from the first strike; the counter-counter strike is a massive counterforce and countervalue strike, using whatever weapons have survived the second strike, and the counter-counter-counter strike is a countervalue strike using whatever weapons are left after the first strike and the counter-counter strike.

There are two versions of the four step sequence, one starting with a Soviet first strike, the other with an American first strike. Call these the SU sequence and the A sequence:

(SUa) In the SU sequence the war begins when the Soviet Union launches a counterforce strike killing, by OTA estimate, some 20,000,-000 Americans. Expected deaths are PE/2 (20,000,000).

(SUb) The United States responds with a massive counterforce and countervalue strike; this is the strike the threat of which was supposed to prevent (SUa) from occurring. Since there is a fifty percent chance that the President's nerve will fail, the probability of (SUb) is PE/4. Since the days of Robert McNamara, the American second strike has been designed to destroy 50 percent of Soviet industry and about 25 percent of its population, for an approximate total of 60,-000,000 Russian deaths. To these deaths we should add approximately 10,000,000 deaths, principally in China and Japan, from fallout drifting west to east from the American second strike. Expected deaths from (SUb) are thus PE/4 (70,000,000).

(SUc) The Soviet Union launches a counter-counter strike against American cities and surviving American forces. This is the action the threat of which was supposed to prevent (SUb) from occurring. What is the probability of (SUc) given (SUb)? The nerve of the Soviet Premier may fail, just as Khrushchev's nerve failed in 1962. On the other hand, the Premier may remember that Khrushchev's failure of nerve cost him his job. It is reasonable to compute the chance of the Premier's failure of nerve as the same as the chance of the American President's (50 percent), in which case the probability of (SUc) is PE/8. The number of deaths from this Soviet counter-counter strike, which will fall on American cities, should be put at at least 40,000,000 (over and above the 20,000,000 who perish in the Soviet first strike). Thus the expected deaths from (SUc) are PE/8 (40,000,000).

(SUd) Thus far 60,000,000 Americans and 60,000,000 Russians have died in the war. Since the Soviets have largely exhausted their strategic weapons in (SUa) and (SUc), they have no threat with which to deter an American counter-counter-counter strike. On the other hand, since the United States is nearly destroyed and since the Soviet Union can no longer fight, there is little reason for any further American action. The President or his survivor will be torn between the futility of the counter-counter-counter strike and the thought that the United States is not yet a clear winner in terms of casualties. Once again, it is reasonable to estimate that the probability of failure to respond as 50 percent. Thus the probability of (SUd) is PE/16. This will be mainly a countervalue strike, but the Russian population is highly scattered. We should estimate deaths from (SUd), then, as at least 20,000,000; this is a conservative estimate, which leaves more than half of the Russian population alive after two full scale countervalue attacks. The expected deaths from (SUd) are thus PE/16 (20,000,-000).

(Aa) In the A sequence, the United States strikes first, launching a massive counterforce strike, destroying a large fraction of Soviet ICBMs, eliminating a good fraction of in-port Soviet missile subs, and a certain percentage of Soviet subs at sea.[30] Since Soviet cities are not

30. Since most Soviet subs leave through the Baltic, tracking of Soviet subs is easier than tracking American subs. Furthermore, the Soviet subs are noisier and therefore more detectable than American Polaris subs, though they may be

hit and the Soviet population is dispersed, such attacks might leave no more than 15,000,000 Soviet dead, but to these deaths we should add approximately 5,000,000 more deaths due to fallout drifting east. Since we have assumed that the chance of an American first strike is the same as the chance of a Soviet first strike, the probability of (Aa) is PE/2, and the expected deaths from (Aa) are Pe/2 (20,000,000).

(Ab) Since under E the Soviets have second-strike capacity, we must assume that at least some Soviet weapons survive, either in hardened silos or in undetected missile submarines. The Soviet Premier knows that if he launches these weapons, the Soviet Union will be devastated by a massive American counter-counter strike. On the other hand, the entire Soviet system is geared to launch this strike in the event of an American attack, and any Premier who simply surrenders after 20,000,000 Russians have died is very likely to be replaced. Given the traditional pragmatism of the Russian leadership, we will assume that the Soviet leaders are twice as likely to understand the futility of second strikes and twice as reluctant to launch the second strike as the American President is in the analogous situation. This makes the probability of (Ab) PE/8. Since Soviet missiles are MIRVed, the effects of the Russian counterstrike, aimed at American industry and cities, will be devastating; we can expect, at a minimum, that 40,000,000 Americans will be killed if even a small number of Russian missiles survive the American first strike. Thus expected deaths from (Ab) are PE/8 (40,000,000).

(Ac) A large fraction of the American weapons held in reserve after (Aa) will survive the Soviet counterstrike; the threat of these weapons, in fact, was supposed to prevent (Ab) from occurring. The President or his survivor, having little to fear from a Soviet counter-counter-counter strike and having 40,000,000 American deaths to revenge, is very likely to order (Ac) in response to (Ab). If we rate the President's likelihood of response at 80 percent, the probability of (Ac) is (4/5) (PE/8), or PE/10. The number of Soviet deaths from this mainly countervalue strike will be at least 40,000,000, with an additional ten million deaths caused in other countries by fallout. Thus the expected deaths from (Ac) are PE/10 (50,000,000).

---

less detectable than Tridents. Some will be hit, but since we are operating under E, we assume that not all are hit.

(Ad) It is highly probable that the Soviet Union will sue for peace after (Ac), provided that there are any leaders left to sue for peace. However, there is a chance that a few Soviet missiles have not been launched in (Ab), in the hope that the threat of launching these missiles will prevent (Ac) from occurring. These missiles might be launched after (Ac) either on command from the Premier or by enterprising lower level commanders seeking revenge for the destruction of the Soviet Union. It is not unreasonable to suppose that there is one chance in four that such an attack might occur, given (Ac), and if even a single thermonuclear warhead exploded over an American city the deaths from (Ad) might run into the millions. The probability of this attack is thus PE/40, but the number of deaths from this attack, if it occurs, are likely to be near 4,000,000. Thus the expected deaths from (Ad) are PE/40 (4,000,000).

At first sight it may appear that these Strangelovian exercises are largely a matter of pulling numbers out of a hat. But in fact these estimates are highly conservative, and though it is not likely that all-out war, should it occur, will reach precisely these targets, it is highly probable that all-out war will not produce results that are substantially *less* than these figures. The numbers of casualties might appear inflated, but they are not inflated if one considers the number of wounded who will die because of the disruption in medical services and the collapse of the economic system.[31] Furthermore, we have been extremely conservative in the high degree of discretion allotted to the American and Soviet leadership. In many scenarios, leadership does not have the authority here assigned to it, and the four stages of nuclear war proceed in quick succession, with the occurrence of each stage generating a high probability that the subsequent stage will occur—the so-called spasm feared by all students of thermonuclear

31. In "Medical Problems of Survivors of Nuclear War," *New England Journal of Medicine*, 12 November 1981, pp. 1226–32, Herbert Abrams and William von Kaenel estimate the effects of a 6559-megaton attack on the United States, taking special note of the consequences of disruption in the American medical system. (The megatonnage of this attack is megatonnage of the so-called CRP-2B model used by the Federal Emergency Planning Agency for civil defense planning in the 1980s.) Abrams and van Kaenel conclude that 133,000,000 Americans will die within two months of such an attack, a figure that far exceeds any estimate of deaths used in this article.

war. If we narrow the range of leadership discretion, the probability that the end stages will be reached rises substantially, and so does the number of expected deaths.[32]

Moral Comparison of E and ND

The total of expected deaths under E is:

(SUa)	PE/2 × 20,000,000	= PE × 10,000,000
(SUb)	PE/4 × 70,000,000	= PE × 17,500,000
(SUc)	PE/8 × 40,000,000	= PE × 5,000,000
(SUd)	PE/16 × 20,000,000	= PE × 1,250,000
(Aa)	PE/2 × 20,000,000	= PE × 10,000,000
(Ab)	PE/8 × 40,000,000	= PE × 5,000,000
(Ac)	PE/10 × 40,000,000	= PE × 4,000,000
(Ad)	PE/40 × 4,000,000	= PE × 100,000
		PE × 52,850,000

For example, if you think that there is one chance in ten of a nuclear war under E, then the expected deaths under E are about 5.3 million.

The total of expected dead under ND is:

PD × 10,000,000

In our estimate, PE is greater than PD, and thus the moral case for unilateral nuclear disarmament is overwhelming. The majority of authors, however, feel that Equivalence, or mutual deterrence, "lowers the chance of nuclear war" compared to ND. These figures show that even if the probability of a Soviet attack were *five times* greater under ND than the probability of either a Soviet or an American first strike under E, Nuclear Disarmament would *still*, on utilitarian grounds, be morally preferable to Equivalence. Furthermore, these

32. Readers who are arithmetically inclined can compute how narrowing the degree of leadership discretion in all-out war will raise the number of expected dead to the point where few could plausibly maintain either a moral or prudential case for Equivalence. Even if we permit leadership a 25 percent chance of failing to respond, the number of expected dead from Equivalence rises to 88,809,500. The defender of deterrence must argue that if Equivalence is prudentially preferred, then if the chance of Soviet attack under Equivalence is 13 percent, the chance of Soviet attack under Disarmament is nearly certain.

figures show that the probability of a *Soviet* first strike against the United States must be *more than ten times* higher under Nuclear Disarmament than under Equivalence before ND ceases to be the morally preferable policy. For reasons given earlier, I rate the chance that the Soviet Union is ten times as likely to attack a nonnuclear United States as it is likely to attack a nuclear United States as very small indeed.

Prudential Comparison of E and ND

The number of expected American deaths under E is:

(SUa)	PE/2 $\times$ 20,000,000	= PE $\times$ 10,000,000
(SUc)	PE/8 $\times$ 40,000,000	= PE $\times$ 5,000,000
(Ab)	PE/8 $\times$ 40,000,000	= PE $\times$ 5,000,000
(Ad)	PE/40 $\times$ 4,000,000	= PE $\times$ 100,000

PE $\times$ 20,100,000

The number of expected American deaths under ND remains:

PD $\times$ 10,000,000

If, as we have argued, PE is greater than PD, and if these damage estimates are probable, there is a decisive prudential case in favor of Nuclear Disarmament. The strategy of Equivalence is not only immoral, but irrational. Anyone who denies that Equivalence is irrational must show that the chance of nuclear war is at least twice as great under Nuclear Disarmament as it is under Equivalence. What is even more astounding, considering the popularity of Equivalence as a preferred rational strategy, is that anyone who wishes to make out a prudential case for Equivalence must show that the chance of Soviet attack under Nuclear Disarmament is *at least four times* as great as the chance of Soviet attack under Equivalence. This is a task from which even the most ardent defender of deterrence may shrink.

VIII. Multilateral Considerations

The preceding conclusions resulted from arguments limited to relations between the United States and the Soviet Union. Do these results change if we consider the present multilateral situation? Is unilateral disarmament still preferable when many nations have bombs? The expansion of the nuclear club does seem to have adversely affected the political movement for nuclear disarmament, which flourished in the late 1950s and early 1960s. If only two nations have nuclear weapons, nuclear disarmament by one may provoke nuclear disarmament in the other, producing the ideal result of general nuclear disarmament. But if many nations possess nuclear weapons, disarmament by one can hardly be expected to provoke disarmament by all of the others, and each armed nation, considering the fact that at least some other nations will continue to retain nuclear arms, may feel compelled to keep its weapons in order to deter the hard-core noncooperators. Even the most ardent supporters of disarmament become disheartened when they consider the difficulties of arranging a simultaneous surrender of nuclear weapons by seven or more independent nation states.

None of the arguments of the preceding sections, however, depends on the assumption that the Soviet Union will disarm if the United States arms, nor do they depend on the assumption that nuclear disarmament by the United States will increase the probability that the Soviet Union will disarm. Since the geographical situation of the Soviet Union makes Soviet disarmament contingent upon disarmament by both NATO and the Chinese, and since it is generally believed by the Soviet leadership that "backwardness" has been the source of Russian catastrophes across the centuries, it is highly unlikely that the Soviet Union will disarm *no matter what* the United States does. The fact remains that there are fewer expected deaths, and fewer expected American deaths, under ND than under E.

There are several considerations which show that the case for disarmament in the multilateral situation is as strong as or stronger than the case for disarmament in the bilateral situation. The case for Nuclear Disarmament is *at least as strong* in the multilateral situation because the multilateral case can legitimately be decomposed into a set of bilateral cases. The main reason why ND is preferable to E in the bilateral case is that the costs of war, if it occurs, are much higher under E than under ND, making ND preferable even if the chance of *a* war is higher under ND than under E. This argument makes no use of special information about the United States and the Soviet Union, and, if it is sound at all, it is also sound for the U.S.-China case, the

China-U.S.S.R. case, the U.S.S.R.-NATO case, and all of the other cases that in sum make up the multilateral problem.

The case for ND in the multilateral situation is *stronger than* the case for ND in the bilateral situation if one considers the import of Richard's theorem, proved in the 1930s, that *if every pair of a triplet of nations is stable, the triplet itself may still be unstable.*[33] For example, even if relations between the United States and the Soviet Union, the Soviet Union and China, and China and the United States are relatively stable, it is possible that the ensemble of these three nations is unstable, producing an arms race, and perhaps even a war. On the other hand, relative stability can be restored by any nation in the triplet that unilaterally withdraws from the nuclear club. Thus unilateral disarmament reduces the chance of war among those nations that do not choose to disarm, a result that recommends itself both prudentially and morally. In sum, if a nation is better off with Nuclear Disarmament in the bilateral case, it is even better off with Nuclear Disarmament in the multilateral case.

IX. FROM MORALS TO POLITICS

Nuclear Disarmament, Superiority, and Equivalence are the nuclear strategies most discussed by theorists, and other strategies are largely variants or specifications of these three. If utilitarianism favors Nuclear Disarmament over Superiority and Equivalence, it favors Nuclear Disarmament *tout court.* For utilitarians, ND is morally right, and ought to be adopted.

It remains to consider whether it is also morally right to *advocate* or *support* Nuclear Disarmament. Support is logically distinct from adoption, and acts of support have their own sets of consequences. It is possible, and by no means paradoxical, that within the utilitarian framework support for the morally right policy may be morally wrong.

The commonest situation where support for the right leads to the wrong is a three-way election in which support for the best candidate

33. Lewis Fry Richardson, *Arms and Insecurity* (Chicago: Quadrangle, 1960), chap. 9. See also E. Gold's "biographical preface" in L.F. Richardson, *Statistics of Deadly Quarrels*, ed. Quincy Wright and C.C. Lienau (Chicago: Quadrangle, 1960), p. xxv.

will elect the worst, while support for the second best outcome will defeat the worst. Moderate liberals whose support for Charles Goodell over Richard Ottinger led to the election of James Buckley in 1972 and whose support for Jacob Javits over Elisabeth Holtzman led to the election of Al d'Amato in 1980 found themselves in each case with their least preferred candidate. In such situations utilitarianism joins hands with a Weberian ethic of responsibility and calls on moral agents to support the second best.

It is often alleged that the competition between S, E, and ND is rather like the Senate races in New York in 1972 and 1980, and many who agree that ND is morally superior to E fear that open advocacy of ND will drain support from E and lead to victory for the Superiority Strategy. The flaw in this reasoning is to compare a three-way election with winners determined by votes to a three-way policy choice with winners determined by the ultimate vector of political pressure. With candidates and votes, support for the extreme steals votes from the center. With policies and pressures, pressure from one extreme helps support the center against pressure from the other. In choosing platforms and policies, Americans have traditionally shied away from extremes, and a three-way race between S, E, and ND places E in the central position historically favored by the American people. A two-way race, which places the "center" between Equivalence and Superiority, allows the supporters of Superiority to argue that their strategy is no more extreme than Equivalence. If the moral principle which evaluates support of strategic policies (as opposed to the policies themselves) determines that support should be exercised in the way most likely to defeat Superiority, there is as much a case for public support of Nuclear Disarmament as there is for Nuclear Disarmament itself.

The author would like to thank the National Endowment for the Humanities for fellowship support during the period of time in which this article was written. Thanks are also due to Mrs. Esther Gutenberg for her help and patience.

GREGORY S. KAVKA   Doubts About Unilateral
                     Nuclear Disarmament

The practice of nuclear deterrence by the United States poses an apparent
dilemma when examined from a utilitarian point of view. Continuation
of this practice risks the gravest of disasters for humankind—a large-
scale nuclear war with the Soviet Union. But its abandonment would
appear to risk, with greater (combined) probability, the lesser utilitarian
disasters of a Soviet nuclear strike or Soviet world-domination by means
of nuclear blackmail. Further, an expected value calculation will not solve
this problem. For reliable estimates of the probabilities and utilities of
the relevant possible outcomes are not available. Hence, in comparing
nuclear deterrence and unilateral nuclear disarmament, the utilitarian
seems trapped between the Scylla of a smaller risk of a worse disaster
(that is, full-scale nuclear war) and the Charybdis of a greater risk of a
smaller disaster (that is, a nuclear strike or Soviet domination via blackmail).[1]

In a recent article,[2] Douglas Lackey seeks to extricate us from this
utilitarian dilemma by denying one of the factual presuppositions that
underlies it. He claims that the probability, P, of a Soviet nuclear strike
or domination via nuclear blackmail, given U.S. unilateral nuclear disarmament, is actually *less* than the probability of a U.S.-Soviet nuclear
war, given a continued policy of deterrence by the United States (pp.
204–5, 221–22). If this is so, unilateral nuclear disarmament by the

1. See my "Deterrence, Utility, and Rational Choice," *Theory and Decision* 12 (March
1980): 41–60.
2. Douglas Lackey, "Missiles and Morals: A Utilitarian Look at Nuclear Deterrence,"
Philosophy & Public Affairs 11 (Summer 1982): 189–231. Page references in the text are
to this article. Though my comments explicitly address only Lackey's utilitarian analysis
of deterrence, they apply to his prudential analysis as well.

United States would involve a *smaller* risk of producing a *lesser* disaster, compared to continued U.S. deterrence. The utilitarian problem is then solved, or dissolved, with an obvious verdict for unilateral nuclear disarmament emerging.

Unfortunately, however, Lackey's solution to this important problem is a pseudosolution based on an implausibly optimistic estimate of P. Lackey describes the probability of continued deterrence leading to nuclear war as "small, but substantial" (p. 208), yet he believes that P is smaller still.[3] A more common view is that P is high, perhaps even close to one. For throughout history nations have been quite inclined to use their power to unilateral advantage, and there is little in the history of the Soviet state to indicate that it is abnormal in this respect. What evidence does Lackey offer to counteract this common view?

He lays much emphasis on the fact that the United States did not use its early atomic monopoly for blackmail or attack (pp. 205 and 212). But there are too many differences between that situation and the one the Soviets would be in now after U.S. unilateral nuclear disarmament, to rely on this precedent. The United States was a democratic nation whose people had just experienced a substantial war, and which was recently allied to the nation it might have employed its weapons against—the U.S.S.R. Technologically, nuclear weapons were much smaller, many fewer, and much less well-tested than they are at present, and the instruments for delivering them were more vulnerable to defensive measures. Militarily, the Soviets had a massive, mobilized, and well-positioned land army that could have readily been used to conquer Europe. This to some degree counterbalanced the military power of early nuclear weapons. Nor was there sufficient appreciation of the power of nuclear weapons to allow leaders to use them most effectively as political-strategic weapons. None of these political, technological, military, and intellectual constraints would apply in the same way to the Soviet Union now, if the United States dismantled its nuclear arsenal.

Might the Soviets' generally cautious military behavior (for example, directly invading only nations on their geographic periphery) be taken as evidence they would not exploit nuclear predominance if they had it? Lackey suggests so with regard to at least one instance—the Soviets'

3. In addition to the pages cited above in the text, see Lackey, "Missiles," pp. 191, 197–98, 206, 210–12, 215, and 218 on the improbability of Soviet attack; and pp. 205, 206, 212, and 215 on the improbability of nuclear blackmail.

failure to attack Chinese nuclear facilities (p. 211). But the moral of that story is not what Lackey takes it to be. Memoirs from the Nixon administration suggest that the Soviets may well have refrained from such an attack only out of concern about the response of the United States, its only equal in nuclear power.[4] From this—and other instances of relatively cautious international behavior—we may not infer how the Soviets would act in the absence of any nuclear equal (or near equal). To do so would be to follow the lead of the apocryphal banker who, upon observing that the bank had never been robbed, did away with locks and guards as unnecessary.

Lackey fails to fully appreciate the force of this point. He writes,

> the Soviet Union has never made the conquest of the United States or a change in its form of government an announced policy goal, and . . . there is no scenario short of fantasy in which it could become a Soviet policy goal. (p. 222)

This may be true, as there is no scenario short of fantasy in which the United States will adopt unilateral nuclear disarmament. But it does not follow that we *would be* safe from Soviet conquest if we practiced unilateral nuclear disarmament, as Lackey seems to suppose. Compare a potential robber's side of our bank case. Lefty may want money and be willing to rob to get it. But as the bank is well guarded and well locked he never adopts robbing the bank as a goal.[5] But should our banker unlock and unguard, we can predict that Lefty will be there with his hands in the till.

Perhaps Lackey believes Soviet leaders are unlikely to attack a nuclearly disarmed United States because they would not have any reason to attack in the absence of a U.S. nuclear threat (p. 221). But, notoriously, the mere expansion of one's power has seemed to numerous political leaders throughout history a good enough reason to undertake aggressive military action. And the Soviets might conceivably attack or employ nuclear blackmail out of loftier motives—to impose lasting peace through world government and to prevent later U.S. nuclear rearmament and possible

4. H. R. Haldeman, *The Ends of Power* (New York: Dell, 1978), pp. 128–35. Also see Marvin Kalb and Bernard Kalb, *Kissinger* (Boston: Little, Brown & Co., 1974), pp. 226–28.

5. Not expecting the bank to unlock and unguard, Lefty never even adopts the conditional goal of robbing it if it does. Like busy Soviet leaders, he does not make contingency plans for fantastical contingencies.

two-sided nuclear war.[6] After all, even so peaceloving and rational an individual as Bertrand Russell advocated, during the time of the U.S. nuclear monopoly, that it adopt such a course toward the Soviet Union for essentially these very reasons.[7]

Much ado is made by Lackey about conventional armament as an effective substitute for nuclear deterrence (pp. 196, 205, and 214). This may well have been so in the early days of atomic weaponry, but not today, given the enormous nuclear arsenals of the superpowers. If a modern superpower were willing to use nuclear attack on a nuclearly disarmed foe to obtain concessions or capitulation, resistance with conventional forces would be quite ineffectual. If these forces massed for defense, or attack, they could be destroyed with tactical nuclear weapons. And they could not defend cities or military bases from nuclear destruction ordered to force compliance with political demands.

There is much reason then to doubt Lackey's sanguine estimate of P. So far, however, we have largely ignored the fact that there are other nuclear powers besides the United States and the Soviet Union. When we take this into account, our estimate of P must increase substantially. For if the United States adopted unilateral nuclear disarmament, it is unlikely that all other nuclear powers—especially China—would follow suit. Their nuclear arsenals would then be tempting targets for Soviet preemptive attack, especially if these countries began to expand their nuclear weaponry to compensate for the removal of the American nuclear umbrella. Lackey, citing a theoretical result of Lewis Richardson, suggests that the fewer the nations armed with nuclear weapons, the smaller the chance of nuclear war (p. 230). But it seems reasonable to give more weight to the specifi historical evidence which suggests, as noted above, that America's nuclear power may be all that has prevented the Soviets from striking the Chinese. Are we not safer relying on our recent experience that mutual deterrence by nearly equal nuclear powers works, than laying humankind open to the uncertainties and instabilities of a

---

6. If, improbably, unilateral nuclear disarmament were ever adopted by the United States, it would surely be over the opposition of powerful domestic forces that might later regain control of U.S. nuclear policy.

7. See Ronald Clark, *The Life of Bertrand Russell* (London: Jonathan Cape, 1975), chap. 19, which includes a number of relevant quotations from articles, speeches, and letters by Russell. See also Bertrand Russell, "The Future of Mankind," in his *Unpopular Essays* (New York: Simon & Schuster, 1950), pp. 34–44.

world of vastly unequal nuclear powers, with the Soviets having nuclear forces much greater than all the others combined?

In sum, a number of considerations indicate that Lackey has seriously underestimated the probability of nuclear attack or nuclear blackmail if the United States should adopt unilateral nuclear disarmament: (1) the general historical tendency of great powers and their leaders to exploit military advantages, (2) disanalogies between past U.S. nuclear dominance and (hypothetical) future Soviet nuclear dominance, (3) the significance of the distinction between current Soviet policy and behavior and what that policy and behavior might become after U.S unilateral nuclear disarmament, (4) the existence of plausible prudential and "moral" motives for Soviet use of nuclear weapons in such circumstances, (5) the ineffectiveness of conventional defense against a vast nuclear arsenal, and (6) the instabilities of a world with multiple unequal nuclear powers. In light of these considerations, it seems clear that the probability, P, of Soviet nuclear attack or blackmail following U.S. unilateral nuclear disarmament exceeds the "small, but substantial" probability of continued U.S. deterrence leading to nuclear war. And the utilitarian dilemma concerning deterrence sketched in the opening paragraph of this paper remains in force.[8]

8. In "Deterrence, Utility, and Rational Choice," I sketch an approach for dealing with this dilemma. Lackey (pp. 202–5) criticizes my position, but his criticisms are largely off-target. He misrepresents the one condition in my analysis that he discusses, confusing two disasters being of "roughly the same *order* of magnitude," that is, the greater not being "a hundred or a thousand times as bad as the lesser" (my terms), with their being "roughly equal in magnitude" (his term). Further, he contends that in comparing policies that risk unequal disasters, it is the *difference* rather than the *ratios* of the magnitudes of the disasters that matters in figuring utilitarian trade-offs with increased chances of avoiding disaster. But this is just wrong.

Consider two choice situations, S_1 and S_2. In each situation, individual members of a base group of persons, numbering 1 in S_1 and 99 in S_2, will suffer equal magnitude disasters if no action is taken. Action may save all from disaster, but if it fails, will cause the base group and an additional person to suffer the disaster. In both S_1 and S_2, the *difference* between the aggregate disasters that might follow from action and inaction is the same (that is, $2 - 1 = 100 - 99$). Yet the *ratios* are quite distinct: 2 in S_1, and 100/99 in S_2. So this can serve as a test of which matters. But it is obvious that, *ceteris paribus*, the action is more worth taking in S_2 than in S_1: we may save 99 at the hazard of harming 1 extra. Thus, contrary to what Lackey asserts, it is ratios rather than differences in magnitude that matter for trade-offs with increased chances of disaster avoidance. As the interested reader may check, the way expected values are calculated confirms the point for all situations of this kind involving risk.

Two final points should be briefly noted. First, even if the risks of continued deterrence *in the form Lackey discusses* were so grave as to make unilateral nuclear disarmament a better option, it does not follow that such disarmament is our best option. For there are a range of policies that retain deterrence but might well reduce the risks of nuclear war which Lackey mentions: initiation by accident, mistake, or escalation (pp. 216–18 and 221). These include significant unilateral peaceful steps that invite Soviet reciprocation; more reasonable negotiation postures on mutual disarmament; willingness to compromise on political differences; a no first use declaration; abrogation of launch on warning procedures, and so on. Adopting such policies might allow us to continue deterrence while greatly reducing the already small (but surely nonnegligible) risk of nuclear war, and it might even eventually lead toward the most desirable of outcomes, mutual (or even multilateral) nuclear disarmament.[9]

Second, and finally, I cannot accept Lackey's judgment that public advocacy of U.S. unilateral nuclear disarmament serves the cause of peace (pp. 230–31). I fear it is more likely to facilitate the ready dismissal and discrediting of the nuclear disarmament movement, both by its foes and by the uncommitted. This movement will flourish more if it avoids excesses of wishful thinking and sticks to the path of reason and moral commitment tempered by realism.

9. Lackey faces a dilemma here. If he admits the Soviets are too unreasonable to mutually disarm on fair or generous terms, he casts doubt on his claim that they are reasonable enough not to attack or blackmail us if we practice unilateral nuclear disarmament. But if the Soviets will disarm on reasonable terms, isn't offering such terms the optimal utilitarian policy?

This paper was written while I was supported by a fellowship for independent study and research from the National Endowment for the Humanities.

DOUGLAS P. LACKEY Disarmament Revisited:
A Reply to Kavka and Hardin

Professor Hardin berates me for neglecting Soviet cooperation; Professor Kavka chides me for depending on it. Logic teaches that my critics cannot both be right.

Professor Hardin says that my account of game theory is out-of-date; that current game theory indicates conditions for rational cooperation; that I am mistaken in arguing that unilateral disarmament dominates deterrence; that cracking an alleged Prisoners' Dilemma with utilitarianism is a simple exercise hardly worth the undertaking; and that throughout I have neglected the problem of how the intentions of policies might be perceived by the opposing side.

In discussing the state of the theory of games it is necessary to distinguish between empirical studies of cooperation and theoretical studies of cooperation. There is, of course, an immense literature of laboratory results, commencing with Rapaport in 1965, concerning how people behave in repeated plays of Prisoners' Dilemma, Chicken, and other games of interest. The results of these studies are mixed, and often it seems that they prove merely that cooperation occurs when people are inclined to cooperate. I would give low marks to any undergraduate who generalized from any of these studies, in which conditions repeat exactly, players and preferences remain constant, and payoffs are palpable and easily comparable, to the arena of international competition and the events of real history.

What I had in mind by "game theory" was the theoretical deductive division of the science, and here the results on cooperation are even more mixed. I think it is generally agreed that repeated play solutions are no help in the original Prisoners' Dilemma, at least in the sense that they cannot solve what made that Dilemma a dilemma. Just as my article went to press, however, certain new results from Steven Brams fell into my hands, which I briefly mentioned in footnote 14. Brams's solutions to Prisoners' Dilemma and Chicken do not require repeated play, but Brams, I believe, still has a problem motivating his players to assume the cooperative strategy. I do not have that problem, since I was concerned only with what morally ought to be done, not with what might be prudent.

Professor Hardin says that utilitarianism obviously prescribes unilateral disarmament, and that forty pages of argument on this point are "overkill." Since the history of the debate about morality and nuclear weapons is largely the history of a dispute between consequentialists (like Kavka) who support deterrence and deontologists who concede a utilitarian case for deterrence but find deterrence contrary to absolute prohibitions, I thought that a utilitarian attack on deterrence would be a bit of a surprise. Furthermore, the utilitarian case for attempted cooperation or for unilateral disarmament does not come so easily. It may turn out that a manifest attempt to cooperate will be exploited by the other side, and the sum of payoffs will be less than what the sum of payoffs would be if there were no manifest attempt to cooperate. In this case, utilitarianism rules against cooperation. Besides, even if both sides are utilitarian and committed to maximizing payoffs of the same sort, they may still disagree about the means of maximizing payoffs. Certainly the Cold War, in which both sides claim to seek maximum freedom and welfare for the world, can be seen in these terms. For this reason I went through the costs and benefits of deterrence in some detail.

I will say little about Hardin's problem of transmitting information. Certainly it is an important problem, but I see no inherent reason why it cannot be solved. Let me note that this is even more of a problem for deterrence than it is for nuclear disarmament. If intentions are misinterpreted under nuclear disarmament, the Soviet Union may act preemptively, but if intentions are misinterpreted under deterrence, the result may be all out nuclear war. Surely the risks of misunderstanding under deterrence are worse than the risks of misunderstanding under unilateral nuclear disarmament. But the risks are still troublesome, and I welcome any concrete suggestions about small steps and unilateral initiatives that might provoke mutual disarmament. The difference between supporters of unilateral disarmament and supporters of bilateral disarmament is that when the small steps are rebuffed, the bilateralist rearms with fervor, whereas the unilateralist proceeds forward on a course he considers morally prescribed.

Professor Kavka argues that I am "implausibly optimistic" about Soviet behavior; that the chance of blackmail under unilateral nuclear disarmament is not less than the chance of nuclear war under deterrence; and that it does disservice to the cause of peace and mutual disarmament to argue for a policy which will never be chosen and which will scare off the public.

Since I wrote my article in dark depression following the Soviet invasion of Afghanistan, and since I argued that the Soviets are little inclined to cooperate, I am a little surprised at being made out to be an optimist on this score. I do not think that the Soviets are saints and I agree that unilateral disarmament poses risks for the United States and for mankind at large. Nevertheless, to make his case for deterrence Kavka assumes (a) that the evil of Soviet world domination is roughly comparable in magnitude to the evil of nuclear war, and (b) that the chance of Soviet domination if the United States disarms is larger than the chance of nuclear war if both nations practice deterrence. I dispute both assumptions. Even if we work with ratios of outcomes rather than differences of outcomes, the disaster of nuclear war seems to me orders of magnitude greater than the disaster of "Soviet world domination" or whatever disaster might emanate from American nuclear disarmament. In either case, the United States ceases to exist, but in the case of nuclear war, a part of the rest of mankind also ceases to exist. If I may hark back to those charming debates of the 1950s, it has always seemed to me that red is better than dead because the red can choose to be dead but the dead cannot choose to be anything at all. Kavka may be indifferent as between these evils, but I doubt that this indifference is generally shared, and if it is not shared, it should not be imposed.

Now, in comparing the probabilities of the outcomes, I am struck by the abundance of reasons for thinking that deterrence will produce nuclear war and the paucity of reasons for thinking that American unilateral disarmament will produce Soviet world domination. Nuclear war under deterrence can be caused by an American accident, an American mistake, an irrational American command, American escalation, Soviet accident, Soviet mistake, an irrational Soviet command, or Soviet escalation, and we must also take into account the long-run prospects of nuclear war given the changing requirements of Assured Destruction, Assured Retaliation, Countervailing Response, or whatever is dictated by strategic fashion as the correct interpretation of second strike capacity. On the other hand, nuclear blackmail requires a motive and an opponent who will cave in, and I am hard put to find a motive and harder put to believe that the world will cave in. Kavka's argument for the blackmail motive is that history teaches that power abhors a vacuum. This is too sweeping a generalization to serve as a predictor: one might as well say that history teaches that arms races lead to war. But even if I concede that the chance of *attempted* blackmail under disarmament is greater than the chance of nuclear war under deterrence, it still seems to me that the chance that such blackmail *will succeed* is less than the chance of nuclear war under deterrence. The Russians will soon be a minority in their own country and are hard pressed to hold on to what they have; before they dominate the world they must first learn how to dominate Afghanistan.

Kavka argues that the danger of deterrence can be reduced by various means. But the dangers of unilateral nuclear disarmament can also be reduced by various means, and it would not be sporting to compare deterrence at its best with disarmament at its worst. While we are patching up deterrence, Kavka says that we should be seeking bilateral arms reductions. But I have little hope that such negotiations will succeed without a reduction of political tensions, and I cannot see how political tensions can be reduced without at least one side ceasing to threaten the other with destruction. In the meantime, it is important that unilateral American steps toward nuclear disarmament not be perpetually struck down by arguments that the "realistic" solution of multilateral disarmament requires an endless succession of new bargaining chips. Unilateral disarmament has its risks, and I am not arguing that the risks are small, only that they are required. Morality is like that.

Kavka and Hardin both argue that if the United States gives up nuclear weapons when the Soviet Union does not, the United States will be instantly impotent. In Hardin's astounding characterization, a United States without nuclear weapons will be magically transformed into another Finland. The future is mysterious but I beg to disagree. The Japanese nowadays have little trouble getting what they want in the world, and I deny that they achieve this because of the American nuclear umbrella. There are many sources of strategic power, and nuclear weapons are by no means a preeminent source. In the scheme of things, I sympathize with Kennan's remark that nuclear devices are the most useless weapons ever invented.

PART IV

The Moral Status
of the Nation-State

MICHAEL WALZER # The Rights of Political
Communities*

AGGRESSION

Aggression is the name we give to the crime of war. We know the crime
because of our knowledge of the peace it interrupts—not the mere absence
of fighting, but peace-with-rights, a condition of liberty and security that
can exist only in the absence of aggression itself. The wrong the aggressor
commits is to force men and women to risk their lives for the sake of their
rights. It is to confront them with the choice: your rights or (some of) your
lives! Groups of citizens respond in different ways to that choice, sometimes
surrendering, sometimes fighting, depending on the moral and material
condition of their state and army. But they are always justified in fighting;
and in most cases, given that harsh choice, fighting is the morally preferred
response. The justification and the preference are very important: they
account for the most remarkable features of the concept of aggression and
for the special place it has in the theory of war.

Aggression is remarkable because it is the only crime that states can
commit against other states: everything else is, as it were, a misdemeanor.
There is a strange poverty in the language of international law. The equiv-
alents of domestic assault, armed robbery, extortion, assault with intent to
kill, murder in all its degrees, have but one name. Every violation of the
territorial integrity or political sovereignty of an independent state is called
aggression. It is as if we were to brand as murder all attacks on a man's
person, all attempts to coerce him, all invasions of his home. This refusal
of differentiation makes it difficult to mark off the relative seriousness of

* Excerpts from *Just and Unjust Wars*, pp. 51–63, 86–101, 106–108, 339–42. Copyright ©
1977 by Basic Books, Inc., Publishers. (Some footnotes have been renumbered and expanded
for completeness.) Reprinted by permission of the publisher.

aggressive acts—to distinguish, for example, the seizure of a piece of land or the imposition of a satellite regime from conquest itself, the destruction of a state's independence (a crime for which Abba Eban, Israel's foreign minister in 1967, suggested the name "policide"). But there is a reason for the refusal. All aggressive acts have one thing in common: they justify forceful resistance, and force cannot be used between nations, as it often can between persons, without putting life itself at risk. Whatever limits we place on the means and range of warfare, fighting a limited war is not like hitting somebody. Aggression opens the gates of hell. Shakespeare's *Henry V* makes the point exactly:[1]

> For never two such kingdoms did contend
> Without much fall of blood, whose guiltless drops
> Are every one a woe, a sore complaint
> 'Gainst him whose wrongs gives edge unto the swords
> That makes such waste in brief mortality.

At the same time, aggression unresisted is aggression still, though there is no "fall of blood" at all. In domestic society, a robber who gets what he wants without killing anyone is obviously less guilty, that is, guilty of a lesser crime, than if he commits murder. Assuming that the robber is prepared to kill, we allow the behavior of his victim to determine his guilt. We don't do this in the case of aggression. Consider, for example, the German seizures of Czechoslovakia and Poland in 1939. The Czechs did not resist; they lost their independence through extortion rather than war; no Czech citizens died fighting the German invaders. The Poles chose to fight, and many were killed in the war that followed. But if the conquest of Czechoslovakia was a lesser crime, we have no name for it. At Nuremberg, the Nazi leadership was charged with aggression in both cases and found guilty in both.[2] Once again, there is a reason for this identity of treatment. We judge the Germans guilty of aggression in Czechoslovakia, I think, because of our profound conviction that they ought to have been resisted—though not necessarily by their abandoned victim, standing alone.

The state that does resist, whose soldiers risk their lives and die, does so because its leaders and people think that they should or that they have to

---

1. *Henry V*, 1:2, ll. 24–28.

2. The judges distinguished "aggressive acts" from "aggressive wars," but then used the first of these as the generic term; see *Nazi Conspiracy and Aggression: Opinion and Judgment* (Washington, D.C., 1947), p. 16.

fight back. Aggression is morally as well as physically coercive, and that is one of the most important things about it. "A conqueror," writes Clausewitz, "is always a lover of peace (as Bonaparte always asserted of himself); he would like to make his entry into our state unopposed; in order to prevent this, we must choose war . . ."[3] If ordinary men and women did not ordinarily accept that imperative, aggression would not seem to us so serious a crime. If they accepted it in certain sorts of cases, but not in others, the single concept would begin to break down, and we would eventually have a list of crimes more or less like the domestic list. The challenge of the streets, "Your money or your life!" is easy to answer: I surrender my money and so I save myself from being murdered and the thief from being a murderer. But we apparently don't want the challenge of aggression answered in the same way; even when it is, we don't diminish the guilt of the aggressor. He has violated rights to which we attach enormous importance. Indeed, we are inclined to think that the failure to defend those rights is never due to a sense of their unimportance, nor even to a belief (as in the street-challenge case) that they are, after all, worth less than life itself, but only to a stark conviction that the defense is hopeless. Aggression is a singular and undifferentiated crime because, in all its forms, it challenges rights that are worth dying for.

THE RIGHTS OF POLITICAL COMMUNITIES

The rights in question are summed up in the lawbooks as territorial integrity and political sovereignty. The two belong to states, but they derive ultimately from the rights of individuals, and from them they take their force. "The duties and rights of states are nothing more than the duties and rights of the men who compose them."[4] That is the view of a conventional British lawyer, for whom states are neither organic wholes nor mystical unions. And it is the correct view. When states are attacked, it is their members who are challenged, not only in their lives, but also in the sum of things they value most, including the political association they have made. We recognize and explain this challenge by referring to their rights. If they were not morally entitled to choose their form of government and shape the

3. Quoted in Michael Howard, "War as an Instrument of Policy," in Herbert Butterfield and Martin Wight, eds, *Diplomatic Investigations* (Cambridge, Mass., 1966), p. 199. Cf. Clausewitz, *On War*, trans. Howard and Paret (Princeton, 1976), p. 370.

4. John Westlake, *Collected Papers*, ed. L. Oppenheim (Cambridge, England, 1914), p. 78.

policies that shape their lives, external coercion would not be a crime; nor
could it so easily be said that they had been forced to resist in self-defense.
Individual rights (to life and liberty) underlie the most important judgments
that we make about war. How these rights are themselves founded I cannot
try to explain here. It is enough to say that they are somehow entailed by
our sense of what it means to be a human being. If they are not natural,
then we have invented them, but natural or invented, they are a palpable
feature of our moral world. States' rights are simply their collective form.
The process of collectivization is a complex one. No doubt, some of the
immediate force of individuality is lost in its course; it is best understood,
nevertheless, as it has commonly been understood since the seventeenth
century, in terms of social contract theory. Hence it is a moral process,
which justifies some claims to territory and sovereignty and invalidates
others.

The rights of states rest on the consent of their members. But this is
consent of a special sort. State rights are not constituted through a series
of transfers from individual men and women to the sovereign or through a
series of exchanges among individuals. What actually happens is harder to
describe. Over a long period of time, shared experiences and cooperative
activity of many different kinds shape a common life. "Contract" is a metaphor for a process of association and mutuality, the ongoing character of
which the state claims to protect against external encroachment. The protection extends not only to the lives and liberties of individuals but also to
their shared life and liberty, the independent community they have made,
for which individuals are sometimes sacrificed. The moral standing of any
particular state depends upon the reality of the common life it protects and
the extent to which the sacrifices required by that protection are willingly
accepted and thought worthwhile. If no common life exists, its own defense
may have no moral justification. But most states do stand guard over the
community of their citizens, at least to some degree: that is why we assume
the justice of their defensive wars. And given a genuine "contract," it makes
sense to say that territorial integrity and political sovereignty can be defended
in exactly the same way as individual life and liberty.[5]

5. The question of when territory and sovereignty can rightly be defended is closely connected
to the question of when individual citizens have an obligation to join the defense. Both hang
on issues in social contract theory. I have discussed the second question at length in my book
Obligations: Essays on Disobedience, War, and Citizenship (Cambridge, Mass., 1970). See
especially "The Obligation to Die for the State" and "Political Alienation and Military Service."
But neither in that book nor in this one do I deal in any detail with the problem of national

It might also be said that a people can defend its country in the same way as men and women can defend their homes, for the country is collectively as the homes are privately owned. The right to territory might be derived, that is, from the individual right to property. But the ownership of vast reaches of land is highly problematic, I think, unless it can be tied in some plausible way to the requirements of national survival and political independence. And these two seem by themselves to generate territorial rights that have little to do with ownership in the strict sense. The case is probably the same with the smaller properties of domestic society. A man has certain rights in his home, for example, even if he does not own it, because neither his life nor his liberty is secure unless there exists some physical space within which he is safe from intrusion. Similarly again, the right of a nation or people not to be invaded derives from the common life its members have made on this piece of land—it had to be made somewhere—and not from the legal title they hold or don't hold. But these matters will become clearer if we look at an example of disputed territory.

The Case of Alsace-Lorraine

In 1870, both France and the new Germany claimed these two provinces. Both claims were, as such things go, well founded. The Germans based themselves on ancient precedents (the lands had been part of the Holy Roman Empire before their conquest by Louis XIV) and on cultural and linguistic kinship; the French on two centuries of possession and effective government.[6] How does one establish ownership in such a case? There is, I think, a prior question having to do with political allegiance, not with legal titles at all. What do the inhabitants want? The land follows the people. The decision as to whose sovereignty was legitimate (and therefore as to whose military presence constituted aggression) belonged by right to the men and women who lived on the land in dispute. Not simply to those who owned the land: the decision belonged to the landless, to town dwellers and factory workers as well, by virtue of the common life they had made. The great majority of these people were apparently loyal to France, and that should

---

minorities—groups of people who do not fully join (or do not join at all) in the contract that constitutes the nation. The radical mistreatment of such people may justify military intervention (see chapter 6 [of *Just and Unjust Wars*]). Short of that, however, the presence of national minorities within the borders of a nation-state does not affect the argument about aggression and self-defense.

6. See Ruth Putnam, *Alsace and Lorraine from Caesar to Kaiser: 58 B.C.-1871 A.D.* (New York, 1915).

have settled the matter. Even if we imagine all the inhabitants of Alsace-Lorraine to be tenants of the Prussian king, the king's seizure of his own land would still have been a violation of their territorial integrity and, through the mediation of their loyalty, of France's too. For tenantry determines only where rents should go; the people themselves must decide where their taxes and conscripts should go.

But the issue was not settled in this way. After the Franco-Prussian war, the two provinces (actually, all of Alsace and a portion of Lorraine) were annexed by Germany, the French conceding German rights in the peace treaty of 1871. During the next several decades, the question was frequently asked, whether a French attack aimed at regaining the lost lands would be justified. One of the issues here is that of the moral standing of a peace treaty signed, as most peace treaties are signed, under duress, but I shall not focus on that. The more important issue relates to the endurance of rights over time. Here the appropriate argument was put forward by the English philosopher Henry Sidgwick in 1891. Sidgwick's sympathies were with the French, and he was inclined to regard the peace as a "temporary suspension of hostilities, terminable at any time by the wronged state . . ." But he added a crucial qualification:[7]

> We must . . . recognize that by this temporary submission of the vanquished . . . a new political order is initiated, which, though originally without a moral basis, may in time acquire such a basis, from a change in the sentiments of the inhabitants of the territory transferred; since it is always possible that through the effects of time and habit and mild government—and perhaps through the voluntary exile of those who feel the old patriotism most keenly—the majority of the transferred population may cease to desire reunion . . . When this change has taken place, the moral effect of the unjust transfer must be regarded as obliterated; so that any attempt to recover the transferred territory becomes itself an aggression . . .

Legal titles may endure forever, periodically revived and reasserted as in the dynastic politics of the Middle Ages. But moral rights are subject to the vicissitudes of the common life.

Territorial integrity, then, does not derive from property; it is simply something different. The two are joined, perhaps, in socialist states where the land is nationalized and the people are said to own it. Then if their country

7. Henry Sidgwick, *The Elements of Politics* (London, 1891), pp. 268, 287.

is attacked, it is not merely their homeland that is in danger but their collective property—though I suspect that the first danger is more deeply felt than the second. Nationalization is a secondary process; it assumes the prior existence of a nation. And territorial integrity is a function of national existence, not of nationalization (any more than of private ownership). It is the coming together of a people that establishes the integrity of a territory. Only then can a boundary be drawn the crossing of which is plausibly called aggression. It hardly matters if the territory belongs to someone else, unless that ownership is expressed in residence and common use.

This argument suggests a way of thinking about the great difficulties posed by forcible settlement and colonization. When barbarian tribes crossed the borders of the Roman Empire, driven by conquerors from the east or north, they asked for land to settle on and threatened war if they didn't get it. Was this aggression? Given the character of the Roman Empire, the question may sound foolish, but it has arisen many times since, and often in imperial settings. When land is in fact empty and available, the answer must be that it is not aggression. But what if the land is not actually empty but, as Thomas Hobbes says in *Leviathan*, "not sufficiently inhabited"? Hobbes goes on to argue that in such a case, the would-be settlers must "not exterminate those they find there but constrain them to inhabit closer together."[8] That constraint is not aggression, so long as the lives of the original settlers are not threatened. For the settlers are doing what they must do to preserve their own lives, and "he that shall oppose himself against [that], for things superfluous, is guilty of the war that thereupon is to follow."[9] It is not the settlers who are guilty of aggression, according to Hobbes, but those natives who won't move over and make room. There are clearly serious problems here. But I would suggest that Hobbes is right to set aside any consideration of territorial integrity-as-ownership and to focus instead on life. It must be added, however, that what is at stake is not only the lives of individuals but also the common life that they have made. It is for the sake of this common life that we assign a certain presumptive value to the boundaries that mark off a people's territory and to the state that defends it.

Now, the boundaries that exist at any moment in time are likely to be arbitrary, poorly drawn, the products of ancient wars. The mapmakers are likely to have been ignorant, drunken, or corrupt. Nevertheless, these lines establish a habitable world. Within that world, men and women (let us assume) are safe from attack; once the lines are crossed, safety is gone. I

8. *Leviathan*, ch. 30.   9. *Leviathan*, ch. 15.

don't want to suggest that every boundary dispute is a reason for war. Sometimes adjustments should be accepted and territories shaped so far as possible to the actual needs of nations. Good borders make good neighbors. But once an invasion has been threatened or has actually begun, it may be necessary to defend a bad border simply because there is no other. We shall see this reason at work in the minds of the leaders of Finland in 1939: they might have accepted Russian demands had they felt certain that there would be an end to them. But there is no certainty this side of the border, any more than there is safety this side of the threshold, once a criminal has entered the house. It is only common sense, then, to attach great importance to boundaries. Rights in the world have value only if they also have dimension.

The Legalist Paradigm

If states actually do possess rights more or less as individuals do, then it is possible to imagine a society among them more or less like the society of individuals. The comparison of international to civil order is crucial to the theory of aggression. I have already been making it regularly. Every reference to aggression as the international equivalent of armed robbery or murder, and every comparison of home and country or of personal liberty and political independence, relies upon what is called the *domestic analogy*.[10] Our primary perceptions and judgments of aggression are the products of analogical reasoning. When the analogy is made explicit, as it often is among the lawyers, the world of states takes on the shape of a political society the character of which is entirely accessible through such notions as crime and punishment, self-defense, law enforcement, and so on.

These notions, I should stress, are not incompatible with the fact that international society as it exists today is a radically imperfect structure. As we experience it, that society might be likened to a defective building, founded on rights; its superstructure raised, like that of the state itself, through political conflict, cooperative activity, and commercial exchange; the whole thing shaky and unstable because it lacks the rivets of authority. It is like domestic society in that men and women live at peace within it (sometimes), determining the conditions of their own existence, negotiating

10. For a critique of this analogy, see the two essays by Hedley Bull, "Society and Anarchy in International Relations," and "The Grotian Conception of International Society," in *Diplomatic Investigations*, chs. 2 and 3.

and bargaining with their neighbors. It is unlike domestic society in that every conflict threatens the structure as a whole with collapse. Aggression challenges it directly and is much more dangerous than domestic crime, because there are no policemen. But that only means that the "citizens" of international society must rely on themselves and on one another. Police powers are distributed among all the members. And these members have not done enough in the exercise of their powers if they merely contain the aggression or bring it to a speedy end—as if the police should stop a murderer after he has killed only one or two people and send him on his way. The rights of the member states must be vindicated, for it is only by virtue of those rights that there is a society at all. If they cannot be upheld (at least sometimes), international society collapses into a state of war or is transformed into a universal tyranny.

From this picture, two presumptions follow. The first, which I have already pointed out, is the presumption in favor of military resistance once aggression has begun. Resistance is important so that rights can be maintained and future aggressors deterred. The theory of aggression restates the old doctrine of the just war: it explains when fighting is a crime and when it is permissible, perhaps even morally desirable.[11] The victim of aggression fights in self-defense, but he isn't only defending himself, for aggression is a crime against society as a whole. He fights in its name and not only in his own. Other states can rightfully join the victim's resistance; their war has the same character as his own, which is to say, they are entitled not only to repel the attack but also to punish it. All resistance is also law enforcement. Hence the second presumption: when fighting breaks out, there must always be some state against which the law can and should be enforced. Someone must be responsible, for someone decided to break the peace of the society of states. No war, as medieval theologians explained, can be just on both sides.[12]

There are, however, wars that are just on neither side, because the idea of justice doesn't pertain to them or because the antagonists are both ag-

11. I shall say nothing here of the argument for nonviolent resistance to aggression, according to which fighting is neither desirable nor necessary. This argument has not figured much in the development of the conventional view. Indeed, it poses a radical challenge to the conventions: if aggression can be resisted, and at least sometimes successfully resisted, without war, it may be a less serious crime than has commonly been supposed. I will take up this possibility and its moral implications in the Afterword [to *Just and Unjust Wars*].

12. See Francisco de Vitoria, *On the Law of War*, trans. John Pawley Bate (Washington, D.C., 1917), p. 177.

gressors, fighting for territory or power where they have no right. The first
case I have already alluded to in discussing the voluntary combat of aris-
tocratic warriors. It is sufficiently rare in human history that nothing more
need be said about it here. The second case is illustrated by those wars that
Marxists call "imperialist," which are not fought between conquerors and
victims but between conquerors and conquerors, each side seeking domin-
ion over the other or the two of them competing to dominate some third
party. Thus Lenin's description of the struggles between "have" and "have-
not" nations in early twentieth century Europe: ". . . picture to yourselves
a slave-owner who owned 100 slaves warring against a slave-owner who
owned 200 slaves for a more 'just' distribution of slaves. Clearly, the application of the term 'defensive' war in such a case . . . would be sheer deception
. . ."[13] But it is important to stress that we can penetrate the deception only
insofar as we can ourselves distinguish justice and injustice: the theory of
imperialist war presupposes the theory of aggression. If one insists that all
wars on all sides are acts of conquest or attempted conquest, or that all
states at all times would conquer if they could, then the argument for justice
is defeated before it begins and the moral judgments we actually make are
derided as fantasies. Consider the following passage from Edmund Wilson's
book on the American Civil War:[14]

> I think that it is a serious deficiency on the part of historians . . . that
> they so rarely interest themselves in biological and zoological phenomena.
> In a recent . . . film showing life at the bottom of the sea, a primitive
> organism called a sea slug is seen gobbling up small organisms through
> a large orifice at one end of its body; confronted with another sea slug of
> an only slightly lesser size, it ingurgitates that, too. Now the wars fought
> by human beings are stimulated as a rule . . . by the same instincts as
> the voracity of the sea slug.

There are no doubt wars to which that image might be fit, though it is not
a terribly useful image with which to approach the Civil War. Nor does it
account for our ordinary experience of international society. Not all states
are sea-slug states, gobbling up their neighbors. There are always groups
of men and women who would live if they could in peaceful enjoyment of
their rights and who have chosen political leaders who represent that desire.
The deepest purpose of the state is not ingestion but defense, and the least

13. Lenin, *Socialism and War* (London, 1940), pp. 10–11.
14. Edmund Wilson, *Patriotic Gore* (New York, 1966), p. xi.

that can be said is that many actual states serve that purpose. When their territory is attacked or their sovereignty challenged, it makes sense to look for an aggressor and not merely for a natural predator. Hence we need a theory of aggression rather than a zoological account.

The theory of aggression first takes shape under the aegis of the domestic analogy. I am going to call that primary form of the theory the *legalist paradigm*, since it consistently reflects the conventions of law and order. It does not necessarily reflect the arguments of the lawyers, though legal as well as moral debate has its starting point here.[15] Later on, I will suggest that our judgments about the justice and injustice of particular wars are not entirely determined by the paradigm. The complex realities of international society drive us toward a revisionist perspective, and the revisions will be significant ones. But the paradigm must first be viewed in its un-revised form; it is our baseline, our model, the fundamental structure for the moral comprehension of war. We begin with the familiar world of individuals and rights, of crimes and punishments. The theory of aggression can then be summed up in six propositions.

1. *There exists an international society of independent states.* States are the members of this society, not private men and women. In the absence of an universal state, men and women are protected and their interests represented only by their own governments. Though states are founded for the sake of life and liberty, they cannot be challenged in the name of life and liberty by any other states. Hence the principle of non-intervention, which I will analyze later on. The rights of private persons can be recognized in international society, as in the UN Charter of Human Rights, but they cannot be enforced without calling into question the dominant values of that society: the survival and independence of the separate political communities.

2. *This international society has a law that establishes the rights of its members—above all, the rights of territorial integrity and political sovereignty.* Once again, these two rest ultimately on the right of men and women to build a common life and to risk their individual lives only when they freely choose to do so. But the relevant law refers only to states, and its details are fixed by the intercourse of states, through complex processes of

15. It is worth noting that the United Nations' recently adopted definition of aggression closely follows the paradigm: see the *Report of the Special Committee on the Question of Defining Aggression* (1974), General Assembly Official Records, 29th session, supplement no. 19 (A/9619), pp. 10–13. The definition is reprinted and analyzed in Yehuda Melzer, *Concepts of Just War* (Leyden, 1975), pp. 26ff.

conflict and consent. Since these processes are continuous, international society has no natural shape; nor are rights within it ever finally or exactly determined. At any given moment, however, one can distinguish the territory of one people from that of another and say something about the scope and limits of sovereignty.

3. *Any use of force or imminent threat of force by one state against the political sovereignty or territorial integrity of another constitutes aggression and is a criminal act.* As with domestic crime, the argument here focuses narrowly on actual or imminent boundary crossings: invasions and physical assaults. Otherwise, it is feared, the notion of resistance to aggression would have no determinate meaning. A state cannot be said to be forced to fight unless the necessity is both obvious and urgent.

4. *Aggression justifies two kinds of violent response: a war of self-defense by the victim and a war of law enforcement by the victim and any other member of international society.* Anyone can come to the aid of a victim, use necessary force against an aggressor, and even make whatever is the international equivalent of a "citizen's arrest." As in domestic society, the obligations of bystanders are not easy to make out, but it is the tendency of the theory to undermine the right of neutrality and to require widespread participation in the business of law enforcement. In the Korean War, this participation was authorized by the United Nations, but even in such cases the actual decision to join the fighting remains a unilateral one, best understood by analogy to the decision of a private citizen who rushes to help a man or woman attacked on the street.

5. *Nothing but aggression can justify war.* The central purpose of the theory is to limit the occasions for war. "There is a single and only just cause for commencing a war," wrote Vitoria, "namely, a wrong received."[16] There must actually have been a wrong, and it must actually have been received (or its receipt must be, as it were, only minutes away). Nothing else warrants the use of force in international society—above all, not any difference of religion or politics. Domestic heresy and injustice are never actionable in the world of states: hence, again, the principle of nonintervention.

6. *Once the aggressor state has been militarily repulsed, it can also be punished.* The conception of just war as an act of punishment is very old, though neither the procedures nor the forms of punishment have ever been firmly established in customary or positive international law. Nor are its

16. *On the Law of War,* p. 170.

purposes entirely clear: to exact retribution, to deter other states, to restrain or reform this one? All three figure largely in the literature, though it is probably fair to say that deterrence and restraint are most commonly accepted. When people talk of fighting a war against war, this is usually what they have in mind. The domestic maxim is, punish crime to prevent violence; its international analogue is, punish aggression to prevent war. Whether the state as a whole or only particular persons are the proper objects of punishment is a harder question, for reasons I will consider later on. But the implication of the paradigm is clear: if states are members of international society, the subjects of rights, they must also be (somehow) the objects of punishment. . . .

[*Editors' note*: Having set forth the "legalist paradigm," Walzer proceeds to revise it. The first revision has to do with the doctrine of preemptive war (see *Just and Unjust Wars*, pp. 74–85), which is not relevant to the debate on intervention and state sovereignty and so is omitted from these excerpts. The next three revisions all have to do with intervention; Walzer's discussion of these begins in the next section.]

. . . The principle that states should never intervene in the domestic affairs of other states follows readily from the legalist paradigm and, less readily and more ambiguously, from those conceptions of life and liberty that underlie the paradigm and make it plausible. But these same conceptions seem also to require that we sometimes disregard the principle; and what might be called the rules of disregard, rather than the principle itself, have been the focus of moral interest and argument. No state can admit to fighting an aggressive war and then defend its actions. But intervention is differently understood. The word is not defined as a criminal activity, and though the practice of intervening often threatens the territorial integrity and political independence of invaded states, it can sometimes be justified. It is more important to stress at the outset, however, that it always has to be justified. The burden of proof falls on any political leader who tries to shape the domestic arrangements or alter the conditions of life in a foreign country. And when the attempt is made with armed force, the burden is especially heavy—not only because of the coercions and ravages that military intervention inevitably brings, but also because it is thought that the citizens of a sovereign state have a right, insofar as they are to be coerced and ravaged at all, to suffer only at one another's hands.

SELF-DETERMINATION AND SELF-HELP

The Argument of John Stuart Mill

These citizens are the members, it is presumed, of a single political community, entitled collectively to determine their own affairs. The precise nature of this right is nicely worked out by John Stuart Mill in a short article published in the same year as the treatise *On Liberty* (1859) and especially useful to us because the individual / community analogy was very much in Mill's mind as he wrote.[17] We are to treat states as self-determining communities, he argues, whether or not their internal political arrangements are free, whether or not the citizens choose their government and openly debate the policies carried out in their name. For self-determination and political freedom are not equivalent terms. The first is the more inclusive idea; it describes not only a particular institutional arrangement but also the process by which a community arrives at that arrangement—or does not. A state is self-determining even if its citizens struggle and fail to establish free institutions, but it has been deprived of self-determination if such institutions are established by an intrusive neighbor. The members of a political community must seek their own freedom, just as the individual must cultivate his own virtue. They cannot be set free, as he cannot be made virtuous, by any external force. Indeed, political freedom depends upon the existence of individual virtue, and this the armies of another state are most unlikely to produce—unless, perhaps, they inspire an active resistance and set in motion a self-determining politics. Self-determination is the school in which virtue is learned (or not) and liberty is won (or not). Mill recognizes that a people who have had the "misfortune" to be ruled by a tyrannical government are peculiarly disadvantaged: they have never had a chance to develop "the virtues needful for maintaining freedom." But he insists nevertheless on the stern doctrine of self-help. "It is during an arduous struggle to become free by their own efforts that these virtues have the best chance of springing up."

Though Mill's argument can be cast in utilitarian terms, the harshness of his conclusions suggests that this is not its most appropriate form. The

17. "A Few Words on Non-Intervention," in J. S. Mill, *Dissertations and Discussions* (New York, 1873), III, 238–63.

Millian view of self-determination seems to make utilitarian calculation unnecessary, or at least subsidiary to an understanding of communal liberty.
He doesn't believe that intervention fails more often than not to serve the
purposes of liberty; he believes that, given what liberty is, it *necessarily*
fails. The (internal) freedom of a political community can be won only by
the members of that community. The argument is similar to that implied
in the well-known Marxist maxim, "The liberation of the working class can
come only through the workers themselves."[18] As that maxim, one would
think, rules out any substitution of vanguard elitism for working class democracy, so Mill's argument rules out any substitution of foreign intervention for internal struggle.

Self-determination, then, is the right of a people "to become free by their
own efforts" if they can, and nonintervention is the principle guaranteeing
that their success will not be impeded or their failure prevented by the
intrusions of an alien power. It has to be stressed that there is no right to
be protected against the consequences of domestic failure, even against a
bloody repression. Mill generally writes as if he believes that citizens get
the government they deserve, or, at least, the government for which they
are "fit." And "the only test . . . of a people's having become fit for popular
institutions is that they, or a sufficient portion of them to prevail in the
contest, are willing to brave labor and danger for their liberation." No one
can, and no one should, do it for them. Mill takes a very cool view of political
conflict, and if many rebellious citizens, proud and full of hope in their own
efforts, have endorsed that view, many others have not. There is no shortage
of revolutionaries who have sought, pleaded for, even demanded outside
help. A recent American commentator, eager to be helpful, has argued that
Mill's position involves "a kind of Darwinian definition [*The Origin of the
Species* was also published in 1859] of self-determination as survival of the
fittest within the national boundaries, even if fittest means most adept in
the use of force."[19] That last phrase is unfair, for it was precisely Mill's point
that force could not prevail, unless it were reinforced from the outside, over
a people ready "to brave labor and danger." For the rest, the charge is
probably true, but it is difficult to see what conclusions follow from it. It is
possible to intervene domestically in the "Darwinian" struggle because the

18. See Irving Howe, ed., *The Basic Writings of Trotsky* (New York, 1963), p. 397.

19. John Norton Moore, "International Law and the United States' Role in Vietnam: A Reply,"
in R. Falk, ed., *The Vietnam War and International Law* (Princeton, 1968), p. 431. Moore
addresses himself specifically to the argument of W. E. Hall, *International Law* (5th ed.,
Oxford, 1904), p. 289–90, but Hall follows Mill closely.

intervention is continuous and sustained over time. But foreign intervention, if it is a brief affair, cannot shift the domestic balance of power in any decisive way toward the forces of freedom, while if it is prolonged or intermittently resumed, it will itself pose the greatest possible threat to the success of those forces.

The case may be different when what is at issue is not intervention at all but conquest. Military defeat and governmental collapse may so shock a social system as to open the way for a radical renovation of its political arrangements. This seems to be what happened in Germany and Japan after World War II, and these examples are so important that I will have to consider later on how it is that rights of conquest and renovation might arise. But they clearly don't arise in every case of domestic tyranny. It is not true, then, that intervention is justified whenever revolution is; for revolutionary activity is an exercise in self-determination, while foreign interference denies to a people those political capacities that only such exercise can bring.

These are the truths expressed by the legal doctrine of sovereignty, which defines the liberty of states as their independence from foreign control and coercion. In fact, of course, not every independent state is free, but the recognition of sovereignty is the only way we have of establishing an arena within which freedom can be fought for and (sometimes) won. It is this arena and the activities that go on within it that we want to protect, and we protect them, much as we protect individual integrity, by marking out boundaries that cannot be crossed, rights that cannot be violated. As with individuals, so with sovereign states: there are things that we cannot do to them, even for their own ostensible good.

And yet the ban on boundary crossings is not absolute—in part because of the arbitrary and accidental character of state boundaries, in part because of the ambiguous relation of the political community or communities within those boundaries to the government that defends them. Despite Mill's very general account of self-determination, it isn't always clear when a community is in fact self-determining, when it qualifies, so to speak, for nonintervention. No doubt there are similar problems with individual persons, but these are, I think, less severe and, in any case, they are handled within the structures of domestic law.[20] In international society, the law provides

20. The domestic analogy suggests that the most obvious way of not qualifying for nonintervention is to be incompetent (childish, imbecilic, and so on). Mill believed that there were incompetent peoples, barbarians, in whose interest it was to be conquered and held in sub-

no authoritative verdicts. Hence, the ban on boundary crossings is subject to unilateral suspension, specifically with reference to three sorts of cases where it does not seem to serve the purposes for which it was established:

—when a particular set of boundaries clearly contains two or more political communities, one of which is already engaged in a large-scale military struggle for independence; that is, when what is at issue is secession or "national liberation;"

—when the boundaries have already been crossed by the armies of a foreign power, even if the crossing has been called for by one of the parties in a civil war, that is, when what is at issue is counter-intervention; and

—when the violation of human rights within a set of boundaries is so terrible that it makes talk of community or self-determination or "arduous struggle" seem cynical and irrelevant, that is, in cases of enslavement or massacre.

The arguments that are made on behalf of intervention in each of these cases constitute the second, third, and fourth revisions of the legalist paradigm. They open the way for just wars that are not fought in self-defense or against aggression in the strict sense. But they need to be worked out with great care. Given the readiness of states to invade one another, revisionism is a risky business.

Mill discusses only the first two of these cases, secession and counter-intervention, though the last was not unknown even in 1859. It is worth pointing out that he does not regard them as exceptions to the nonintervention principle, but rather as negative demonstrations of its reasons. Where these reasons don't apply, the principle loses its force. It would be more exact, from Mill's standpoint, to formulate the relevant principle in this way: *always act so as to recognize and uphold communal autonomy*. Nonintervention is most often entailed by that recognition, but not always,

jection by foreigners. "Barbarians have no rights as a *nation* [i.e., as a political community] . . ." Hence utilitarian principles apply to them, and imperial bureaucrats legitimately work for their moral improvement. It is interesting to note a similar view among the Marxists, who also justified conquest and imperial rule at certain stages of historical development. (See Shlomo Avineri, ed., *Karl Marx on Colonialism and Modernization*, New York, 1969.) Whatever plausibility such arguments had in the nineteenth century, they have none today. International society can no longer be divided into civilized and barbarian halves; any line drawn on developmental principles leaves barbarians on both sides. I shall therefore assume that the self-help test applies equally to all peoples.

and then we must prove our commitment to autonomy in some other way, perhaps even by sending troops across an international frontier. But the morally exact principle is also very dangerous, and Mill's account of the argument is not at this point an account of what is actually said in everyday moral discourse. We need to establish a kind of *a priori* respect for state boundaries; they are, as I have argued before, the only boundaries communities ever have. And that is why intervention is always justified as if it were an exception to a general rule, made necessary by the urgency or extremity of a particular case. The second, third, and fourth revisions have something of the form of stereotyped excuses. Interventions are so often undertaken for "reasons of state" that have nothing to do with self-determination that we have become skeptical of every claim to defend the autonomy of alien communities. Hence the special burden of proof with which I began, more onerous than any we impose on individuals or governments pleading self-defense: intervening states must demonstrate that their own case is radically different from what we take to be the general run of cases, where the liberty or prospective liberty of citizens is best served if foreigners offer them only moral support. And that is how I shall characterize Mill's argument (though he characterizes it differently) that Great Britain ought to have intervened in defense of the Hungarian Revolution of 1848 and 1849.

SECESSION

The Hungarian Revolution

For many years before 1848, Hungary had been a part of the Hapsburg Empire. Formally an independent kingdom, with a Diet of its own, it was effectively ruled by the German authorities in Vienna. The sudden collapse of those authorities during the March Days—symbolized by the fall of Metternich—opened the way for liberal nationalists in Budapest. They formed a government and demanded home rule within the Empire; they were not yet secessionists. Their demand was initially accepted, but controversy developed over the issues that have always plagued federalist schemes: the control of tax revenue, the command of the army. As soon as "order" was restored in Vienna, efforts began to reassert the centralist character of the regime, and these soon took the familiar form of military repression. An imperial army invaded Hungary, and the nationalists fought back. The Hungarians were now rebels or insurgents; they quickly established what international lawyers call their belligerent rights by defeating the Austrians and taking control of much of old Hungary. In the course of the war, the new government shifted leftwards; in April 1849, a republic was proclaimed under the presidency of Lajos Kossuth.[21]

The revolution might be described, in contemporary terms, as a war of national liberation, except that the boundaries of old Hungary included a very large Slavic population, and the Hungarian revolutionaries seem to have been as hostile to Croat and Slovene nationalism as the Austrians were to their own claims for communal autonomy. But this is a difficulty that I am going to set aside, for it did not appear as such at the time; it did not enter into the moral reflections of liberal observers like Mill. The Hungarian Revolution was greeted with enthusiasm by such men, especially in France, Britain, and the United States, and its emissaries were eagerly received. Governmental response was different, in part because nonintervention was the general rule to which all three governments subscribed, in part because the first two were also committed to the European balance of power and therefore to the integrity of Austria. In London, Palmerston was formal and cold: "The British government has no knowledge of Hungary except as one of the component parts of the Austrian Empire."[22] The Hungarians sought only diplomatic recognition, not military intervention, but any British dealings with the new government would have been regarded by the Austrian regime as an interference in its internal affairs. Recognition, moreover, had commercial consequences that might have engaged the British more closely on the side of Hungary, for the revolutionaries hoped to purchase military supplies on the London market. Despite this, the establishment of formal ties, once the Hungarians had demonstrated that "a sufficient portion of them" were committed to independence and willing to fight for it, would not have been difficult to justify in Millian terms. There can be no doubt of the existence (though there was a reason to doubt the extent) of the Hungarian political community; it was one of the oldest nations in Europe, and its recognition as a sovereign state would not have violated the moral rights of the Austrian people. Military supply to insurgent armies is indeed a complex issue, and I will come back to it with reference to another case, but none of the complexities are apparent here. Soon enough, however, the Hungarians needed far more than guns and ammunition.

21. For a brief survey, see Jean Sigmann, *1848: The Romantic and Democratic Revolutions in Europe*, trans. L. F. Edwards (New York, 1973), ch. 10.
22. Charles Sproxton, *Palmerston and the Hungarian Revolution* (Cambridge, 1919), p. 48.

In the summer of 1849, the Austrian emperor asked for the help of Tsar Nicholas I, and Hungary was invaded by a Russian army. Writing ten years later, Mill argued that the British should have responded to this intervention with an intervention of their own.[23]

> It might not have been right for England (even apart from the question of prudence) to have taken part with Hungary in its noble struggle against Austria; although the Austrian government in Hungary was in some sense a foreign yoke. But when, the Hungarians having shown themselves likely to prevail in this struggle, the Russian despot interposed, and joining his force to that of Austria, delivered back the Hungarians, bound hand and foot, to their exasperated oppressors, it would have been an honorable and virtuous act on the part of England to have declared that this should not be, and that if Russia gave assistance to the wrong side, England would aid the right.

The qualification "in some sense a foreign yoke" with regard to Austrian rule in Hungary is curious, for whatever its meaning, it must also qualify the nobility and rightness of the Hungarian struggle for independence. Since Mill does not intend the latter qualification, we need not take the former seriously. The clear tendency of his argument is to justify assistance to a secessionist movement at the same time as it justifies counter-intervention—indeed, to assimilate the one to the other. In both cases, the rule against interference is suspended because a foreign power, morally if not legally alien, is already interfering in the "domestic" affairs, that is, in the self-determinations of a political community.

Mill is right, however, to suggest that the issue is easier when the initial interference involves the crossing of a recognized frontier. The problem with a secessionist movement is that one cannot be sure that it in fact represents a distinct community until it has rallied its own people and made some headway in the "arduous struggle" for freedom. The mere appeal to the principle of self-determination isn't enough; evidence must be provided that a community actually exists whose members are committed to independence and ready and able to determine the conditions of their own existence.[24] Hence the need for political or military struggle sustained over

23. "Non-Intervention," p. 261–62.
24. See S. French and A. Gutman, "The Principle of National Self-determination," in Held, Morgenbesser, and Nagel, eds., *Philosophy, Morality, and International Affairs* (New York, 1974), pp. 138–53.
There is a further issue here, having to do with the natural resources that are sometimes

time. Mill's argument doesn't cover inarticulate and unrepresented peoples, or fledgling movements, or risings quickly suppressed. But imagine a small nation successfully mobilized to resist a colonial power but slowly being ground down in the unequal struggle: Mill would not insist, I think, that neighboring states stand by and watch is inevitable defeat. His argument justifies military action against imperial or colonial repression as well as against foreign intervention. Only domestic tyrants are safe, for it is not our purpose in international society (nor, Mill argues, is it possible) to establish liberal or democratic communities, but only independent ones. When it is required for the sake of independence, military action is "honorable and virtuous," though not always "prudent." I should add that the argument also applies to satellite regimes and great powers: designed for the first Russian intervention in Hungary (1849), it precisely fits the second (1956).

But the relation between virtue and prudence in such cases is not easy to make out. Mill's meaning is clear enough: to threaten war with Russia might have been dangerous to Britain and hence inconsistent "with the regard which every nation is bound to pay to its own safety." Now, whether or not it actually was dangerous was surely for the British to decide, and we would judge them harshly only if the risks they declined to run were very slight indeed. Even if counter-intervention is "honorable and virtuous," it is not morally required, precisely because of the dangers it involves. But one can make much more of prudence than this. Palmerston was concerned with the safety of Europe, not only of England, when he decided to stand by the Austrian empire. It is perfectly possible to concede the justice of the Millian position, and yet opt for nonintervention on what are currently called "world order" principles.[25] So justice and prudence are (with a certain worldly relish) set in opposition to one another in a way that Mill never imagined they could be. He thought, naively perhaps, that the world would

---

at stake in seccessionist struggles. I have argued that "the land follows the people" (*Just and Unjust Wars*], chapter 4). But the will and capacity of the people for self-determination may not establish a right to secede if the secession would remove not only land but also vitally needed fuel and mineral resources from some larger political community. The Katangan controversy of the early 1960s suggests the possible difficulties of such cases—and invites us to worry also about the motives of intervening states. But what was missing in Katanga was a genuine national movement capable, on its own, of "arduous struggle." (See Conor C. O'Brien, *To Katanga and Back*, New York, 1962.) Given the existence of such a movement, I would be inclined to support secession. It would then be necessary, however, to raise more general questions about distributive justice in international society.

25. This is the general position of R. J. Vincent, *Nonintervention and World Order* (Princeton, 1974), esp. ch. 9.

be more orderly if none of its political communities were oppressed by foreign rule. He even hoped that Britain would one day be powerful enough, and have the necessary "spirit and courage," to insist "that not a gun [should] be fired in Europe by the soldiers of one Power against the revolted subjects of another," and to put itself "at the head of an alliance of free peoples . . ." Today, I suppose, the United States has succeeded to those old-fashioned liberal pretensions, though in 1956 its leaders, like Palmerston in 1849, thought it imprudent to enforce them.

It might also be said that the United States had (and has) no right to enforce them, given the self-serving ways in which its government defines freedom and intervention in other parts of the world. Mill's England was hardly in a better position. Had Palmerston contemplated a military move on behalf of the Hungarians, Count Schwarzenberg, Metternich's successor, was prepared to remind him of "unhappy Ireland." "Wherever revolt breaks out within the vast limits of the British Empire," Schwarzenberg wrote to the Austrian ambassador in London, "the English government always knows how to maintain the authority of the law . . . even at the price of torrents of blood. It is not for us," he went on, "to blame her."[26] He sought only reciprocity, and that kind of reciprocity among great powers is undoubtedly the very essence of prudence.

To set prudence and justice so radically at odds, however, is to misconstrue the argument for justice. A state contemplating intervention or counter-intervention will for prudential reasons weigh the dangers to itself, but it must also, *and for moral reasons*, weigh the dangers its action will impose on the people it is designed to benefit and on all other people who may be affected. An intervention is not just if it subjects third parties to terrible risks: the subjection cancels the justice. If Palmerston was right in believing that the defeat of Austria would shatter the peace of Europe, a British intervention ensuring that defeat would not have been "honorable and virtuous" (however noble the Hungarian struggle). And clearly, an American threat of atomic war in 1956 would have been morally as well as politically irresponsible. Thus far prudence can be, and has to be, accommodated within the argument for justice. But it should be said that this deference to third party rights is not at the same time a deference to the local political interests of the great powers. Nor does it involve the acceptance of a Schwarzenbergian reciprocity. Britain's recognition of Austria's imperial claims does not entitle it to a similar recognition. The prudential acceptance of a Russian

26. Sproxton, p. 109.

sphere of influence in Eastern Europe does not entitle the United States to a free hand in its own sphere. Against national liberation and counter-intervention, there are no prescriptive rights.

CIVIL WAR

If we describe the Hungarian Revolution as Mill did, assuming that Palmerston was wrong, ignoring the claims of Croats and Slovenes, it is virtually a paradigm case for intervention. It is also, so described, an historically exceptional, indeed, it is now an hypothetical case. For these circumstances don't often arise in history: a national liberation movement unambiguously embodying the claims of a single, unified political community; capable at least initially of sustaining itself on the battlefield; challenged by an un-ambiguously foreign power; whose intervention can however be deterred or defeated without risking a general war. More often history presents a tangle of parties and factions, each claiming to speak for an entire community, fighting with one another, drawing outside powers into the struggle in secret, or at least unacknowledged, ways. Civil war poses hard problems, not because the Millian standard is unclear—it would require a strict stand-offishness—but because it can be and routinely is violated by degrees. Then it becomes very difficult to fix the point at which a direct and open use of force can plausibly be called a counter-intervention. And it is difficult also to calculate the effects of such a use of force on the already distressed inhabitants of the divided state and on the whole range of possible third parties.

In such cases, the lawyers commonly apply a qualified version of the self-help test.[27] They permit assistance to the established government—it is after all, the official representative of communal autonomy in international society—so long as it faces nothing more than internal dissension, rebellion, and insurgency. But as soon as the insurgents establish control over some substantial portion of the territory and population of the state, they acquire belligerent rights and an equality of status with the government. Then the lawyers enjoin a strict neutrality. Now, neutrality is conventionally regarded as an optative condition, a matter of choice, not of duty. So it is with regard to wars between states, but in civil wars there seem to be very good (Millian) reasons for making it obligatory. For once a community is effectively divided, foreign powers can hardly serve the cause of self-determination by acting

27. See, for example, Hall, *International Law*, p. 293.

militarily within its borders. The argument has been succinctly put by Montague Bernard, whose Oxford lecture "On the Principle of Non-intervention" ranks in importance with Mill's essay: "Of two things, one: the interference in the case supposed either turns the balance, or it does not. In the latter event, it misses its aim; in the former, it gives the superiority to the side which would not have been uppermost without it and establishes a sovereign, or a form of government, which the nation, if left to itself, would not have chosen."[28]

As soon as one outside power violates the norms of neutrality and non-intervention, however, the way is open for other powers to do so. Indeed, it may seem shameful not to repeat the violation—as in the case of the Spanish Civil War, where the noninterventionist policies of Britain, France, and the United States did not open the way for a local decision, but simply allowed the Germans and Italians to "turn the balance."[29] Some military response is probably required at such moments if the values of independence and community are to be sustained. But though that response upholds values shared throughout international society, it cannot accurately be described as law enforcement. Its character is not readily explicable within the terms of the legalist paradigm. For counter-intervention in civil wars does not aim at punishing or even, necessarily, at restraining the intervening states. It aims instead at holding the circle, preserving the balance, restoring some degree of integrity to the local struggle. It is as if a policeman, instead of breaking up a fight between two people, should stop anyone else from interfering or, if he cannot do that, should give proportional assistance to the disadvantaged party. He would have to have some notions about the value of the fight, and given the ordinary conditions of domestic society, those would be strange notions for him to have. But in the world of states they are entirely appropriate; they set the standards by which we judge between actual and pretended counter-interventions.

The American War in Vietnam

I doubt that it is possible to tell the story of Vietnam in a way that will command general agreement. The official American version—that the struggle began with a North Vietnamese invasion of the South, to which the

28. "On the Principle of Non-Intervention" (Oxford, 1860), p. 21.

29. See Hugh Thomas, *The Spanish Civil War* (New York, 1961), ch. 31, 40, 48, 58; Norman J. Padelford, *International Law and Diplomacy in the Spanish Civil Strife* (New York, 1939) is an incredibly naive defense of the nonintervention agreements.

United States responded in accordance with its treaty obligations—follows the legalist paradigm closely, but is on its surface unbelievable. Fortunately, it seems to be accepted by virtually no one and need not detain us here. I want to pursue a more sophisticated version of the American defense, which concedes the existence of a civil war and describes the U.S. role, first, as assistance to a legitimate government, and secondly, as counter-intervention, a response to covert military moves by the North Vietnamese regime.[30] The crucial terms here are "legitimate" and "response." The first suggests that the government on behalf of which our counter-intervention was undertaken had a local status, a political presence independent of ourselves, and hence that it could conceivably win the civil war if no external force was brought to bear. The second suggests that our own military operations followed upon and balanced those of another power, in accordance with the argument I have put forward. Both these suggestions are false, but they point to the peculiarly confined character of counter-intervention and indicate what one has to say (at least) when one joins in the civil wars of other states.

The Geneva Agreement of 1954, ending the first Vietnamese war, established a temporary frontier between the North and the South, and two temporary governments on either side of the line, pending elections scheduled for 1956.[31] When the South Vietnamese government refused to permit these elections, it clearly lost whatever legitimacy was conferred by the agreements. But I shall not dwell on this loss, nor on the fact that some sixty states nevertheless recognized the sovereignty of the new regime in the South and opened embassies in Saigon. I doubt that foreign states, whether they act independently or collectively, sign treaties or send ambassadors, can establish or disestablish the legitimacy of a government. What is crucial is the standing of that government with its own people. Had the new regime been able to rally support at home, Vietnam today would have joined the dual states of Germany and Korea, and Geneva 1954 would be remembered only as the setting for another cold war partition. But what is the test of popular support in a country where democracy is unknown and elections are routinely managed? The test, for governments as for in-

---

30. A useful statement of this position can be found in the essay by John Norton Moore already cited. For an example of the official view, see Leonard Meeker, "Vietnam and the International Law of Self-Defense" in the same volume, pp. 318–32.

31. I shall follow the account of G. M. Kahin and John W. Lewis, *The United States in Vietnam* (New York, 1967).

surgents, is self-help. That doesn't mean that foreign states cannot provide assistance. One assumes the legitimacy of new regimes; there is, so to speak, a period of grace, a time to build support. But that time was ill-used in South Vietnam, and the continuing dependence of the new regime on the U.S. is damning evidence against it. Its urgent call for military intervention in the early 1960's is more damning evidence still. One must ask of President Diem a question first posed by Montague Bernard: "How can he impersonate [represent] his people who is begging the assistance of a foreign power in order to reduce them to obedience?"[32] Indeed, it was never a successful impersonation.

The argument might be put more narrowly: a government that receives economic and technical aid, military supply, strategic and tactical advice, and is still unable to reduce its subjects to obedience, is clearly an illegitimate government. Whether legitimacy is defined sociologically or morally, such a government fails to meet the most minimal standards. One wonders how it survives at all. It must be the case that it survives because of the outside help it receives and for no other, no local reasons. The Saigon regime was so much an American creature that the U.S. government's claim to be committed to it and obligated to ensure its survival is hard to understand. It is as if our right hand were committed to our left. There is no independent moral or political agent on the other side of the bond and hence no genuine bond at all. Obligations to one's creatures (except insofar as they pertain to the personal safety of individuals) are as insignificant politically as obligations to oneself are insignificant morally. When the U.S. did intervene militarily in Vietnam, then, it acted not to fulfill commitments to another state, but to pursue policies of its own contrivance.

Against all this, it is argued that the popular base of the South Vietnamese government was undermined by a systematic campaign of subversion, terrorism, and guerrilla war, largely directed and supplied from the North. That there was such a campaign, and that the North was involved in it, is clearly true, though the extent and timing of the involvement are very much in dispute. If one were writing a legal brief, these matters would be critically important, for the American claim is that the North Vietnamese were illegally supporting a local insurgency, with both men and material, at a time when the U.S. was still providing only economic assistance and military supply to a legitimate government. But that claim, whatever its legal force, somehow misses the moral reality of the Vietnamese case. It would be better to say

32. "On the Principle of Non-Intervention," p. 16.

that the U.S. was literally propping up a government—and shortly a series
of governments—without a local political base, while the North Vietnamese
were assisting an insurgent movement with deep roots in the countryside.
We were far more vital to the government than they were to the insurgents.
Indeed, it was the weakness of the government, its inability to help itself
even against its internal enemies, that forced the steady escalation of American involvement. And that fact must raise the most serious questions about
the American defense: for counter-intervention is morally possible only on
behalf of a government (or a movement, party, or whatever) that has already
passed the self-help test.

I can say very little here about the reasons for insurgent strength in the
countryside. Why were the communists able, and the government unable,
to "impersonate" Vietnamese nationalism? The character and scope of the
American presence probably had a great deal to do with this. Nationalism
is not easily represented by a regime as dependent as Saigon was on foreign
support. It is also important that North Vietnamese moves did not similarly
brand those they benefited as foreign agents. In nations divided as Vietnam
was, infiltration across the dividing line is not necessarily regarded as outside
interference by the men and women on the other side. The Korean War
might look very different than it does if the Northerners had not marched
in strength across the 38th parallel, but had made covert contact, instead,
with a Southern rebellion. In contrast to Vietnam, however, there was no
rebellion—and there was considerable support for the government—in
South Korea.[33] These cold war dividing lines have the usual significance of
an international border only insofar as they mark off, or come in time to
mark off, two political communities within each of which individual citizens
feel some local loyalty. Had South Vietnam taken shape in this way, American military activity, in the face of large-scale Northern connivance at
terrorism and guerrilla war, might have qualified as counter-intervention.
At least, the name would have been an arguable one. As it is, it is not.

It remains an issue whether the American counter-intervention, had it
been such, could rightly have assumed the size and scope of the war we
eventually fought. Some notion of symmetry is relevant here, though it
cannot be fixed absolutely in arithmetic terms. When a state sets out to
maintain or restore the integrity of a local struggle, its military activity should
be roughly equivalent to that of the other intervening states. Counter-in-

33. See Gregory Henderson, *Korea: The Politics of the Vortex* (Cambridge, Mass., 1968),
ch. 6.

tervention is a balancing act. I have made this point before, but it is worth emphasizing, for it reflects a deep truth about the meaning of responsiveness: *the goal of counter-intervention is not to win the war.* That this is not an esoteric or obscure truth is suggested by President Kennedy's well-known description of the Vietnam War. "In the final analysis," Kennedy said, "it is their war. They are the ones who have to win it or lose it. We can help them, we can give them equipment, we can send our men out there as advisors, but they have to win it—the people of Vietnam against the Communists . . ."[34] Though this view was reiterated by later American leaders, it is not, unhappily, a definitive exposition of American policy. In fact, the United States failed in the most dramatic way to respect the character and dimensions of the Vietnamese civil war, and we failed because we could not win the war as long as it retained that character and was fought within those dimensions. Searching for a level of conflict at which our technological superiority could be brought to bear, we steadily escalated the struggle, until finally it was an American war, fought for American purposes, in someone else's country.

Humanitarian Intervention

A legitimate government is one that can fight its own internal wars. And external assistance in those wars is rightly called counter-intervention only when it balances, and does no more than balance, the prior intervention of another power, making it possible once again for the local forces to win or lose on their own. The outcome of civil wars should reflect not the relative strength of the intervening states, but the local alignment of forces. There is another sort of case, however, where we don't look for outcomes of that sort, where we don't want the local balance to prevail. If the dominant forces within a state are engaged in massive violations of human rights, the appeal to self-determination in the Millian sense of self-help is not very attractive. That appeal has to do with the freedom of the community taken as a whole; it has no force when what is at stake is the bare survival or the minimal liberty of (some substantial number of) its members. Against the enslavement or massacre of political opponents, national minorities, and religious sects, there may well be no help unless help comes from outside. And when a government turns savagely upon its own people, we must doubt the very

34. Kahin and Lewis, p. 146.

existence of a political community to which the idea of self-determination might apply. . . .

Governments and armies engaged in massacres are readily identified as criminal governments and armies (they are guilty, under the Nuremberg code of "crimes against humanity"). Hence humanitarian intervention comes much closer than any other kind of intervention to what we commonly regard, in domestic society, as law enforcement and police work. At the same time, however, it requires the crossing of an international frontier, and such crossings are ruled out by the legalist paradigm—unless they are authorized, I suppose, by the society of nations. In the cases I have considered, the law is unilaterally enforced; the police are self-appointed. Now, unilateralism has always prevailed in the international arena, but we worry about it more when what is involved is a response to domestic violence rather than to foreign aggression. We worry that, under the cover of humanitarianism, states will come to coerce and dominate their neighbors; once again, it is not hard to find examples. Hence many lawyers prefer to stick to the paradigm. That doesn't require them, on their view, to deny the (occasional) need for intervention. They merely deny legal recognition to that need. Humanitarian intervention "belongs in the realm not of law but of moral choice, which nations, like individuals must sometimes make . . ."[35] But that is only a plausible formulation if one doesn't stop with it, as lawyers are likely to do. For moral choices are not simply *made*; they are also judged, and so there must be criteria for judgment. If these are not provided by the law, or if legal provision runs out at some point, they are nevertheless contained in our common morality, which doesn't run out, and which still needs to be explicated after the lawyers have finished. . . .

Humanitarian intervention is justified when it is a response (with reasonable expectations of success) to acts "that shock the moral conscience of mankind." The old-fashioned language seems to me exactly right. It is not the conscience of political leaders that one refers to in such cases. They have other things to worry about and may well be required to repress their normal feelings of indignation and outrage. The reference is to the moral convictions of ordinary men and women, acquired in the course of their everyday activities. And given that one can make a persuasive argument in terms of those convictions, I don't think that there is any moral reason to

35. Thomas M. Franck and Nigel S. Rodley, "After Bangladesh: The Law of Humanitarian Intervention by Military Force," 67 *American Journal of International Law* 304 (1973).

adopt that posture of passivity that might be called waiting for the UN (waiting for the universal state, waiting for the messiah . . .).

> Suppose . . . that a great power decided that the only way it could continue to control a satellite state was to wipe out the satellite's entire population and recolonize the area with "reliable" people. Suppose the satellite government agreed to this measure and established the necessary mass extermination apparatus . . . Would the rest of the members of the U.N. be compelled to stand by and watch this operation merely because [the] requisite decision of U.N. organs was blocked and the operation did not involve an "armed attack" on any [member state] . . . ?[36]

The question is rhetorical. Any state capable of stopping the slaughter has a right, at least, to try to do so. The legalist paradigm indeed rules out such efforts, but that only suggests that the paradigm, unrevised, cannot account for the moral realities of military intervention.

The second, third, and fourth revisions of the paradigm have this form: states can be invaded and wars justly begun to assist secessionist movements (once they have demonstrated their representative character), to balance the prior interventions of other powers, and to rescue peoples threatened with massacre. In each of these cases we permit or, after the fact, we praise or don't condemn these violations of the formal rules of sovereignty, because they uphold the values of individual life and communal liberty of which sovereignty itself is merely an expression. The formula is, once again, permissive, but I have tried in my discussion of particular cases to indicate that the actual requirements of just interventions are constraining indeed. And the revisions must be understood to include the constraints. Since the constraints are often ignored, it is sometimes argued that it would be best to insist on an absolute rule of nonintervention (as it would be best to insist on an absolute rule of a nonanticipation). But the absolute rule will also be ignored, and we will then have no standards by which to judge what happens next. In fact, we do have standards, which I have tried to map out. They reflect deep and valuable, though in their applications difficult and problematic, commitments to human rights.

36. Julius Stone, *Aggression and World Order*, (Berkeley, 1968), p. 99.

DAVID LUBAN   Just War and
                              Human Rights

Doctrines of just war have been formulated mainly by theologians
and jurists in order to provide a canon applicable to a variety of practical situations. No doubt these doctrines originate in a moral understanding of violent conflict. The danger exists, however, that when the
concepts of the theory are adopted into the usage of politics and diplomacy their moral content is replaced by definitions which are merely
convenient. If that is so, the concepts of the traditional theory of just
war could be exactly the wrong starting point for an attempt to come
to grips with the relevant moral issues.

This is the case, I wish to argue, with the moral assessment of the
justice of war (*jus ad bellum*).[1] My argument is in four parts. First I
show that the dominant definition in international law is insensitive to
one morally crucial dimension of politics. Secondly, I connect this argument with classical social contract theory. Thirdly, I propose an alternative definition which attempts to base itself more firmly on the
moral theory of human rights. And finally, I apply this definition to
two hard cases.

I

Just War as Defense Against Aggression

International law does not speak of just or unjust war as such, but
rather of legal or illegal war. For the purpose of the present discussion

1. I follow the traditional distinction between the justice of war, that is, which
side is in the right with respect to the issues over which they are fighting, and
justice in war (*jus in bello*), which pertains to the way the war is fought.

I shall assume that the latter distinction expresses a theory of just war and treat the two distinctions as equivalent. The alternative would be to claim that international law is simply irrelevant to the theory of just war, a claim which is both implausible and question-begging.

Several characterizations of illegal war exist in international law. The Kellogg-Briand Pact of 1928, for example, condemns any use of war as an instrument of national policy except in the case of self-defense; and Brierly maintained that it did not lapse among it signers.[2] It is a very wide criterion for unjust war—wider, it may at first appear, than the United Nations Charter, which reads:

> All members shall refrain in their international relations from the threat or use of force against the territorial integrity or political independence of any State, or in any other manner inconsistent with the purposes of the United Nations.[3]

Presumably an act of war could exist which violated neither the political independence nor the territorial integrity of any state—say, a limited sea war. Or, to take another example, two states could agree to settle an issue by fighting a series of prearranged battles with prior agreements protecting their political independence and territorial integrity. Such acts would be barred by the Kellogg-Briand Pact; whether they are prohibited by Article 2(4) depends on how one reads the phrase "inconsistent with the purposes of the United Nations." I believe that on the most plausible reading, they would be prohibited.[4] Moreover, they would most likely constitute violations of the *jus cogens*, the overriding principles of general international law.[5] Thus, Article 2(4) is in fact roughly equivalent to the Kellogg-Briand Pact.

In any case, the provisions of Article 2(4) are subsumed under the definition of aggression adopted by the UN General Assembly in 1974. It includes the clause:

> Aggression is the use of armed force by a State against the sovereignty, territorial integrity or political independence of another

2. J. L. Brierly, *The Law of Nations*, 6th ed., ed. Humphrey Waldock (Oxford: Oxford University Press, 1963), p. 409.

3. Article 2(4), quoted in Brierly, p. 415.

4. This is Brierly's claim, p. 409. The relevant Article of the Charter is 1(1).

5. This point was suggested to me by Professor Boleslaw Boczek.

State, or in any other manner inconsistent with the Charter of the
United Nations.[6]

Aggression, in other words, is *armed intervention* in a state's affairs. That
this is a characterization of unjust war may be seen from the fact that it
terms aggression "the most serious and dangerous form of the illegal use
of force."[7] The definition of aggression differs from Article 2(4) in that it
includes a reference to sovereignty not present in the latter. This does not,
however, mean that it is a wider characterization of unjust war than Article
2(4), for an armed attack on a state's sovereignty would be barred by the
latter's catchall phrase "inconsistent with the purposes of the United Nations." Thus, the definition of aggression is not really an emendation of
Article 2(4). Rather, it should be viewed as an attempt to conceptualize and
label the offense at issue in Article 2(4). It attempts to give a sharp statement
of principle.

Matters are further complicated by the fact that the General Assembly in 1946 adopted the Charter of the Nuremberg Tribunal as UN
policy. Article 6 of this Charter includes among the crimes against
peace "waging of a war of aggression or a war in violation of international treaties, agreements, or assurances. . . ."[8] This appears to be
wider in scope than the definition of aggression, in that a war of
aggression is only one type of criminal war. However, an argument
similar to the one just given can be made here. Wars in violation of
international treaties, agreements, or assurances are without question
"inconsistent with the Charter of the United Nations," and hence fall
under the definition of aggression; the Nuremberg Charter and the
definition of aggression are thus extensionally equivalent.

It appears, then, that the definition of aggression captures what is
essential in the Kellogg-Briand Pact, Article 2(4) of the UN Charter,
and the relevant clause in the Nuremberg Charter. Thus, we may say
that the UN position boils down to this:

(1) A war is unjust if and only if it is aggressive.

6. Quoted in Yehuda Melzer, *Concepts of Just War* (Leyden: A. W. Sijthoff,
1975), pp. 28-29.
7. Ibid.
8. Quoted in Ian Brownlie, *Principles of Public International Law*, 2nd ed.
(Oxford: Clarendon Press, 1973), p. 545.

This gives us a characterization of unjust war, which is half of what we want. The other half emerges from Article 51 of the UN Charter:

> Nothing in the present Charter shall impair the inherent right of individual or collective self-defense if an armed attack occurs against a member of the United Nations. . . .[9]

This tells us, at least in part, what a just war is. Thus, we have

(2) A war is just if it is a war of self-defense (against aggression).

We note that "just" and "unjust" do not, logically speaking, exhaust the possibilities, since it is (just barely) possible that a war which is not fought in self-defense also does not threaten the sovereignty, territorial integrity, or political independence of any state, nor violate international treaties, agreements, or assurances. Now the expression "just war" suggests "permissible war" rather than "righteous war"; if so, then any war which is not specifically proscribed should be just. It is perhaps better, then, to make the two characterizations exhaustive of the possibilities. This can be done in two ways. The first is to permit wars that are not fought in self-defense against aggression, provided that they are not themselves aggressive wars—and we have just seen that it is in theory possible for a war to be neither defensive nor aggressive.

A definition more in the spirit of the UN Charter, however, would ban every war except wars of self-defense. To do this, we must modify (2) to

(2') A war is just if and only if it is a war of self-defense (against aggression).

Then we must expand (1) to

(1') A war is unjust if and only if it is not just.

Finally, we conjoin (1') to (2').

Thus, (1') and (2') capture pretty much what we want, namely the extant conception of *jus ad bellum*. In what follows I will refer to the conjunction of (1') and (2') as "the UN definition," although it must be emphasized that it is not formulated in these words in any United Nations document.

9. Quoted in Melzer, *Concepts of Just War*, p. 18. I have omitted a clause which does not bear on the present argument.

The UN Definition and the Doctrine of Sovereignty: A Critique

As it is formulated in the UN definition, the crime of aggressive war is a crime of state against state. Each state, according to international law, has a duty of non-intervention into the affairs of other states: indeed, this includes not just military intervention, but, in Lauterpacht's widely accepted definition, any "dictatorial interference in the sense of action amounting to the denial of the independence of the State."[10] At the basis of this duty lies the concept of state sovereignty, of which in fact the duty of non-intervention is considered a "corollary."[11] Now the concept of sovereignty has been interpreted in a multitude of ways, and has at different times covered a multitude of sins (in such forms as the notorious doctrine that sovereign states are above the law and entitled to do anything); but in its original use by Bodin, it meant that there can be only one ultimate source of law in a nation, namely the sovereign.[12] This doctrine suffices to explain why intervention is a crime, for "dictatorial interference" of one state in another's affairs in effect establishes a second legislator.

The doctrine does not, however, explain why the duty of non-intervention is a moral duty. For the recognition of a state as sovereign means in international law only that it in fact exercises sovereign power,[13] and it is hard to see how that fact could confer moral rights on it. Might, or so we are told, does not make right. Rather, one should distinguish mere *de facto* exercise of sovereign power from legitimate exercise of it. The natural argument would then be that the duty of non-intervention exists only toward states which are legitimate (in the sense of the term employed in normative political theory).

Before accepting this argument, however, we must consider another possibility, namely that the duty of non-intervention in a state's affairs is not a duty owed to that state, but to the community of nations as a whole. This, in fact, seems to be one idea behind the United Nations Charter. The experience of World War II showed the disas-

10. Hersch Lauterpacht, *International Law and Human Rights* (London: Stevens, 1950), p. 167.

11. The term is used in Brownlie, *Public International Law*, p. 280.

12. Brierly, *Law of Nations*, pp. 7-16. See Bodin, *République* (n.p.: Scientia Aalen, 1961), Book One, Chap. 8.

13. This is discussed in Brownlie, chap. 5, pp. 89-108.

trous nature of escalating international violence, and an absolute ban on the initiation of warfare is justified on what we would now call rule-utilitarian grounds: regardless of the moral stature of a state, or the empirical likelihood of escalation in a given case, military intervention in the state's affairs is forbidden for the sake of international security.

I want to reject this argument as the basis for a theory of just war, however. For by giving absolute primacy to the world community's interest in peace, it does not really answer the question of when a war is or can be just; rather, it simply refuses to consider it. Obviously, the dangers posed by a war in the volatile political configuration of the nuclear era must weigh heavily into the question of *jus ad bellum*. But to make this the only factor is to refuse a priori to consider the merits of particular issues, and this is simply to beg the question of *jus ad bellum*.

Thus, I return to the claim that a state must be legitimate in order for a moral duty of non-intervention in its affairs to exist. If this is so, it pulls the rug out from under the UN definition, which is simply indifferent to the question of legitimacy, and thus to the whole moral dimension of the issue. We may put this in more graphic terms. When State *A* recognizes State *B*'s sovereignty it accepts a duty of non-intervention in *B*'s internal affairs. In other words, it commits itself to pass over what *B* actually does to its own people unless *B* has entered into international agreements regulating its domestic behavior; and even in this case *A* cannot intervene militarily to enforce these agreements.[14]

14. On the relation of international agreements with the duty of non-intervention, particularly in the case of human rights, see Louis Henkin, "Human Rights and 'Domestic Jurisdiction,'" in Thomas Buergenthal, ed., *Human Rights, International Law and the Helsinki Accords* (New York: Universe Books, 1977), pp. 21-40, and Thomas Buergenthal, "Domestic Jurisdiction, Intervention, and Human Rights: The International Law Perspective," in Peter G. Brown and Douglas Maclean, eds., *Human Rights and U.S. Foreign Policy* (Lexington, Mass.: Lexington Books, 1979), pp. 111-120. Both agree that even when the right of domestic jurisdiction over human rights has been "signed away" by a state, military intervention against it is proscribed. This doctrine, a product of the United Nations era, has replaced the nineteenth-century doctrine which permitted humanitarian intervention on behalf of oppressed peoples. The legal issues are discussed in the readings collected in Richard B. Lillich and Frank C. Newman, eds., *International Human Rights: Problems of Law and Policy* (Bos-

No matter if *B* is repulsively tyrannical; no matter if it consists of the
most brutal torturers or sinister secret police; no matter if its ruling
generals make its primary export bullion shipped to Swiss banks. If *A*
recognizes *B*'s sovereignty it recognizes *B*'s right to enjoy its excesses
without "dictatorial interference" from outside.

Really, however, the point retains its force no matter what the
character of *B*. The concept of sovereignty is morally flaccid, not because it applies to illegitimate regimes, but because it is insensitive to
the entire dimension of legitimacy.

Can the UN definition be repaired, then, by restricting the concepts
of sovereignty and aggression to legitimate states? This would certainly be a step in the right direction; but the attempt underlines a puzzle
about the whole strategy of defining *jus ad bellum* as a crime against
states. Wars are not fought by states, but by men and women. There
is, therefore, a conceptual lacuna in such a definition. It can be bridged
only by explaining how a crime against a state is also a crime against
its citizens, that is, by relating men and women to their states in a
morally cogent fashion. This, I take it, is what the concept of legitimacy is supposed to do. A legitimate state has a right against aggression because people have a right to their legitimate state. But if so we
should be able to define *jus ad bellum* directly in terms of human
rights, without the needless detour of talk about states. Nor is this
simply a question of which terms are logically more basic. If the rights
of states are derived from the rights of humans, and are thus in a
sense one kind of human rights, it will be important to consider their
possible conflicts with other human rights. Thus, a doctrine of *jus ad
bellum* formulated in terms of human rights may turn out not to consider aggression the sole crime of war. Indeed, this is what I shall argue in Section III.

First, however, it will be helpful to consider more closely the connection between a state's rights and those of its citizens. For I have

---

ton: Little, Brown and Company, 1979), pp. 484-544. The case analyzed there
is India's 1971 intervention into Bangladesh; on this see also Oriana Fallaci's
interview with Zulfikar Ali Bhutto, in *Interview With History* (Boston: Hough-
ton Mifflin Co., 1976), pp. 182-209.

criticized the UN definition (and the doctrine of sovereignty) by suggesting that its focus on the former shows indifference to the latter.

II

Contract, Nation and State

This argument may be clarified by examining social contract theory, the canonical modern account of legitimacy. The key feature of contract theory for our present discussion is its conception of the rights of political communities, particularly their right against aggression. According to contract theory, a political community is made legitimate by the consent (tacit or explicit) of its members; it thereby acquires rights which derive from the rights of its members. Thus the rights of political communities are explained by two rather harmless assumptions: that people have rights, and that those rights may be transferred through freely given consent. Contract theory, then, appears to offer a particularly clear account of how aggression against a political community is a crime against its members.

However, it is important to note that the term "political community" has two radically distinct meanings, corresponding to two very different conceptions of the social contract. The seventeenth-century theorists distinguished between a contract by which people bind themselves into a community prior to any state—Locke's version—and a contract by which people set a sovereign over them—Hobbes' version. Let us call the former a "horizontal" and the latter a "vertical" contract.[15]

A horizontal contract may be explicit: Arendt, in introducing the terms, suggests the Mayflower Compact as a paradigm case of a horizontal contract to which consent was explicitly rendered. More often, however, the consent is given tacitly through the process of everyday living itself. In Walzer's words:

15. I adopt this terminology from Hannah Arendt, "Civil Disobedience," in *Crises of the Republic* (New York: Harcourt, Brace, Jovanovich, 1972), pp. 85-87. See also her *On Revolution* (New York: Viking, 1965), pp. 169-171. It appears also in Michael Walzer, "The Problem of Citizenship," *Obligations* (New York: Simon and Schuster, 1970), p. 207.

Over a long period of time, shared experiences and cooperative activity of many different kinds shape a common life. 'Contract' is a
metaphor for a process of association and mutuality. . . .[16]

Such a contract gives rise to a *people* or, as I shall say in order to
emphasize the people's existence as a political community, to a *nation*.
But only the vertical contract can legitimate a *state*. A state is an on-
going institution of rule over, or government of, its nation. It is a
drastic error to confuse the two; for while every government loudly
asserts, "Le peuple, c'est moi!" it is clear that this is never literally true
and seldom plausible even as a figure of speech. And it is equally obvious what ulterior motives and interests lie behind the assertion.

A state's rights can be established only through a vertical contract,
which according to social-contract theory means nothing more or less
than that the state is legitimate. This, too, requires consent, and this
will be consent over and above that which establishes the horizontal
contract. For the nation is prior to the state. Political communities,
not sets of atomic individuals, consent to be governed. Of course it is
the typical argument of totalitarianism, with its idolatry of the state,
to deny this. For example, Giovanni Gentile, the "philosopher of
fascism," says:

For it is not nationality that creates the State, but the State which
creates nationality, by setting the seal of actual existence on it. It
is through the *conquest* of unity and independence that the nation
gives proof of its political will, and establishes its existence as a
State.[17]

Gentile had in mind Italy's struggle for unity in the Risorgimento;
evidently, he believed that until the Italian state was established the
nation as such did not exist. But what, then, gave "proof of its political will"? Gentile calls it the nation, and he is right, although this is
inconsistent with his original contention that before the state the nation did not exist. A national liberation movement comes about when
a people acts as a political community, that is, as a nation; its state

16. Walzer, *Just and Unjust Wars* (New York: Basic Books, 1977), p. 54.
17. Giovanni Gentile, *Genesis and Structure of Society*, trans. H. S. Harris
(Urbana: University of Illinois Press, 1966), pp. 121-122.

comes later if it comes at all. The nation is the more-or-less permanent social basis of any state that governs it.

The relevance of these distinctions for just-war theory is this: clearly, aggression violates a state's rights only when the state possesses these rights. According to contract theory this entails that the state has been legitimated by the consent of its citizens. An illegitimate state, that is, one governing without the consent of the governed is, therefore, morally if not legally estopped from asserting a right against aggression. The *nation* possesses such a right, to be sure, but the state does not. Thus we have returned to the argument of the preceding section, which in our present terminology amounts to the claim that the concept of sovereignty systematically and fallaciously confuses a nation and its state, granting illegitimate states a right to which they are not entitled.

Curiously, Walzer himself falls prey to this confusion in his theory of just war. He attempts to give a contractarian justification of the UN definition, grounding the rights of states in a social contract based on tacit consent as characterized above ("shared experiences and cooperative activity of many kinds shape a common life"). This form of consent, however, can only refer to the horizontal contract, and can thus ground only the rights of nations, not of states. As Gerald Doppelt points out, "Walzer's theory seems to operate on two levels: on the *first* level, he implicitly identifies the state with the established government . . .; on the *second* level, he identifies the state with the people, nation, or political community—not its *de facto* government. . . ."[18] This is precisely a confusion of vertical with horizontal contracts. Doppelt goes on to criticize Walzer on grounds quite similar to those suggested by my argument: an illegitimate and tyrannical state cannot derive sovereign rights against aggression from the rights of its own oppressed citizens, when it itself is denying them those same rights.

The question which we are facing is this: what sort of evidence shows that consent to a state has indeed been rendered? I shall not attempt to give a general answer here, since the issue is quite com-

18. Gerald Doppelt, "Walzer's Theory of Morality in International Relations," *Philosophy & Public Affairs* 8, no. 1 (Fall 1978): 9.

plex. Two things, however, are clear. The first is that the mere existence of the nation cannot be sufficient evidence of the required sort:
it would then legitimate any pretender. This is why Walzer's contract
in no way establishes a state's rights, contrary to his claim. The second is that clear evidence can exist that a state is *not* based on consent and hence *not* legitimate.

An example drawn from the recent Nicaraguan revolution will il-
lustrate this. On 22 August 1978 a band of Sandinista guerrillas took
over the National Palace in Nicaragua, holding virtually the entire
parliament hostage. They demanded and received the release of political prisoners, a large ransom, and free passage to Panama. Newspapers reported that as the guerrillas drove to the airport the streets
were lined with cheering Nicaraguans. Within two days a general
strike against the government of Anastasio Somoza Debayle had shut
down the country; it was unusual in that it had the support of Nicaragua's largest business association, and thus seemed to voice a virtually unanimous rejection of the Somoza regime. Soon armed insurrection began. In the city of Matagalpa the barricades were manned
mainly by high school students and other youths. Somoza responded
by ordering the air force to bomb Matagalpa; the Matagalpans sent
delegates to the bishopric to ask the church to intervene on their behalf with the government. The rebellion spread; at this point American newspapers were routinely referring to the Nicaraguan events as
a struggle between the Nicaraguan people and the National Guard
(the army). In a press statement strongly reminiscent of Woody
Allen's *Bananas*, Somoza stated that his was the cause of Nicaraguan
freedom, since he enjoyed the support of virtually the entire National
Guard. By October the uprising was crushed—albeit temporarily—by
sheer force of arms.

I do not pretend to possess a detailed understanding of Nicaraguan
politics. However, it does not take a detailed understanding to realize
that when the populace of a capital city cheers the guerrillas who have
taken their own parliament hostage, when labor unions and business
associations are able to unite in a general strike, and when a large
city's residents must ask for third-party intervention to prevent their
own government from bombing them to rubble, the government in

question enjoys neither consent nor legitimacy. The evidence, I submit, is more than sufficient to back this claim.

It might be objected that this example shows only that the Somoza régime was illegitimate, not the Nicaraguan state as such. The distinction between regime and state, however, is simply this: the regime is a particular distribution of men and women over the leadership posts which the state institutionalizes. (I shall ignore the complication that replacements can be made in some posts without the regime changing.) If this is so, then the objection amounts to the claim that the Nicaraguan people might consent to an institutional structure involving a leadership position with Somoza's powers—that is, that they might consent to a dictatorial structure which they could change only through armed struggle. It is clear that this claim possesses vanishingly small plausibility; ultimately, I believe it rests on the question-begging assumption that a nation always consents to some state or other.

This example underlines the moral impotence of the concept of sovereignty. For other states continued to recognize the sovereignty of the Somoza regime and thus committed themselves to a policy of non-intervention in the state's war against its nation. No doubt such decisions were discreet; they were certainly not moral.[19]

Other examples are—unfortunately—not hard to find. One thinks of the Organization of African Unity's frosty reception of Tanzania's "aggression" in Uganda, despite the notorious illegitimacy of Idi Amin's regime.[20] The point is graphically illustrated as well by the United States government's response to the conquest of Cambodia by Vietnam in January 1979. The Carter administration had frequently pinpointed the regime of Pol Pot and Ieng Sary as the worst human rights violator in the world, and some reports suggested that the "auto-genocide" in Cambodia was the most awful since the Holocaust.[21] Nevertheless, the State Department denounced Vietnam for aggression and violation of Cambodia's territorial integrity and sovereignty;

19. Walzer would, it seems, agree; see *Just and Unjust Wars*, p. 98.
20. See *Amnesty International Report 1978* (London: Amnesty International Publications, 1979), pp. 89-92, and Amnesty's *Human Rights in Uganda* (London: Amnesty International Publications, 1978).
21. See *Amnesty International Report 1978*, pp. 167-170, for detailed instances.

and this despite the fact that the Vietnamese-installed regime's first announcement concerned the restoration of human rights in Cambodia.[22] I shall discuss this issue more fully in Section IV.

The Modern Moral Reality of War

Modern international law is coeval with the rise of the European nation-state in the seventeenth and eighteenth centuries. As the term suggests, it is within the historical context of nation-states that a theory will work whose tendency is to equate the rights of nations with the rights of states. It is plausible to suggest that an attack on the French state amounts to an attack on the French nation (although even here some doubts are possible: a Paris Communard in 1871 would hardly have agreed). But when nations and states do not characteristically coincide, a theory of *jus ad bellum* which equates unjust war with aggression, and aggression with violations of state sovereignty, removes itself from the historical reality of war.

World politics in our era is marked by two phenomena: a breakup of European hegemony in the Third World which is the heritage of nineteenth-century imperialism; and maneuvering for hegemony by the (neo-imperialist) superpowers, perhaps including China. The result of this process is a political configuration in the Third World in which states and state boundaries are to an unprecedented extent

22. ". . . A profound moral and political issue is at stake. Which is the greater evil: the continuation of a tyrannical and murderous regime, or a flagrant violation of national sovereignty? . . . the Carter Administration . . . decided without hesitation . . . that the violation of Cambodia's sovereignty was a greater enormity than the Cambodian regime's violations of human rights. . . ." Henry Kamm, "The Cambodian Dilemma," *The New York Times Magazine*, 4 February 1979, pp. 54-55. Evidently, this view was shared by the United Nations, which voted recently to seat a delegation from the deposed Pol Pot government rather than the Vietnam-supported Heng Samrin regime, on the grounds that no matter how unappetizing the behavior of the former, it would be wrong to condone aggression by recognizing the latter.

In citing these examples I am not entering any large moral claims on behalf of Vietnam or Tanzania, both of which are accountable for their share of human rights violations. Here I am in agreement with Walzer (*Just and Unjust Wars*, p. 105) that pure motives and clean hands are not necessary to morally justify an intervention. The present essay was written in early 1979, before the current Cambodian famine, in which it appears that the policies of Vietnam may be just as horrifying as those of the Khmer Rouge.

the result of historical accident (how the European colonial powers parceled up their holdings) and political convenience (how the contending superpowers come to terms with each other). In the Third World the nation-state is the exception rather than the rule. Moreover, a large number of governments possess little or no claim to legitimacy. As a result of these phenomena, war in our time seems most often to be revolutionary war, war of liberation, civil war, border war between newly established states, or even tribal war, which is in fact a war of nations provoked largely by the noncongruence of nation and state.

In such circumstances a conception of *jus ad bellum* like the one embodied in the UN definition fails to address the moral reality of war. It reflects a theory that speaks to the realities of a bygone era. The result is predictable. United Nations debates—mostly ineffectual in resolving conflicts—and discussions couched in terms of aggression and defense, have deteriorated into cynical and hypocritical rhetoric and are widely recognized as such. Nor is this simply one more instance of the well-known fact that politicians lie in order to dress up their crimes in sanctimonious language. For frequently these wars are fought for reasons which are recognizably moral. It is just that their morality cannot be assessed in terms of the categories of the UN definition; it must be twisted and distorted to fit a conceptual Procrustes' bed.

III

Human Rights and the New Definition

What, then, are the terms according to which the morality of war is to be assessed? In order to answer this question, let me return to my criticism of the contractarian derivation of the rights of states from the rights of individuals. States—patriots and Rousseau to the contrary—are not to be loved, and seldom to be trusted. They are, by and large, composed of men and women enamored of the exercise of power, men and women whose interests are consequently at least slightly at variance with those of the rest of us. When we talk of the rights of a state, we are talking of rights—"privileges" is a more accurate word—which those men and women possess over and above the general rights of man; and this is why they demand a special justification.

Just War and
Human Rights

I have not, however, questioned the framework of individual rights as an adequate language for moral discourse. It is from this framework that we may hope to discover the answer to our question. Although I accept the vocabulary of individual rights for the purpose of the present discussion, I do not mean to suggest that its propriety cannot be questioned. Nevertheless, talk of individual rights does capture much of the moral reality of contemporary politics, as talk of sovereignty and states' rights does not. This is a powerful pragmatic reason for adopting the framework.

To begin, let me draw a few elementary distinctions. Although rights do not necessarily derive from social relations, we do not have rights apart from them, for rights are always claims on other people. If I catch pneumonia and die, my right to life has not been violated unless other humans were directly or indirectly responsible for my infection or death. To put this point in syntactic terms, a right is not to be thought of as a one-place predicate, but rather a two-place predicate whose arguments range over the class of beneficiaries and the class of obligors. A human right, then, will be a right whose beneficiaries are all humans and whose obligors are all humans in a position to effect the right. (The extension of this latter class will vary depending on the particular beneficiary.)[23] Human rights are the demands of all of humanity on all of humanity. This distinguishes human rights from, for example, civil rights, where the beneficiaries and obligors are specified by law.

By a *socially basic human right* I mean a right whose satisfaction is necessary to the enjoyment of any other rights.[24] Such rights deserve to be called "basic" because, while they are neither intrinsically

23. Other analyses of the concept of "human right" are possible. Walzer, for example, makes the interesting suggestion that the beneficiary of human rights is not a person but humanity itself (*Just and Unjust Wars*, p. 158). Such an analysis has much to recommend it, but it does not concern us here, for humanity will still enjoy its rights through particular men and women.

24. I take this concept from Henry Shue, "Foundations for a Balanced U.S. Policy on Human Rights: The Significance of Subsistence Rights" (College Park, Maryland: Center for Philosophy and Public Policy Working Paper HRFP-1, 1977), pp. 3-4. Shue discusses it in detail in *Basic Rights: Subsistence, Affluence, and U.S. Foreign Policy* (Princeton, NJ: Princeton University Press, 1980), chap. 1.

more valuable nor more enjoyable than other human rights, they are means to the satisfaction of all rights, and thus they must be satisfied even at the expense of socially non-basic human rights if that is necessary. In Shue's words, "Socially basic human rights are everyone's minimum reasonable demands upon the rest of humanity." He goes on to argue that socially basic human rights include security rights—the right not to be subject to killing, torture, assault, and so on—and subsistence rights, which include the rights to healthy air and water, and adequate food, clothing, and shelter.[25]

Such rights are worth fighting for. They are worth fighting for not only by those to whom they are denied but, if we take seriously the obligation which is indicated when we speak of human rights, by the rest of us as well (although how strictly this obligation is binding on "neutrals" is open to dispute). This does not mean that any infringement of socially basic human rights is a *casus belli*: here as elsewhere in the theory of just war the doctrine of proportionality applies. But keeping this reservation in mind we may formulate the following, to be referred to henceforth as the "new definition":

(3)   A just war is (i) a war in defense of socially basic human rights (subject to proportionality); or (ii) a war of self-defense against an unjust war.

(4)   An unjust war is (i) a war subversive of human rights, whether socially basic or not, which is also (ii) not a war in defense of socially basic human rights.

I shall explain. The intuition here is that any proportional struggle for socially basic human rights is justified, even one which attacks the non-basic rights of others. An attack on human rights is an unjust war *unless* it is such a struggle. This is why clause (4) (ii) is necessary: without it a war could be both just and unjust. Clause (3) (ii) is meant to capture the moral core of the principle of self-defense, formulated above as (2). And it is worth noting that clause (4) (i) is an attempt to reformulate the concept of aggression as a crime against people rather than states; an aggressive war is a war against human rights. Since the rights of nations may be human rights (I

25. Ibid., pp. 3, 6-12.

shall not argue the pros or cons of this here), this notion of aggression may cover ordinary cases of aggression against nations.

Let me emphasize that (3) and (4) refer to *jus ad bellum*, not *jus in bello*. When we consider the *manner* in which wars are fought, of course, we shall always find violations of socially basic human rights. One might well wonder, in that case, whether a war can ever be justified. Nor is this wonder misplaced, for it addresses the fundamental horror of war. The answer, if there is to be one, must emerge from the doctrine of proportionality; and here I wish to suggest that the new definition is able to make sense of this doctrine in a way which the UN definition is not.[26] For the UN definition would have us measure the rights of states against socially basic human rights, and this may well be a comparison of incommensurables. Under the new definition, on the other hand, we are asked only to compare the violations of socially basic human rights likely to result from the fighting of a war with those which it intends to rectify. Now this comparison, like the calculus of utilities, might be Benthamite pie-in-the-sky; but if it is nonsense, then proportionality under the UN definition is what Bentham once called the theory of human rights: "nonsense on stilts."

IV

Two Hard Cases

The new definition differs in extension from the UN definition in two ways: on the one hand, an aggressive war may be intended to defend socially basic human rights, and thus be just according to (3); on the other, a war of self-defense may be fought in order to preserve a status quo which subverts human rights, and thus be unjust according to (4). But, I suggest, this is no objection, because (3) and (4) accord more with the moral reality of war in our time than (1) and (2) or (1') and (2').

26. The new definition also allows us to make sense of an interesting and plausible suggestion by Melzer, namely that a just war (in the sense of *jus ad bellum*) conducted in an unjust way (*jus in bello*) becomes unjust (*jus ad bellum*), in other words, that the *jus ad bellum* is "anchored" in the *jus in bello*. On the new definition this would follow from the fact that a war conducted in a sufficiently unjust way would violate proportionality. See Melzer, pp. 87-93.

There are two situations which are of particular interest for the theory of *jus ad bellum* because they exhibit marked differences between the UN definition and the new definition. The first concerns a type of economic war, the second an armed intervention in a state's internal affairs.

What I have in mind in the first case is a war for subsistence. Consider this example: *A* and *B* are neighboring countries of approximately the same military capability, separated by a mountain range. *A* is bordered by the ocean and receives plentiful rainfall; however, the mountains prevent rain clouds from crossing over to *B*, which is consequently semi-arid. One year the lack of rain causes a famine in *B* which threatens millions of lives. *A*, on the other hand, has a large food surplus; but for a variety of cultural, historical, and economic reasons it makes none of this food available to *B*. Can *B* go to war with *A* to procure food?

According to the UN definition such a war would constitute an aggression, and consequently be unjust; but according to (3), since the war would be an attempt to procure socially basic human rights for *B*'s people, it would be just. Indeed, *A* is morally obligated to give food to *B*, and assuming that *B*'s sole purpose in fighting is to procure food, a defense by *A* would be an unjust war.

This, I suggest, is a position fully in accord with moral decency. Indeed, it is interesting to note that Walzer adopts a similar position, despite the fact that it runs counter to his basic argument concerning the criminality of aggression. Discussing the case of barbarian tribes who, driven west by invaders, demanded land from the Roman Empire on which to settle, Walzer quotes Hobbes with approval: "he that shall oppose himself against [those doing what they must do to preserve their own lives], for things superfluous, is guilty of the war that thereupon is to follow."[27] A fight for life is a just fight.

An important qualification must be made to this argument, however. If *A* itself has a food shortage it cannot be obligated to provide food to *B*, for its own socially basic human rights are in jeopardy.

27. Walzer, *Just and Unjust Wars*, p. 57. See also Charles R. Beitz, *Political Theory in International Relations* (Princeton: Princeton University Press, 1979), pp. 175-176.

Thus *B* loses its claim against *A*. And if a third nation, *C*, can supply food to *A* or *B* but not both, it is unclear who has a right to it. Socially basic human rights can conflict, and in such cases the new definition of just war will not yield clear-cut answers. Nor, however, do we have reason to expect that clear-cut answers might exist.

There are less clear examples. What about a fight against impoverishment? In the 1960s and 1970s Great Britain and Iceland were repeatedly embroiled in a conflict over fishing grounds. This resulted in an act of war on the part of Iceland, namely, a sea attack on British ships. Of course, Iceland's belligerence may have been merely theatrical; moreover, on Iceland's interpretation of the limits of fisheries jurisdiction, she was simply defending her own right, since the British vessels were within the two-hundred mile fisheries zone claimed by Iceland. But the moral issue had to do with the fact that Iceland's economy is built around the fishing industry, and thus a threat to this industry presented a threat of impoverishment. Now no socially basic human rights are at issue here: impoverishment is not starvation. Nevertheless, there is a certain moral plausibility to the Icelanders' position, and it clearly resembles the position of country *B* in our previous example. But if we weaken the definition of unjust war to include struggles against economic collapse, the door is opened to allowing any economic war. For example, do industrialized countries have a right to go to war for OPEC oil?

One way to handle this would be to claim that while nations have no socially basic right to any given economic level beyond subsistence, they do possess a socially basic right not to have their economic position worsened at a catastrophic rate. There is a certain plausibility to this suggestion, inasmuch as a collapsing economy will undoubtedly cause social disruption sufficient to prevent the enjoyment of other rights. The point is nevertheless debatable. Without pretending to settle it, I would, however, claim that we are now on the right moral ground for carrying out the debate, whereas a discussion couched in terms of aggression and sovereignty would miss the point completely.

The other case I wish to discuss concerns foreign intervention into a country's internal affairs. The point is that if such an intervention is on behalf of socially basic human rights it is justified according to the new definition.

Here again it will be useful to look at Walzer's position. He begins by endorsing an argument of Mill's which is based on the right of national self-determination. Mill's point is that this is a right of nations to set their own house in order *or fail to* without outside interference. If a people struggles against a dictatorship but loses, it is still self-determining; whereas if it wins due to the intervention of an outside power, its right to self-determination has been violated. Walzer admits only three exceptions: (i) a secession, when there are two or more distinct political communities contending within the same national boundary; (ii) a situation in which another foreign power has already intervened; and (iii) a situation in which human rights violations of great magnitude—massacres or enslavements—are occurring. Only in these cases may intervention be justified.[28]

Now Mill's argument employs a somewhat Pickwickian conception of self-determination. A self-determining people, it suggests, fights its own battles, even if it loses them. But then one might infer that a self-determining people fights its own wars as well, even if it loses them. Thus, a nation's conquest by a foreign power would become an instance of its self-determination.[29] Surely the fact that it is a foreign rather than a domestic oppressor is not a morally relevant factor, for that would imply that oppressions can be sorted on moral grounds according to the race or nationality of the oppressor. Yet something is clearly wrong with an argument which leads to this doublethink concept of self-determination.[30]

The problem with Mill's position is that it takes the legitimacy of states too much at face value. "Mill generally writes as if he believes that citizens get the government they deserve. . . ."[31] That is, somehow oppression of domestic vintage carries a prima facie claim to legitimacy which is not there in the case of foreign conquest. It seems that Mill suspects that the state would not be there if the people did not secretly want it. This seems to me to be an absurd, and at times even

28. Walzer, *Just and Unjust Wars*, pp. 87-91.

29. As Walzer expressly denies, p. 94.

30. I take Doppelt to be making a similar point when he suggests that a people can be "aggressed" against by its own state as well as by a foreign state, "Walzer's Theory," p. 8. My argument in this section is quite in sympathy with Doppelt's, pp. 10-13.

31. Walzer, p. 88.

obscene view, uncomfortably reminiscent of the view that women are raped because secretly they want to be. The only argument for Mill's case, I believe, is the improbable claim that the fact that people are not engaged in active struggle against their state shows tacit consent. Even granting this, however, there remains one case in which Mill's position is unacceptable on its own terms. That is when there is overwhelming evidence that the state enjoys no legitimacy—when there is active and virtually universal struggle against it. Such struggles do not always succeed, and after each bloody suppression the possibility of another uprising grows less. Heart and flesh can bear only so much. In such a case an argument against intervention based on the people's right of self-determination is merely perverse. It makes the "self" in "self-determination" mean "other"; it reverses the role of people and state. One thinks of Brecht's poem "Die Lösung," written after the rebellion of East German workers in 1953: "After the rebellion of the seventeenth of June . . . one could read that the people had forfeited the government's confidence and could regain it only by redoubling their work efforts. Would it not be simpler for the government to dissolve the people and elect another one?"[32] I might add that in fact Walzer grants the point: "a state (or government) established against the will of its own people, ruling violently, may well forfeit its right to defend itself even against a foreign invasion."[33] Thus, it would appear that in such a case intervention is morally justified, even in the absence of massacres and slavery.

And, to make a long story short, the new definition will endorse this view. For the kind of evidence which demonstrates a government's illegitimacy must consist of highly visible signs that it does not enjoy consent, for example, open insurrection or plain repression. And this necessitates violations of security rights, which are socially basic human rights. Obedience which is not based on consent is based on coercion; thus the more obvious it is that a government is illegitimate, the more gross and widespread will its violations of security rights be, reaching even those who do not actively oppose it. This is akin to a

32. Quoted by Hannah Arendt, *Men in Dark Times* (New York: Harcourt, Brace and World, 1968), p. 213.

33. Walzer, *Just and Unjust Wars*, p. 82 n.

law of nature. And thus an intervention becomes morally justified, or even morally urgent.

No definition of just war is likely to address all of the difficult cases adequately—and there is no realm of human affairs in which difficult cases are more common. Seat-of-the-pants practical judgment is a necessary supplement to one's principles in such matters: in this respect I fully agree with Walzer that "The proper method of practical morality is casuistic in character."[34] Thus, while I do not doubt that troubling examples may be brought against the new definition, it seems to me that if it corresponds with our moral judgments in a large number of actual cases, and can be casuistically stretched to address others, it serves its purpose. My claim is that, whatever its deficiencies, the new definition of *jus ad bellum* offered in (3) and (4) is superior to the existing one in this respect.

34. Ibid., p. xvi.

Some of the ideas in Sections II and III were suggested to me by George Friedman. I received helpful criticism of an early draft of this paper from Boleslaw Boczek and my colleagues Douglas Maclean and Henry Shue. Any resemblance between my remaining mistakes and their beliefs is wholly accidental. Finally, I wish to thank the Editors of *Philosophy & Public Affairs*, who spared the reader some rococo diction and bad arguments.

MICHAEL WALZER   The Moral Standing of
                        States: A Response
                        to Four Critics

I

The argument of *Just and Unjust Wars* has been criticized in a number of ways, most of them overtly political in character, as if in paraphrase of Clausewitz's famous maxim: writing about war is a continuation of writing about politics. . . .[1] That is not an entirely false maxim; indeed, it contains, as will be apparent below, unavoidable truth. And yet it is the purpose of a *theory* of just war to produce principles that, however they apply in this or that case, cannot be conscripted permanently into the service of any particular political creed or of any state or party. They are critical principles, and they open all states and parties to moral criticism. The principles I have put forward are of this sort, and I am less concerned—at least in this journal—to defend the casuistic judgments through which they were worked out than the overall structure of the argument.

But there is one set of criticisms to which I want to respond here because it does raise deep questions about the overall structure. Four writers, in substantial reviews or articles, have adopted the same position, developed it in somewhat different ways, arrived at a common conclusion: that *Just and Unjust Wars*, despite its putative foundation in a theory of individual rights, is ultimately "statist" in character. "The rights of states, and not the rights of individuals," says Wasserstrom, "come in the end to enjoy an exalted, primary status within the moral critique of aggression."[2] The book, says Doppelt, "furnishes

1. Michael Walzer, *Just and Unjust Wars* (New York, 1977).
2. Richard Wasserstrom, *Harvard Law Review* 92 (December 1978): 544.

a rhetoric of morality in international relations which places the rights of de facto states above those of individuals."[3] Beitz and Luban, while trying to suggest what an alternative morality might look like, make similar arguments.[4] The criticism of these writers rests in places upon a misreading of my own position, but it rests more largely upon significant philosophical disagreements about the nature of political life. And so it is worth pursuing.

The immediate issue is the doctrine of non-intervention, a feature of *jus ad bellum*, the part of the theory that explains the criminality of aggressive war. Wasserstrom, Doppelt, Beitz, and Luban all argue that the theory as I have formulated it (1) protects states that should not be protected against foreign intervention and (2) does so on grounds that are either inadequate or incoherent. The theory has, on their view, conservative implications, and what it conserves is the authority or sovereignty of illegitimate, that is tyrannical, regimes. They, on the other hand, are more open, given certain qualifications about proportionality, to an activist and interventionist politics aimed at overthrowing such regimes and maximizing the enjoyment of individual rights. This is not a line of criticism that I anticipated with any clarity. My own worries had a different focus: I thought the theory might be too permissive with regard to secessionist movements and foreign support for such movements. Hence, in responding now, I shall have to enlarge upon the argument of the book, and at one or two points, indicated below, I shall have to amend or qualify the argument. But the basic position remains intact. The state is presumptively, though by no means always in practice, the arena within which self-determination is worked out and from which, therefore, foreign armies have to be excluded.

II

The real subject of my argument is not the state at all but the political community that (usually) underlies it. And I will compound my

3. Gerald Doppelt, "Walzer's Theory of Morality in International Relations," *Philosophy & Public Affairs* 8, no. 1: 26.

4. Charles R. Beitz, "Bounded Morality: Justice and the State in World Politics," *International Organization* 33: 405-424; David Luban, "Just War and Human Rights," *Philosophy & Public Affairs* 9, no. 2: 161-181.

putative conservatism by saying at the outset that that community rests most deeply on a contract, Burkeian in character, among "the living, the dead, and those who are yet to be born." It is hard, therefore, to imagine the assembly at which it was ratified. Contract, as I wrote in the book, is a metaphor. The moral understanding on which the community is founded takes shape over a long period of time. But the idea of communal integrity derives its moral and political force from the rights of contemporary men and women to live as members of a historic community and to express their inherited culture through political forms worked out among themselves (the forms are never entirely worked out in a single generation). I shall describe later on, with several examples, how these individual rights are violated when communal integrity is denied, even if the denial is benevolent in intention.

The members of the community are bound to one another. That is Luban's "horizontal" contract, and it constitutes the only form of political obligation.[5] There is no "vertical" or governmental contract—at least, not one that is mutually binding. Though the community requires a government, it is not the case that the citizens are bound to the government to defend it against foreigners. Rather, the government is bound to the citizens to defend them against foreigners. That is what it is for, or one of the things it is for. The citizens defend one another and their common life; the government is merely their instrument. But sometimes this instrument is turned against the citizens: perhaps it still defends them against foreigners, but it also constrains and represses their common life; it denies their civil liberties; it imposes religious uniformity; it blocks attempts at self-help against political or economic oppression. It is a tyrannical government. Now it is the claim of my four critics, if I understand them correctly, that such a government, because it has no standing with its own people (no moral claim upon their allegiance), has no standing in international society either. It is an outlaw government, without rights, or it is simply an ugly government, with something less than the usual complement of rights, subject to attack by anyone capable of attacking it and altering (for the better) the conditions of its rule. That is a large claim, for countries with tyrannical governments make up the

5. Luban, p. 167.

greater part of international society. But it is a false claim—false not only in the law, as the law currently stands, but false morally too, for reasons I shall come to below. The international standing of governments derives only indirectly from their standing with their own citizens. The derivation is complex because it is mediated by foreigners and because foreigners are not confronted (as citizens are) by a naked government, but by a state.

The state is constituted by the union of people and government, and it is the state that claims against all other states the twin rights of territorial integrity and political sovereignty. Foreigners are in no position to deny the reality of that union, or rather, they are in no position to attempt anything more than speculative denials. They don't know enough about its history, and they have no direct experience, and can form no concrete judgments, of the conflicts and harmonies, the historical choices and cultural affinities, the loyalties and resentments, that underlie it. Hence their conduct, in the first instance at least, cannot be determined by either knowledge or judgment. It is, or it ought to be, determined instead by a morally necessary presumption: that there exists a certain "fit" between the community and its government and that the state is "legitimate." It is not a gang of rulers acting in its own interests, but a people governed in accordance with its own traditions. This presumption is simply the respect that foreigners owe to a historic community and to its internal life. Like other presumptions in morality and law, it can be rebutted and disregarded, and what I have called "the rules of disregard" are as important as the presumption itself. So long as it stands, however, the boundaries of international society stand with it. This first presumption entails a second: that if a particular state were attacked, its citizens would think themselves bound to resist, and would in fact resist, because they value their own community in the same way that we value ours or in the same way that we value communities in general. The general valuation is, of course, crucial to the argument, but I won't stop to defend it until I am in a position to consider alternatives. In any case, it is the expectation of resistance that establishes the ban on invasion.

The obligation of citizens to fight for the state is something very different from the expectation that they will in fact fight. The expectation arises, or ought to arise, from the mere existence of a state, any state—with important exceptions to which I will come later. The obligation arises from the existence of a state of a certain sort, shaped to the requirements of moral and political philosophy. Now, this particular state is of that sort, or not; the obligation is real, or it isn't. These are questions open to argument, and foreigners, even foreign officials, are free to argue that the citizens of a particular state have no such obligations, and then to make further arguments about consent, freedom, participation, and so on. But they are not free to act on such arguments and go to war against a state whose citizens are not (so the foreigners think) bound to fight. They cannot claim that such states are literally indefensible. For as long as substantial numbers of citizens believe themselves bound and are prepared, for whatever reasons, to fight, an attack upon their state would constitute aggression. And again, foreigners are required (with exceptions . . .) to assume the belief and the preparedness, whether the obligation is real or not.

In a footnote in *Just and Unjust Wars*, I wrote that "the question of when territory and sovereignty can rightly be defended is closely connected to the question of when individual citizens have an obligation to join the defense." Doppelt takes this sentence to say that the citizens of a *sovereign* state, whatever its character and whatever their convictions about its character, are bound to fight on its behalf.[6] I meant only to suggest, as I went on to say, that both questions "hang on issues in social contract theory" (and to point readers to the arguments that I put forward in *Obligations*). But the sentence is misleading. In fact, a state whose citizens are not bound to fight may still find citizens ready to fight against an invading army, and it can hardly be doubted that these citizens (with exceptions . . .) have a right to fight and that the invaders are guilty of aggressive war. If no citizens come forward, or if they immediately surrender, then the state simply isn't defended. And then the invasion is a lesser crime than the crime we commonly call aggression, or it isn't a crime at all.[7]

6. Doppelt, p. 14.

7. This claim parallels the argument in *Just and Unjust Wars* (p. 330) about non-violence. If citizens choose civil rather than military resistance, then the criminality of the aggressor is diminished, for he has evidently not forced them to fight, risk their lives, and die for their rights. If the invaders are welcomed by a clear majority of the people, then it would be odd to accuse them of any

Nothing in my book was meant to suggest that citizens are bound to one another to defend tyrannical states (and they certainly are not bound to their tyrants). They are as free not to fight as they are free to rebel. But that freedom does not easily transfer to foreign states or armies and become a right of invasion or intervention; above all, it does not transfer at the initiative of the foreigners.

Hence states can be presumptively legitimate in international society and actually illegitimate at home. The doctrine of legitimacy has a dual reference. It is this dualism to which I referred when I wrote in *Just and Unjust Wars* that intervention is not justified whenever revolution is.[8] The two justifications do not coincide because they are addressed to different audiences. First, then, a state is legitimate or not depending upon the "fit" of government and community, that is, the degree to which the government actually represents the political life of its people. When it doesn't do that, the people have a right to rebel. But if they are free to rebel, then they are also free not to rebel—because they (or the greater number of them) judge rebellion to be imprudent or uncertain of success or because they feel that "slowness and aversion . . . to quit their old Constitutions," which Locke noted in his *Second Treatise*. That is, they still believe the government to be tolerable, or they are accustomed to it, or they are personally loyal to its leaders. And so arguments about legitimacy in this first sense of the word must be addressed to the people who make up a particular community. Anyone can make such arguments, but only subjects or citizens can act on them.

The second set of arguments concerns the presumptive legitimacy of states in international society. These arguments too can be made by anyone, including subjects and citizens, but they are properly addressed to foreigners, for it is foreigners who must decide whether to intervene or not. They are not to intervene unless the absence of "fit" between the government and community is radically apparent. Intervention in any other case usurps the rights of subjects and citizens. Wasserstrom asks: If the established government already

---

crime at all. But it is almost certain that such a welcome will be extended only in circumstances that make for the three exceptions that I take up below. And then the invasion will be blameless even before it is welcomed.

8. *Just and Unjust Wars*, p. 89.

deprives subjects and citizens of their rights, how can an attack narrowly aimed at that government add to the deprivation?[9] But the tyranny of established governments gives rise to a right of revolution, held individually by each subject or citizen, rightly exercised by any group of them, of which they cannot be deprived. When invasions are launched by foreign armies, even armies with revolutionary intentions, and even when revolution is justified, it is entirely plausible to say that the rights of subjects and citizens have been violated. Their "slowness" has been artificially speeded up, their "aversion" has been repudiated, their loyalties have been ignored, their prudential calculations have been rejected—all in favor of someone else's conceptions of political justice and political prudence. But this argument, Wasserstrom and Doppelt claim, suggests a Hobbesian theory of legitimacy: any Leviathan state that is stable, that manages successfully to control its own people, is therefore legitimate.[10] In a sense, that is right. In international society, Leviathan states, and many other sorts of states too, enjoy the rights of territorial integrity and political sovereignty. It has to be said, however, that Hobbes' argument is directed to the subjects of Leviathan, and it is not my intention, not by any means, to recommend its acceptance by that audience.

The first kind of legitimacy is or is likely to be singular in character. The judgments we make reflect our democratic values and suggest that there is only one kind of legitimate state or only a narrow range of legitimacy. Given an illiberal or undemocratic government, citizens are always free to rebel, whether they act on that right or not, and whether they believe themselves to have it or not. Their opinions are not relevant, for whatever they think, we can argue that such a government does not and cannot represent the political community.[11] But the second kind of legitimacy is pluralist in character. Here the judgments we make reflect our recognition of diversity and our respect

9. Wasserstrom, p. 540.

10. Wasserstrom, p. 542; Doppelt, p. 16.

11. Hence the Italian nationalist Mazzini was wrong to say (in his opening address to Young Europe in 1847) that "There is no international question as to forms of government, but only a national question." Instead, a simple distinction holds. The philosophical question is indeed international (or transnational or universal), but the political question can only rightly be answered by some national process of decision making.

for communal integrity and for different patterns of cultural and political development. And now the opinions of the people, and also their habits, feelings, religious convictions, political culture, and so on, do matter, for all these are likely to be bound up with, and partly explanatory of, the form and character of their state. That's why states objectively illegitimate are able, again and again, to rally subjects and citizens against invaders. In all such cases, though the "fit" between government and community is not of a democratic sort, there is still a "fit" of some sort, which foreigners are bound to respect.

The confusion of these two kinds of legitimacy, or the denial of the distinction between them, is the fundamental error of these four writers. They insist that the theory of *Just and Unjust Wars* requires me to call tyrannical states legitimate. My actual claim is that foreign officials must act as if they were legitimate, that is, must not make war against them. My critics are uneasy with the politics of *as if*, more uneasy with the presumption that underlies it, and most uneasy, I think, with the pluralism that that presumption mandates. They are committed to the view that the first kind of legitimacy is the only kind, and they are prepared to press international society toward a kind of reiterated singularity—the same government or roughly the same sort of government for every political community. But I won't try to address their positive arguments until I have worked through the cases where I am prepared to allow intervention and until I have indicated the far greater extent of their own allowance.

III

Though the concept of state sovereignty is, as Luban says, "insensitive" to legitimacy in its first sense, it is not insensitive to "the entire dimension of legitimacy," for there is such a thing as an illegitimate state even in international society, and there are cases when sovereignty can be disregarded.[12] These are the rules of disregard as I describe them in *Just and Unjust Wars*.[13] First, when a particular state includes more than one political community, when it is an

12. Luban, p. 166.
13. The following paragraphs summarize the argument of *Just and Unjust Wars*, pp. 89-108.

empire or a multinational state, and when one of its communities or
nations is in active revolt, foreign powers can come to the assistance
of the rebels. Struggles for secession or national liberation justify or
may justify intervention because in such cases there is no fit at all
between government and community, and the state cannot claim,
once the rebellion has reached certain proportions, even a presumptive
legitimacy. While some citizens will probably feel bound to resist an
intervention, it can be assumed that the citizens of the rebellious nation won't resist, and hence military action on their behalf does not
count as aggression.

Second, when a single community is disrupted by civil war, and
when one foreign power intervenes in support of this or that party,
other powers can rightfully intervene in support of the other party.
Counter-interventions of this sort can be defended without reference
to the moral character of the parties. Hence it may be the case that a
foreign state has a right to intervene even when, given certain political
principles, that would not be the right thing to do (similarly, the right
may exist where intervention isn't the wise or prudent thing to do).
Some of my critics object to the neutrality of the rule, but that kind
of neutrality is a feature of all the rules of war; without it there could
be no rules at all but only permissions addressed to the Forces of Good
entitling them to do whatever is necessary (though only what is *necessary*) to overcome their enemies.

Third, interventions can be justified whenever a government is
engaged in the massacre or enslavement of its own citizens or subjects.[14] In such cases, the usual presumption is reversed, and we ought
to assume either that there is no "fit" between the government and
the community or that there is no community. I think that I would

14. For reasons I cannot understand, Doppelt takes me to mean by "enslavement" the "forced resettlement of masses of people" (p. 7), referring to a discussion of Spanish policy in Cuba in 1898. But all that I say about Spanish policy
is that it was carried out "with so little regard for the health of the people
involved that thousands of them suffered and died" (*Just and Unjust Wars*, p.
102). No, by "enslavement" I mean enslavement: the dictionary definition will
do well enough. I offer no examples because, so far as I know, enslavement
has never been made the occasion for (even the pretext for) a military intervention. Hence Doppelt's reference to the American South (p. 20) is otiose.
Slaves are not to be conceived of as participants in any social or political process
of self-determination.

now add to massacre and enslavement the expulsion of very large numbers of people (not simply the retreat of political opponents after a revolution or the transfer of populations that sometimes follows upon national liberation struggles—though these can be brutal enough). The example of Bangladesh which I used in the book to suggest the meaning of massacre may also be used to suggest the meaning of expulsion. The Indian intervention might as easily have been justified by reference to the millions of refugees as by the reference to the tens of thousands of murdered men and women. The purpose of stressing these extreme forms of oppression is, of course, to rule out intervention in cases of "ordinary" oppression. By democratic standards, most states throughout human history have been oppressive (and illegitimate), but those are not necessarily or usually the standards by which they are judged among their own people. On the other hand, we can always assume that murder, slavery, and mass expulsion are condemned, at least by their victims.

I will consider now some examples suggested by my critics—and first, the example of South Africa, referred to briefly by Wasserstrom and more extensively by Doppelt.[15] It is important to both these writers to assimilate the treatment of blacks in South Africa to the category of ordinary oppression so that they can challenge the limits set by the three exceptions. But politically active blacks do not, in fact, talk about their own situation in this manner. Their arguments fall readily into the structure of the theory I have presented; they claim that South Africa is an exceptional case in two different ways.[16] (1) They describe black South Africans as near-slaves, virtual slaves, in-effect-slaves, and true (for the moment at least) to the logic of that description, they call for measures short of military intervention—economic boycott, for example. But it would not, I think, be an unreasonable extension of the argument to hold that, from a moral standpoint, in-effect-slaves (if that description is accurate) and legal slaves count in the same way and that foreign intervention on behalf of either is justifiable.[17] (2) They describe the struggle of black South

15. Wasserstrom, p. 544; Doppelt, pp. 20, 23-25.
16. I can't refer authoritatively here to any body of South African literature; my reference is to arguments made in leaflets and at political meetings in the United States.
17. It is a problem, of course, that even ordinary oppression can be and

Africans as a struggle for national liberation. This is especially plausible since it parallels the official position of the South African government: that blacks are a separate nation and that they are not entitled to full citizenship in the Republic of South Africa. The policy of apartheid turns internal revolution into national liberation, even though the actual separation of the races is not such as to make possible a black secession. And so it opens the possibility of external support for the subject people. I would guess that if such support ever takes military forms, it will be defended in one or another of these two ways.

But South Africa is a stalking horse for a larger argument which is better examined in a case where my critics would permit intervention and the theory of *Just and Unjust Wars* would prohibit it. Consider secondly, then, the recent revolution in Nicaragua, which Luban treats in some detail.[18] The *Sandinista* struggle in Nicaragua extended over many years and culminated in two periods of civil war, the first of which (in August and September of 1978) resulted in a defeat for the rebels. The fighting was resumed in the summer of 1979, and the Somoza government was overthrown. What happened in the months between the two military campaigns usefully illustrates the meaning of self-determination under conditions of political oppression. During that time, the rebels regrouped, re-armed (with some outside help) and, what is most important for us, negotiated a significant broadening of the revolutionary "front." In the course of those negotiations, they were required to commit themselves in fairly explicit ways as to the character of the regime they hoped to establish. Now, had there been a foreign intervention at the time of the first campaign, aimed at rescuing the rebels from defeat, as Luban believes there should have been, this internal process of bargaining and commitment would have been cut short. And then the character of the new regime would have been determined by the intervening state together with whatever faction of rebels it chose to

commonly is described in the language of enslavement—as in the Marxist phrase "wage slavery." But that only suggests the importance of drawing a line that protests internal political and social processes (not against philosophical criticism or domestic resistance and revolution but only) against military intervention.

18. Luban, pp. 170-171.

support. It is my claim that such an intervention would have violated the right of Nicaraguans as a group to shape their own political institutions and the right of individual Nicaraguans to live under institutions so shaped. Wasserstrom is wrong, then, to say that this individual right comes to nothing more than the right to live in "a civil society of almost any sort."[19] It is, in this case, the right to live in a civil society of a Nicaraguan sort.

But what if the *Sandinistas*, facing defeat in September 1978 had asked for foreign military intervention? Can the right of revolution transfer at the initiative of the revolutionaries? It does exactly that in the case of a national liberation struggle, when the revolutionaries are themselves, in a sense, at war with foreigners and are assumed to have the support of their own people. But in the case of revolution and civil war, no such assumption is possible. In principle, revolutionaries who enjoy the active and visible support of a clear majority of their own people can invite foreign armies to intervene on their behalf. But I do not believe that revolutionaries are ever in that position until they are well beyond the point where they need foreign help. All that they need then is that there be no help for the government. The case that Mill envisioned in his essay on non-intervention is more realistic: a group of rebels fighting for the freedom of the people and claiming their passive support, hard-pressed militarily, asks for the help of some foreign state. The rebels, Mill argued, must mobilize their own (putative) supporters, not some alien army.[20] Only a popular mobilization will pave the way for the establishment of a free government. I would add that only such a mobilization, which makes foreign assistance superfluous, could also make it justifiable.

In practice, the request for foreign help is an admission of domestic weakness. It is probably for that reason that the *Sandinistas* never asked for help (except for equipment to match what the government was receiving or had received). They thought themselves to have, or they thought themselves capable of achieving, majority support. And they were "unrealistic" in the same way I am, according to Wasserstrom. "It is surprisingly unrealistic to suppose that a modern state cannot control its citizens effectively without their genuine con-

19. Wasserstrom, p. 542.
20. See the discussion of Mill's argument, *Just and Unjust Wars*, pp. 87-91.

sent."[21] The *Sandinistas* believed, at the least, that the Somoza government could not control its citizens against their active opposition. They wanted their own victory to build upon and reflect that opposition, that is, to be a popular victory. And that is what foreigners should want too, if they are committed to Nicaraguan self-determination.

In most civil wars, it just isn't possible to determine whether the government or the rebels (or which faction among the rebels) has majority support. Most citizens hide if they can, or profess to support whatever forces control the territory in which they live, or try to guess who will win and join the winners as early as possible. And then, the right of revolution can't and doesn't transfer to foreigners, whatever invitations are offered. Foreign states can't join a civil war, when no other states have joined, simply because they admire the principles of the party that has invited them in or even because they believe that that party would, under ideal conditions, win a free election. If they intervene successfully, the party on whose behalf they have intervened will certainly win the elections, but the conditions will not be ideal. In any case, they have no right to make their own principles or their own beliefs definitive for other people.

But if the eventual outcome, writes Doppelt, "reflects nothing but the balance of internal military might, I see no more reason for calling this process one of 'self-determination' . . . than I do for denying that it is self-determination on the mere basis that foreign troops have played some role in it."[22] In fact, however, there is no such thing as a bare "balance of internal military might." Armies and police forces are social institutions; soldiers and policemen come from families, villages, neighborhoods, classes. They will not fight cohesively, with discipline, or at length unless the regime for which they are fighting has some degree of social support. A civil war is the sign of a divided society. As an extended insurrection indicates popular support for the rebels (that's why the Viet Cong, despite the claims of the United States Government, could not have been sustained entirely from North Vietnam), so an extended resistance to insurrection indicates popular support for the government. That support may be ignorant, passive,

21. Wasserstrom, p. 542.
22. Doppelt, p. 13.

bewildered; it may reflect nothing more than the people's "slowness and aversion" to change. Still, no foreigner can rightly override it. Of course, the actual outcome of a particular struggle will also reflect factors "irrelevant from a moral point of view." There is no way to guarantee the "right" result. But foreign troops are more irrelevant than any local factor, for their strength depends upon the character of their own government and community, their historical traditions, loyalties, and so on, and bears no relation at all to the history and culture of the people whose fate they are determining.

I am inclined to doubt that the issues raised in the last few paragraphs are, in any simple sense, empirical issues. At any rate, they are not susceptible to empirical resolution. We have no reliable indices of popular sentiment in time of civil war. For more or less similar reasons, it is virtually impossible to judge the strength or likely endurance of some established tyranny. There is no point at which foreigners can point to a tyrannical regime and say, "Self-determination has clearly failed; there is nothing to do but intervene." For revolution often comes unexpectedly, as it came to the Iran of the Shah, a sudden upsurge of previously invisible political currents. Intervention denies the political significance of such currents or it denies their moral significance. These are not denials that can be empirically justified. They are instead principled denials of self-determination itself—because it is too slow or too costly, or because its outcome is not foreknown, or because the likely outcome is thought to be unattractive. Underlying all such reasons, however, there must be some alternative principle. The alternative figures only implicitly in Doppelt's article; it is called "reform intervention" by Beitz;[23] Luban provides its formulas; and Wasserstrom gives it an appropriate theoretical label: "the utilitarianism of rights."[24] This principle poses a radical challenge to communal integrity, and I want now to consider it in some detail.

23. Beitz, p. 413.
24. The notion of a "utilitarianism of rights" was first formulated by Robert Nozick in *Anarchy, State, and Utopia* (New York, 1974), p. 28. Nozick goes on to argue, on Kantian grounds, that rights must be understood as constraints on action rather than as goals of a maximizing politics. Though I don't share his views as to the substance of a rights theory, the same conception of its structure underlies my own position in *Just and Unjust Wars*.

IV

It is easiest to begin with Luban's formulas, the most important of which is simply this: "A just war is (1) a war in defense of socially basic human rights (subject to proportionality). . . ."[25] Socially basic rights include security rights, against tyrannical governments as well as against foreign invaders, and subsistence rights. Luban would not justify a war fought for the sake of democracy or social justice, though Doppelt and Beitz apparently would.[26] Still, this is a far-reaching license. Or something more than a license: since socially basic rights "are the demands of all of humanity on all of humanity," it might be Luban's view that we are bound to fight all the just wars we are able to fight—up to the point of exhaustion and incapacity. Then "the utilitarianism of rights" would have the same consequence as ordinary utilitarianism, leaving us no time to ourselves. But I won't pursue this line of argument.

If rights don't require us to intervene, however, then it is difficult to see why they should be called rights (in Luban's sense) or why Luban should object to my own argument, which would also permit interventions against governments that murdered or starved their own people. I suspect that he is reaching for a wider permissiveness —as the others certainly are—not only against governments that violate his list of rights, narrowly conceived, but against all repressive governments and against all governments that are or seem to be indifferent to the poverty of their people. Hence, the phrase "in de-

25. Luban, p. 175.
26. I am not sure, however, that Beitz means to defend *military* intervention. Reviewing a book on war, he certainly seems to do so. But in his own book, he introduces a similar argument by saying that he wishes "to bracket the case of military intervention" and talk only of "policies of interference that . . . fall short of the actual use of violence" (*Political Theory and International Relations*, Princeton, 1979, p. 72). For myself, I was concerned in *Just and Unjust Wars* only with military intervention, but the arguments I constructed do rule out any external determination of domestic constitutional arrangements (as an example below will suggest). I don't, however, mean to rule out every effort by one state to influence another or every use of diplomatic and economic pressure. Drawing the line is sure to be difficult, but the precise location of the line is not at issue here, for all my critics, with only the possible exception of Beitz, are ready for "the actual use of violence" in other people's countries, in order to do them good.

fense of rights," though technically correct, is politically misleading. Since these are rights that people don't, in the relevant cases, enjoy and may not know themselves to have, the actual purpose of just wars might be better described: to establish or enforce rights, or to maximize their effectiveness, or to enlarge the population for which they are effective. Maximizing rights is very much like maximizing well-being—hence "the utilitarianism of rights"—though with the important proviso that the maximization can be pursued only up to a certain point by military force. But any extra enjoyment of rights, like any extra well-being, probably wouldn't balance the costs of the fighting anyway.

To whom is this far-reaching license granted? Who is to make the crucial calculations? In principle, I suppose, the license is extended to any and all foreigners; in practice, today, to the officials of foreign states; tomorrow, perhaps, to some set of global bureaucrats acting by themselves or as advisers to and agents of a Universal Assembly. Now, why them? And here a more serious sort of rights argument properly begins. Rights are in an important sense distributive principles. They distribute decision-making authority. When we describe individual rights, we are assigning to individuals a certain authority to shape their own lives, and we are denying that officials, even well-meaning officials, are authorized to interfere. The description of communal rights makes a similar assertion and a similar denial. In the individual case, we fix a certain area for personal choice; in the communal case, we fix a certain area for political choice. Unless these areas are clearly marked out and protected, both sorts of choices are likely to become problematic.

But unless they are democratically made, my critics might argue, political choices are already problematic and can't plausibly count as the free choices of the community. The area within which tyrants, oligarchs, ruling classes, priestly castes, and military cliques make their choices isn't worth protecting. Only liberal or democratic states have rights against external intervention. This claim plays on a (pretended) domestic equivalent: that only the uncoerced choices of minimally rational individuals are protected against intervention. But it is not the sign of some collective derangement or radical incapacity for a political community to produce an authoritarian regime. Indeed, the history, culture, and religion of the community may be such that authoritarian regimes come, as it were, naturally, reflecting a widely shared world view or way of life. Such views and ways may be wrong or badly conceived; they are not necessarily insane. The authoritarian regime is not, to be sure, freely chosen, but then no set of political institutions is ever freely chosen from the full range of alternatives by a single set of people at a single moment in time. Institutions have histories; they are the products of protracted struggles. And it can't be the case that communities are protected against intervention only if those struggles have a single philosophically correct or universally approved outcome (or one of a small number of correct or approved outcomes). That would not be the same thing as protecting only free individuals; it would be more like protecting only individuals who had arrived at certain opinions, life styles, and so on.

The difference between my own views and those of my critics may be sharpened if we consider a hypothetical case designed to neutralize the proportionality qualification and all the other issues raised by the use of force and to focus exclusively on the question of communal integrity. Imagine, then, a country called Algeria in which a group of revolutionaries come to power pledged to create a democratic and secular state, with equal rights for all citizens. The regime they actually create, or which is created as a result of their struggles with one another, is very different: a military dictatorship and a religious "republic," without civil and political liberties, and brutally repressive, not only because a new political elite has established itself and resists all challenges but also because women have been returned to their traditional religious subordination to patriarchal authority. It is clear, however, that this regime (in contrast to the one the revolutionaries originally had in mind) has deep roots in Algerian history and draws importantly upon Algerian political and religious culture. It is not a democratic regime; its popularity has never been tested in a democratic way; but there can be no doubt that it is an Algerian regime. Now, imagine further that the Swedish government had in its possession a wondrous chemical which, if introduced into the water supply of Algeria, would turn all Algerians, elites and masses, into Swedish-style social democrats. It would wipe out of their minds their own political and religious culture (though it would leave them with no sense of loss). And it would provide them instead with the knowledge, capacity, and will to create a new regime in which basic security rights, political and civil liberties too, would be respected, women would be treated as equals, and so on. Should they use the chemical? Do they have a right to use it? The force of the argument depends upon the reader's readiness to value Swedish social-democracy far above Algerian "socialism." I assume that valuation, and yet I am certain that the Swedes should not use the chemical. They should not use it because the historical religion and politics of the Algerian people are values for the Algerian people (even though individual Algerians have not chosen their religion and politics from among a range of alternatives) which our valuation cannot override. It may seem paradoxical to hold that the Algerian people have a right to a state within which their rights are violated. But that is, given the case as I have described it, the only kind of state that they are likely to call their own.

Nor would the case be different if there were a democratic political movement or a feminist movement within Algeria. For foreigners cannot judge the relative strength of such movements or allow them to substitute themselves for the people as a whole, not until they have won sufficient support to transform Algerian politics on their own. That may be a long process; it will certainly involve compromises of different sorts; and the movements if and when they win will be different from what they were when they began. All that is Algerian self-determination, a political process that also has value, even if it isn't always pretty, and even if its outcome doesn't conform to philosophical standards of political and social justice.

Individual rights may well derive, as I am inclined to think, from our ideas about personality and moral agency, without reference to political processes and social circumstances. But the enforcement of rights is another matter. It is not the case that one can simply proclaim a list of rights and then look around for armed men to enforce it. Rights are only enforceable within political communities where they have been collectively recognized, and the process by which they come to be recognized is a political process which requires a political arena. The globe is not, or not yet, such an arena. Or rather, the only global community is pluralist in character, a community of nations, not of humanity, and the rights recognized within it have been minimal and largely negative, designed to protect the integrity of nations and to regulate their commercial and military transactions.

Beitz seems to believe that this pluralist world order has already been transcended and that communal integrity is a thing of the past. In a world of increasing interdependence, he argues, it is an "evident falsity" to claim "that states are relatively self-enclosed arenas of political development."[27] Just as no man is an island, so no state is an island—not even Britain, Japan, or Singapore. We are all involved in one another's politics, responsible for one another, and open (it seems) to one another's interventions. I don't know what evidence might be presented for this view, what sorts of comparisons might be drawn with what previous historical periods. Perfect self-enclosure has probably never existed. Relative self-enclosure seems to me an evident truth. Anyone doubting it would have to account on psychological grounds for the enormous importance colonial peoples attach to their recently won independence and the enormous importance revolutionary groups attach to the seizure of power in their own political communities. In fact, psychological explanations are quite unnecessary. Political power within a particular community remains the critical factor in shaping the fate of the members. Of course, that fate (like all fates) is shaped within political and economic limits, and these can be more or less narrow; there are some states with relatively little room for maneuver. And yet, even economically dependent states, locked into international markets they can't control, can dramatically alter the conditions of their dependence and the character of their domestic life. Surely the histories of Yugoslavia since World War II, of Cuba since 1960, and of Iran over the last two years, suggest strongly that what actually happens within a country is a function, above all, of local political processes. An internal decision (or an internal revolution) can turn a country around in a way no decision by another country, short of a decision to invade, can possibly do.

So the political community with its government, that is, the state, is still the critical arena of political life. It has not been transcended, and there are two important reasons, I think, for hesitating a long time before attempting the transcendence. The first reason is pru-

27. Beitz, pp. 422-423.

dential. If the outcome of political processes in particular communal arenas is often brutal, then it ought to be assumed that outcomes in the global arena will often be brutal too. And this will be a far more effective and therefore a far more dangerous brutality, for there will be no place left for political refuge and no examples left of political alternatives.

The second reason has to do with the very nature of political life. Politics (as distinct from mere coercion and bureaucratic manipulation) depends upon shared history, communal sentiment, accepted conventions—upon some extended version of Aristotle's "friendship." All this is problematic enough in the modern state; it is hardly conceivable on a global scale. Communal life and liberty requires the existence of "relatively self-enclosed arenas of political development." Break into the enclosures and you destroy the communities. And that destruction is a loss to the individual members (unless it rescues them from massacre, enslavement, or expulsion), a loss of something valuable, which they clearly value, and to which they have a right, namely their participation in the "development" that goes on and can only go on within the enclosure. Hence the distinction of state rights and individual rights is simplistic and wrongheaded. Against foreigners, individuals have a right to a state of their own. Against state officials, they have a right to political and civil liberty. Without the first of these rights, the second is meaningless: as individuals need a home, so rights require a location.

V

My own argument is perhaps best understood as a defense of politics, while that of my critics reiterates what I take to be the traditional philosophical dislike for politics. This dislike is most readily recognized in utilitarian argument, commonly addressed to real or imaginary bureaucrats. But it is also apparent among rights theorists, whenever the enforcement of rights is assigned to authorities who stand outside the political arena or who are allowed (or required) to act even in the absence of prior consent. Some such assignment, I don't doubt, is necessary even to my own argument, as the three exceptions suggest, and so it might be said that the question is only where to draw the line between external (bureaucratic or military) enforcement, on the one hand, and political decision-making, on the other. But I suspect that the disagreement goes deeper than that formulation allows. It has to do with the respect we are prepared to accord and the room we are prepared to yield to the political process itself, with all its messiness and uncertainty, its inevitable compromises, and its frequent brutality. It has to do with the range of outcomes we are prepared to tolerate, to accept as presumptively legitimate, though not necessarily to endorse. "For Walzer," writes Doppelt, states that possess the collective right of sovereignty "may violate the individual rights of all or some group of [their] citizens."[28] No, I do not give out permissions of that sort; obviously, I oppose all such violations. But I don't believe that the opposition of philosophers is a sufficient ground for military invasion. Perhaps, indeed, like Prince Hamlet, we are born to set things right, but we do that, or try to do it, by making arguments, not by summoning up armies.

28. Doppelt, p. 25.

DAVID LUBAN

The Romance of the Nation-State

The theory I espoused in "Just War and Human Rights" entitles nations to wage war to enforce basic human rights.[1] This entitlement stems from the cosmopolitan nature of human rights. The rights of security and subsistence, with which I was concerned, are necessary for the enjoyment of any other rights at all; no one can do without them. Basic rights, therefore, are universal. They are no respecters of political boundaries, and require a universalist politics to implement them, even when this means breaching the wall of state sovereignty.

Since the time of the French Revolution, which linked the Rights of Man with the demand for national sovereignty, cosmopolitan theories have been criticized by appealing to the ideology of nationalism. National sovereignty, it was thought, gives people their most important entitlement: a state that expresses their traditions, history and unity—their "national soul."[2] Attack the state, and you attack the soul of its people. The cosmopolitan vision of humanity is really a flattening universalism, a philosopher's conceit. As Herder says, "Every nation has its own core of happiness just as every sphere has its center of gravity! . . . Philosopher in a northern valley, with the infant's scales of your century in your hand, do you know better than Providence?"[3]

1. See *Philosophy & Public Affairs* 9, no. 2 (Winter 1980): 160-181.

2. See Hannah Arendt, *The Origins of Totalitarianism*, rev. ed. (New York: Meridian, 1958), pp. 230-231.

3. "Auch eine Philosophie der Geschichte zur Bildung der Menschheit," *Werke*, ed. Suphan, vol. 5, pp. 501 ff.; quoted in Ernst Cassirer, *The Philosophy of the Enlightenment*, trans. Koelln and Pettegrove (Princeton: Princeton University Press, 1951), pp. 232-233. See also Cassirer, *The Myth of the State* (New Haven:

Nationalism may have originated as an ideology of liberation and tolerance; in our century it is drenched in blood. What Mazzini began, Il Duce ended; other examples are equally obvious and equally painful. The violence of modern nationalism and its indifference to basic human rights arises, I believe, from the conviction that the only right which matters politically is the right to a unified nation-state. Its picture of the nation-state, however, is a myth. It emphasizes a nation's commonality, affinity, shared language and traditions and history, what Mazzini called "unanimity of mind."[4] The picture glosses over intramural class conflict, turmoil, violence, and repression; these it represents as the reflection of inscrutable processes akin to national destiny.[5] This view I shall call the Romance of the Nation-State. In place of respect for people it sets respect for peoples; in place of universalism, relativism.

What disturbs me about Walzer's essay is its acceptance of the premises of nationalism.[6] Walzer embodies his anti-cosmopolitanism in five theses: (1) that nations are comparatively self-enclosed (p. 227); (2) that "the state is constituted by the union of people and government" (p. 212); (3) that the political and moral status of a nation is aptly characterized by the metaphor of the social contract; (4) that "the only global community is . . . a community of nations, not of humanity" (p. 226); and (5) that the main moral principle of international politics is "pluralism": respect for the integrity of nations and their states; in particular, respect for their right to choose political forms which from our point of view are morally deficient.

Yale University Press, 1946), pp. 176-186; Isaiah Berlin, *Against the Current* (New York: Viking, 1979), chaps. 1, 13; and Berlin, *Vico and Herder* (New York: Viking, 1976).

4. For this citation, together with a short survey of nineteenth-century nationalist ideology, see Victor Alba, *Nationalists Without Nations* (New York: Praeger, 1968), pp. 5-17.

5. Even Mill seems to subscribe to this, for according to Walzer it is his idea "that citizens get the government they deserve, or, at least, the government for which they are 'fit,'" *Just and Unjust Wars* (New York: Basic Books, 1977), p. 88.

6. Parenthetical references in the text are to Walzer, "The Moral Standing of States: A Response to Four Critics," *Philosophy & Public Affairs* 9, no. 3 (Spring 1980).

This is a molecular theory of world politics, in which self-contained nation-states are the units of moral regard: molecular, because each is bound together from within and presents itself as a unit from without. The fourth and fifth theses yield the anti-cosmopolitan international morality that underlies Walzer's theory of *jus ad bellum*; these theses depend, however, on the first three, which represent the Romance of the Nation-State.

The social contract metaphor is central to this myth. It suggests reciprocity, coincident interests, mutual obligation, formal equality of the parties. But the presence of these features is not a conceptual truth about the nation-state, nor, I think, a factual one. The metaphor and the myth, I shall argue, lead Walzer to a deficient account of human rights and a blindness to the threat physical repression poses to political processes.

The controversial thesis of Walzer's essay is this: he believes that states which oppress their people may, nevertheless, be considered legitimate in international society, as long as they do not fall under what he calls the "rules of disregard." Intervention is allowable in a nation when a national minority is seceding from it; when a foreign power has intervened in a civil war it is fighting; or when it is massacring, enslaving, or expelling large numbers of people. In these instances, Walzer argues, "the absence of 'fit' between the government and community is radically apparent" (p. 214). The rest of the time we are obliged to act *as if* states are legitimate. Walzer calls this "the politics of *as if*" (p. 216); its leading principle is "a morally necessary presumption: that there exists a certain 'fit' between the community and its government and that the state is 'legitimate'" (p. 212). Hard as it is for liberal democrats to believe, foreigners may want their tyranny—there may be a "fit" between government and people.

What supports this presumption? According to Walzer, foreigners just can't judge an alien culture's fit with its government. "They don't know enough about its history, and they have no direct experience, and can form no concrete judgments of the conflicts and harmonies, the historical choices and cultural affinities, the loyalties and resentments, that underlie it" (p. 212).

I find no plausibility in this. True, if we don't know enough about a foreign culture to judge its "fit" with its government, we should give it the benefit of the doubt and presume the fit is there. But why presume we are ignorant? We aren't, usually. There are, after all, experts, experienced travelers, expatriates, scholars, and spies; libraries have been written about the most remote cultures. Bafflingly, Walzer does not mention the obvious sources of information even to dismiss them. He seems to take as an a priori truth—it is part of the Romance of the Nation-State—that without "direct experience" a member of one culture cannot, ultimately, know what it's really like to be a member of another. But this is of a piece with "no man can really know what it's like to be a woman" or "you can't know what it's really like to be me": even granting their validity, we don't assume that such considerations preclude making true judgments about other people. That is more like solipsism than pluralism, and if it were true it would spell the end, not the principle, of politics.

Of course Walzer is right that the lack of fit between government and people should be "radically apparent" to justify intervening, because intervention based on a misperception is horribly wrong. But what does it take to make things radically apparent? In my view, Walzer's rules of disregard set the threshold too high; what he calls "ordinary oppression" can make the lack of fit apparent enough. Let us look at ordinary oppression in a medium-size dictatorship. Each year there are a few score executions, a few hundred tortures, a few thousand political imprisonments, a few million people behaving cautiously because they know that a single slip will bring the police. The police and army believe that if the government falls they are dead men; it is the bargain they accepted to escape the poverty of their villages. They take their foreign-made fighters, small arms, and pepper gas and hope for the best.

If this is a "union of people and government," why are the jails so full? Surely all those strapped to the torture table are not misfits in their own culture. I think we should aim at a more common-sense explanation than Walzer's of why people put up with the regime, such as the idea that they are afraid of being "disappeared" (to use a phrase

current in Argentina and the Philippines). The government fits the
people the way the sole of a boot fits a human face: after a while the
patterns of indentation match with uncanny precision.

It was central to my argument in "Just War and Human Rights"
that under ordinary oppression peoples' socially basic human rights
are violated—not, to be sure, on the scale envisioned in Walzer's third
rule of disregard, which refers to what the Nuremberg court called
"crimes against humanity," but systematically enough to define the
state's political physiognomy and justify intervention. Walzer's theory
of intervention as aggression is also based on individual rights, but
those that control are the rights emphasized by nationalism: to fight
for the homeland and to live under institutions formed by one's fellow-
nationals. They are rights to a nation-state, not claims against it.

This difference is illustrated by Walzer's analysis of the recent
Nicaraguan revolution. He emphasizes the fact that in the wake of
their initial defeat the *Sandinistas* were forced to clarify their program
and solidify their political base. This is indeed an instance of self-determination, and if Walzer's position is that, other things being equal,
it is better that it should happen than not, he is undoubtedly right. Let
us not forget, though, that other things were not equal. Fifty thousand
people were killed in the second round of revolution, Nicaragua's
productive capacity was ravaged, and Somoza's followers had an additional year to strip the country of everything they could crate. Because
of this, the new government has been forced to make a number of
deals that have weakened its political base. Neither should we dismiss as unimportant the fact that Nicaraguans had to live under an
oppressive regime one year longer. We cannot ignore, as Walzer's
theory does, the cost in blood, the bottom line in an account that
makes socially basic human rights its guiding concept.

The problem with Walzer's argument is this. Human rights accrue
to people no matter what country they live in and regardless of history
and traditions. If human rights exist at all, they set a moral limit to
pluralism. For this reason Walzer's appeal to pluralism begs the question, for making pluralism the overriding value is incompatible from
the outset with a theory that grants universal human rights.

Rights, moreover, are crucial values for us—as Walzer points out, they are deeply connected with our notions of personality and moral agency. Thus, when murders, tortures, imprisonments go unchecked, more so when their perpetrators (the worst people in the world) are treated *as if* they are legitimate, the common humanity of all of us is stained. In this way, the politics of *as if*, in which we acknowledge rights but turn our backs on their enforcement (p. 226), fails to take our values seriously. It raises politics above moral theory.

Walzer sees it differently. He claims that he is defending politics while his critics are expressing "the traditional philosophical dislike for politics." This, he says, is because we are unwilling to tolerate unwanted outcomes of "the political process itself, with all its messiness and uncertainty, its inevitable compromises, and its frequent brutality"; we would restrict the outcomes by force of arms (p. 31).

But why is this less political than standing by while an uprising against a repressive regime is crushed by force of arms? Repression is itself an attempt to restrict, or rather, to eliminate the political process. It subjects politics to the essentially apolitical technology of violence, the "great unequalizer." Intervention, when it is just, should restore self-determination, not deny it. In this respect it is similar to counter-intervention of the sort countenanced by Walzer's second rule of disregard—an analogy which is particularly apposite in view of the fact that military technology is usually provided to repressive regimes by foreign powers.

Walzer dismisses the ability of sheer force to stifle the political process because force cannot prevail against the united community, while if the community is not united intervention would be wrong. But a united community is a rare political achievement, particularly under conditions of class oppression and terror, and I think it is wrong to make it the yardstick of politics—doing so is another metamorphosis of the Romance of the Nation-State. One might doubt whether in a civil war an intervener can know which side to support. But the entitlement to intervene derives from the cosmopolitan character of human rights; one intervenes, then, on behalf of socially basic human rights, for it is these which enable people to enjoy their political rights. Walzer's hands-off approach, on the other hand, waiting for the day when the nation unites, simply yields to guns and tanks.

PART V

International Humanitarianism
and Distributive Justice

PETER SINGER

Famine, Affluence, and Morality

As I write this, in November 1971, people are dying in East Bengal from lack of food, shelter, and medical care. The suffering and death that are occurring there now are not inevitable, not unavoidable in any fatalistic sense of the term. Constant poverty, a cyclone, and a civil war have turned at least nine million people into destitute refugees; nevertheless, it is not beyond the capacity of the richer nations to give enough assistance to reduce any further suffering to very small proportions. The decisions and actions of human beings can prevent this kind of suffering. Unfortunately, human beings have not made the necessary decisions. At the individual level, people have, with very few exceptions, not responded to the situation in any significant way. Generally speaking, people have not given large sums to relief funds; they have not written to their parliamentary representatives demanding increased government assistance; they have not demonstrated in the streets, held symbolic fasts, or done anything else directed toward providing the refugees with the means to satisfy their essential needs. At the government level, no government has given the sort of massive aid that would enable the refugees to survive for more than a few days. Britain, for instance, has given rather more than most countries. It has, to date, given £14,750,000. For comparative purposes, Britain's share of the nonrecoverable development costs of the Anglo-French Concorde project is already in excess of £275,000,000, and on present estimates will reach £440,000,000. The implication is that the British government values a supersonic transport mo than thirty times as highly as it values the lives of the nine million refugees. Australia is another country which, on a per capita basis, is well up in the "aid to Bengal" table. Australia's aid, however, amounts to less than one-twelfth of the cost of Sydney's new opera house. The total amount given, from all sources, now stands at about £65,000,000. The estimated cost of keeping the refugees alive for one year is £464,000,000. Most of the refugees have now been in the camps for more than six months. The World Bank has said that India needs a minimum of £300,000,000 in assistance from other countries before the end of the year. It seems obvious that assistance on this scale will not be forthcoming. India will be forced to choose between letting the refugees starve or diverting funds from her own development program, which will mean that more of her own people will starve in the future.[1]

These are the essential facts about the present situation in Bengal. So far as it concerns us here, there is nothing unique about this situation except its magnitude. The Bengal emergency is just the latest and most acute of a series of major emergencies in various parts of the world, arising both from natural and from man-made causes. There are also many parts of the world in which people die from malnutrition and lack of food independent of any special emergency. I take Bengal as my example only because it is the present concern, and because the size of the problem has ensured that it has been given adequate publicity. Neither individuals nor governments can claim to be unaware of what is happening there.

What are the moral implications of a situation like this? In what follows, I shall argue that the way people in relatively affluent countries react to a situation like that in Bengal cannot be justified; indeed, the whole way we look at moral issues—our moral conceptual scheme —needs to be altered, and with it, the way of life that has come to be taken for granted in our society.

In arguing for this conclusion I will not, of course, claim to be morally neutral. I shall, however, try to argue for the moral position

---

1. There was also a third possibility: that India would go to war to enable the refugees to return to their lands. Since I wrote this paper, India has taken this way out. The situation is no longer that described above, but this does not affect my argument, as the next paragraph indicates.

that I take, so that anyone who accepts certain assumptions, to be made explicit, will, I hope, accept my conclusion.

I begin with the assumption that suffering and death from lack of food, shelter, and medical care are bad. I think most people will agree about this, although one may reach the same view by different routes. I shall not argue for this view. People can hold all sorts of eccentric positions, and perhaps from some of them it would not follow that death by starvation is in itself bad. It is difficult, perhaps impossible, to refute such positions, and so for brevity I will henceforth take this assumption as accepted. Those who disagree need read no further.

My next point is this: if it is in our power to prevent something bad from happening, without thereby sacrificing anything of comparable moral importance, we ought, morally, to do it. By "without sacrificing anything of comparable moral importance" I mean without causing anything else comparably bad to happen, or doing something that is wrong in itself, or failing to promote some moral good, comparable in significance to the bad thing that we can prevent. This principle seems almost as uncontroversial as the last one. It requires us only to prevent what is bad, and not to promote what is good, and it requires this of us only when we can do it without sacrificing anything that is, from the moral point of view, comparably important. I could even, as far as the application of my argument to the Bengal emergency is concerned, qualify the point so as to make it: if it is in our power to prevent something very bad from happening, without thereby sacrificing anything morally significant, we ought, morally, to do it. An application of this principle would be as follows: if I am walking past a shallow pond and see a child drowning in it, I ought to wade in and pull the child out. This will mean getting my clothes muddy, but this is insignificant, while the death of the child would presumably be a very bad thing.

The uncontroversial appearance of the principle just stated is deceptive. If it were acted upon, even in its qualified form, our lives, our society, and our world would be fundamentally changed. For the principle takes, firstly, no account of proximity or distance. It makes no moral difference whether the person I can help is a neighbor's child ten yards from me or a Bengali whose name I shall never know, ten thousand miles away. Secondly, the principle makes no distinction between cases in which I am the only person who could possibly do anything and cases in which I am just one among millions in the same position.

I do not think I need to say much in defense of the refusal to take proximity and distance into account. The fact that a person is physically near to us, so that we have personal contact with him, may make it more likely that we *shall* assist him, but this does not show that we *ought* to help him rather than another who happens to be further away. If we accept any principle of impartiality, universalizability, equality, or whatever, we cannot discriminate against someone merely because he is far away from us (or we are far away from him). Admittedly, it is possible that we are in a better position to judge what needs to be done to help a person near to us than one far away, and perhaps also to provide the assistance we judge to be necessary. If this were the case, it would be a reason for helping those near to us first. This may once have been a justification for being more concerned with the poor in one's own town than with famine victims in India. Unfortunately for those who like to keep their moral responsibilities limited, instant communication and swift transportation have changed the situation. From the moral point of view, the development of the world into a "global village" has made an important, though still unrecognized, difference to our moral situation. Expert observers and supervisors, sent out by famine relief organizations or permanently stationed in famine-prone areas, can direct our aid to a refugee in Bengal almost as effectively as we could get it to someone in our own block. There would seem, therefore, to be no possible justification for discriminating on geographical grounds.

There may be a greater need to defend the second implication of my principle—that the fact that there are millions of other people in the same position, in respect to the Bengali refugees, as I am, does not make the situation significantly different from a situation in which I am the only person who can prevent something very bad from occurring. Again, of course, I admit that there is a psychological difference between the cases; one feels less guilty about doing nothing if one can

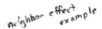

point to others, similarly placed, who have also done nothing. Yet this can make no real difference to our moral obligations.[2] Should I consider that I am less obliged to pull the drowning child out of the pond if on looking around I see other people, no further away than I am, who have also noticed the child but are doing nothing? One has only to ask this question to see the absurdity of the view that numbers lessen obligation. It is a view that is an ideal excuse for inactivity; unfortunately most of the major evils—poverty, overpopulation, pollution—are problems in which everyone is almost equally involved.

The view that numbers do make a difference can be made plausible if stated in this way: if everyone in circumstances like mine gave £5 to the Bengal Relief Fund, there would be enough to provide food, shelter, and medical care for the refugees; there is no reason why I should give more than anyone else in the same circumstances as I am; therefore I have no obligation to give more than £5. Each premise in this argument is true, and the argument looks sound. It may convince us, unless we notice that it is based on a hypothetical premise, although the conclusion is not stated hypothetically. The argument would be sound if the conclusion were: if everyone in circumstances like mine were to give £5, I would have no obligation to give more than £5. If the conclusion were so stated, however, it would be obvious that the argument has no bearing on a situation in which it is not the case that everyone else gives £5. This, of course, is the actual situation. It is more or less certain that not everyone in circumstances like mine will give £5. So there will not be enough to provide the needed food, shelter, and medical care. Therefore by giving more than £5 I will prevent more suffering than I would if I gave just £5.

It might be thought that this argument has an absurd consequence. Since the situation appears to be that very few people are likely to give

2. In view of the special sense philosophers often give to the term, I should say that I use "obligation" simply as the abstract noun derived from "ought," so that "I have an obligation to" means no more, and no less, than "I ought to." This usage is in accordance with the definition of "ought" given by the *Shorter Oxford English Dictionary*: "the general verb to express duty or obligation." I do not think any issue of substance hangs on the way the term is used; sentences in which I use "obligation" could all be rewritten, although somewhat clumsily, as sentences in which a clause containing "ought" replaces the term "obligation."

substantial amounts, it follows that I and everyone else in similar circumstances ought to give as much as possible, that is, at least up to the point at which by giving more one would begin to cause serious suffering for oneself and one's dependents—perhaps even beyond this point to the point of marginal utility, at which by giving more one would cause oneself and one's dependents as much suffering as one would prevent in Bengal. If everyone does this, however, there will be more than can be used for the benefit of the refugees, and some of the sacrifice will have been unnecessary. Thus, if everyone does what he ought to do, the result will not be as good as it would be if everyone did a little less than he ought to do, or if only some do all that they ought to do.

The paradox here arises only if we assume that the actions in question—sending money to the relief funds—are performed more or less simultaneously, and are also unexpected. For if it is to be expected that everyone is going to contribute something, then clearly each is not obliged to give as much as he would have been obliged to had others not been giving too. And if everyone is not acting more or less simultaneously, then those giving later will know how much more is needed, and will have no obligation to give more than is necessary to reach this amount. To say this is not to deny the principle that people in the same circumstances have the same obligations, but to point out that the fact that others have given, or may be expected to give, is a relevant circumstance: those giving after it has become known that many others are giving and those giving before are not in the same circumstances. So the seemingly absurd consequence of the principle I have put forward can occur only if people are in error about the actual circumstances—that is, if they think they are giving when others are not, but in fact they are giving when others are. The result of everyone doing what he really ought to do cannot be worse than the result of everyone doing less than he ought to do, although the result of everyone doing what he reasonably believes he ought to do could be.

If my argument so far has been sound, neither our distance from a preventable evil nor the number of other people who, in respect to that evil, are in the same situation as we are, lessens our obligation to mitigate or prevent that evil. I shall therefore take as established the principle I asserted earlier. As I have already said, I need to assert it only in its qualified form: if it is in our power to prevent something very bad from happening, without thereby sacrificing anything else morally significant, we ought, morally, to do it.

The outcome of this argument is that our traditional moral categories are upset. The traditional distinction between duty and charity cannot be drawn, or at least, not in the place we normally draw it. Giving money to the Bengal Relief Fund is regarded as an act of charity in our society. The bodies which collect money are known as "charities." These organizations see themselves in this way—if you send them a check, you will be thanked for your "generosity." Because giving money is regarded as an act of charity, it is not thought that there is anything wrong with not giving. The charitable man may be praised, but the man who is not charitable is not condemned. People do not feel in any way ashamed or guilty about spending money on new clothes or a new car instead of giving it to famine relief. (Indeed, the alternative does not occur to them.) This way of looking at the matter cannot be justified. When we buy new clothes not to keep ourselves warm but to look "well-dressed" we are not providing for any important need. We would not be sacrificing anything significant if we were to continue to wear our old clothes, and give the money to famine relief. By doing so, we would be preventing another person from starving. It follows from what I have said earlier that we ought to give money away, rather than spend it on clothes which we do not need to keep us warm. To do so is not charitable, or generous. Nor is it the kind of act which philosophers and theologians have called "supererogatory"—an act which it would be good to do, but not wrong not to do. On the contrary, we ought to give the money away, and it is wrong not to do so.

I am not maintaining that there are no acts which are charitable, or that there are no acts which it would be good to do but not wrong not to do. It may be possible to redraw the distinction between duty and charity in some other place. All I am arguing here is that the present way of drawing the distinction, which makes it an act of charity for a man living at the level of affluence which most people in the "developed nations" enjoy to give money to save someone else from starvation, cannot be supported. It is beyond the scope of my argument to consider whether the distinction should be redrawn or abol-

[Handwritten marginal notes: "spending money this way, put them in that position" ; "LOTTERY example" ; "spending $1 to win to more to give"]

ished altogether. There would be many other possible ways of drawing the distinction—for instance, one might decide that it is good to make other people as happy as possible, but not wrong not to do so.

Despite the limited nature of the revision in our moral conceptual scheme which I am proposing, the revision would, given the extent of both affluence and famine in the world today, have radical implications. These implications may lead to further objections, distinct from those I have already considered. I shall discuss two of these.

One objection to the position I have taken might be simply that it is too drastic a revision of our moral scheme. People do not ordinarily judge in the way I have suggested they should. Most people reserve their moral condemnation for those who violate some moral norm, such as the norm against taking another person's property. They do not condemn those who indulge in luxury instead of giving to famine relief. But given that I did not set out to present a morally neutral description of the way people make moral judgments, the way people do in fact judge has nothing to do with the validity of my conclusion. My conclusion follows from the principle which I advanced earlier, and unless that principle is rejected, or the arguments shown to be unsound, I think the conclusion must stand, however strange it appears.

It might, nevertheless, be interesting to consider why our society, and most other societies, do judge differently from the way I have suggested they should. In a well-known article, J. O. Urmson suggests that the imperatives of duty, which tell us what we must do, as distinct from what it would be good to do but not wrong not to do, function so as to prohibit behavior that is intolerable if men are to live together in society.[3] This may explain the origin and continued existence of the present division between acts of duty and acts of charity. Moral attitudes are shaped by the needs of society, and no doubt society needs people who will observe the rules that make social existence tolerable. From the point of view of a particular society, it is

3. J. O. Urmson, "Saints and Heroes," in *Essays in Moral Philosophy*, ed. Abraham I. Melden (Seattle and London, 1958), p. 214. For a related but significantly different view see also Henry Sidgwick, *The Methods of Ethics*, 7th edn. (London, 1907), pp. 220-221, 492-493.

we are all human beings

essential to prevent violations of norms against killing, stealing, and so on. It is quite inessential, however, to help people outside one's own society.

If this is an explanation of our common distinction between duty and supererogation, however, it is not a justification of it. The moral point of view requires us to look beyond the interests of our own society. Previously, as I have already mentioned, this may hardly have been feasible, but it is quite feasible now. From the moral point of view, the prevention of the starvation of millions of people outside our society must be considered at least as pressing as the upholding of property norms within our society.

It has been argued by some writers, among them Sidgwick and Urmson, that we need to have a basic moral code which is not too far beyond the capacities of the ordinary man, for otherwise there will be a general breakdown of compliance with the moral code. Crudely stated, this argument suggests that if we tell people that they ought to refrain from murder and give everything they do not really need to famine relief, they will do neither, whereas if we tell them that they ought to refrain from murder and that it is good to give to famine relief but not wrong not to do so, they will at least refrain from murder. The issue here is: Where should we drawn the line between conduct that is required and conduct that is good although not required, so as to get the best possible result? This would seem to be an empirical question, although a very difficult one. One objection to the Sidgwick-Urmson line of argument is that it takes insufficient account of the effect that moral standards can have on the decisions we make. Given a society in which a wealthy man who gives five percent of his income to famine relief is regarded as most generous, it is not surprising that a proposal that we all ought to give away half our incomes will be thought to be absurdly unrealistic. In a society which held that no man should have more than enough while others have less than they need, such a proposal might seem narrow-minded. What it is possible for a man to do and what he is likely to do are both, I think, very greatly influenced by what people around him are doing and expecting him to do. In any case, the possibility that by spreading the idea that we ought to be doing very much more than we are to relieve famine we shall bring about a general breakdown of moral behavior seems remote. If the stakes are an end to widespread starvation, it is worth the risk. Finally, it should be emphasized that these considerations are relevant only to the issue of what we should require from others, and not to what we ourselves ought to do.

The second objection to my attack on the present distinction between duty and charity is one which has from time to time been made against utilitarianism. It follows from some forms of utilitarian theory that we all ought, morally, to be working full time to increase the balance of happiness over misery. The position I have taken here would not lead to this conclusion in all circumstances, for if there were no bad occurrences that we could prevent without sacrificing something of comparable moral importance, my argument would have no application. Given the present conditions in many parts of the world, however, it does follow from my argument that we ought, morally, to be working full time to relieve great suffering of the sort that occurs as a result of famine or other disasters. Of course, mitigating circumstances can be adduced—for instance, that if we wear ourselves out through overwork, we shall be less effective than we would otherwise have been. Nevertheless, when all considerations of this sort have been taken into account, the conclusion remains: we ought to be preventing as much suffering as we can without sacrificing something else of comparable moral importance. This conclusion is one which we may be reluctant to face. I cannot see, though, why it should be regarded as a criticism of the position for which I have argued, rather than a criticism of our ordinary standards of behavior. Since most people are self-interested to some degree, very few of us are likely to do everything that we ought to do. It would, however, hardly be honest to take this as evidence that it is not the case that we ought to do it.

It may still be thought that my conclusions are so wildly out of line with what everyone else thinks and has always thought that there must be something wrong with the argument somewhere. In order to show that my conclusions, while certainly contrary to contemporary Western moral standards, would not have seemed so extraordinary at other times and in other places, I would like to quote a passage from a writer not normally thought of as a way-out radical, Thomas Aquinas.

Now, according to the natural order instituted by divine providence, material goods are provided for the satisfaction of human needs. Therefore the division and appropriation of property, which proceeds from human law, must not hinder the satisfaction of man's necessity from such goods. Equally, whatever a man has in superabundance is owed, of natural right, to the poor for their sustenance. So Ambrosius says, and it is also to be found in the *Decretum Gratiani*: "The bread which you withhold belongs to the hungry; the clothing you shut away, to the naked; and the money you bury in the earth is the redemption and freedom of the penniless."[4]

I now want to consider a number of points, more practical than philosophical, which are relevant to the application of the moral conclusion we have reached. These points challenge not the idea that we ought to be doing all we can to prevent starvation, but the idea that giving away a great deal of money is the best means to this end.

It is sometimes said that overseas aid should be a government responsibility, and that therefore one ought not to give to privately run charities. Giving privately, it is said, allows the government and the noncontributing members of society to escape their responsibilities.

This argument seems to assume that the more people there are who give to privately organized famine relief funds, the less likely it is that the government will take over full responsibility for such aid. This assumption is unsupported, and does not strike me as at all plausible. The opposite view—that if no one gives voluntarily, a government will assume that its citizens are uninterested in famine relief and would not wish to be forced into giving aid—seems more plausible. In any case, unless there were a definite probability that by refusing to give one would be helping to bring about massive government assistance, people who do refuse to make voluntary contributions are refusing to prevent a certain amount of suffering without being able to point to any tangible beneficial consequence of their refusal. So the onus of showing how their refusal will bring about government action is on those who refuse to give.

4. *Summa Theologica*, II-II, Question 66, Article 7, in *Aquinas, Selected Political Writings*, ed. A. P. d'Entreves, trans. J. G. Dawson (Oxford, 1948), p. 171.

I do not, of course, want to dispute the contention that governments of affluent nations should be giving many times the amount of genuine, no-strings-attached aid that they are giving now. I agree, too, that giving privately is not enough, and that we ought to be campaigning actively for entirely new standards for both public and private contributions to famine relief. Indeed, I would sympathize with someone who thought that campaigning was more important than giving oneself, although I doubt whether preaching what one does not practice would be very effective. Unfortunately, for many people the idea that "it's the government's responsibility" is a reason for not giving which does not appear to entail any political action either.

Another, more serious reason for not giving to famine relief funds is that until there is effective population control, relieving famine merely postpones starvation. If we save the Bengal refugees now, others, perhaps the children of these refugees, will face starvation in a few years' time. In support of this, one may cite the now well-known facts about the population explosion and the relatively limited scope for expanded production.

This point, like the previous one, is an argument against relieving suffering that is happening now, because of a belief about what might happen in the future; it is unlike the previous point in that very good evidence can be adduced in support of this belief about the future. I will not go into the evidence here. I accept that the earth cannot support indefinitely a population rising at the present rate. This certainly poses a problem for anyone who thinks it important to prevent famine. Again, however, one could accept the argument without drawing the conclusion that it absolves one from any obligation to do anything to prevent famine. The conclusion that should be drawn is that the best means of preventing famine, in the long run, is population control. It would then follow from the position reached earlier that one ought to be doing all one can to promote population control (unless one held that all forms of population control were wrong in themselves, or would have significantly bad consequences). Since there are organizations working specifically for population control, one would then support them rather than more orthodox methods of preventing famine.

A third point raised by the conclusion reached earlier relates to the question of just how much we all ought to be giving away. One pos-

sibility, which has already been mentioned, is that we ought to give
until we reach the level of marginal utility—that is, the level at which,
by giving more, I would cause as much suffering to myself or my
dependents as I would relieve by my gift. This would mean, of course,
that one would reduce oneself to very near the material circumstances
of a Bengali refugee. It will be recalled that earlier I put forward both
a strong and a moderate version of the principle of preventing bad
occurrences. The strong version, which required us to prevent bad
things from happening unless in doing so we would be sacrificing
something of comparable moral significance, does seem to require
reducing ourselves to the level of marginal utility. I should also say
that the strong version seems to me to be the correct one. I proposed
the more moderate version—that we should prevent bad occurrences
unless, to do so, we had to sacrifice something morally significant—
only in order to show that even on this surely undeniable principle a
great change in our way of life is required. On the more moderate
principle, it may not follow that we ought to reduce ourselves to the
level of marginal utility, for one might hold that to reduce oneself and
one's family to this level is to cause something significantly bad to
happen. Whether this is so I shall not discuss, since, as I have said,
I can see no good reason for holding the moderate version of the principle rather than the strong version. Even if we accepted the principle
only in its moderate form, however, it should be clear that we would
have to give away enough to ensure that the consumer society,
dependent as it is on people spending on trivia rather than giving to
famine relief, would slow down and perhaps disappear entirely. There
are several reasons why this would be desirable in itself. The value
and necessity of economic growth are now being questioned not only
by conservationists, but by economists as well.[5] There is no doubt, too,
that the consumer society has had a distorting effect on the goals and
purposes of its members. Yet looking at the matter purely from the
point of view of overseas aid, there must be a limit to the extent to
which we should deliberately slow down our economy; for it might be
the case that if we gave away, say, forty percent of our Gross National
Product, we would slow down the economy so much that in absolute

5. See, for instance, John Kenneth Galbraith, *The New Industrial State* (Boston, 1967); and E. J. Mishan, *The Costs of Economic Growth* (London, 1967).

terms we would be giving less than if we gave twenty-five percent of the much larger GNP that we would have if we limited our contribution to this smaller percentage.

I mention this only as an indication of the sort of factor that one would have to take into account in working out an ideal. Since Western societies generally consider one percent of the GNP an acceptable level for overseas aid, the matter is entirely academic. Nor does it affect the question of how much an individual should give in a society in which very few are giving substantial amounts.

It is sometimes said, though less often now than it used to be, that philosophers have no special role to play in public affairs, since most public issues depend primarily on an assessment of facts. On questions of fact, it is said, philosophers as such have no special expertise, and so it has been possible to engage in philosophy without committing oneself to any position on major public issues. No doubt there are some issues of social policy and foreign policy about which it can truly be said that a really expert assessment of the facts is required before taking sides or acting, but the issue of famine is surely not one of these. The facts about the existence of suffering are beyond dispute. Nor, I think, is it disputed that we can do something about it, either through orthodox methods of famine relief or through population control or both. This is therefore an issue on which philosophers are competent to take a position. The issue is one which faces everyone who has more money than he needs to support himself and his dependents, or who is in a position to take some sort of political action. These categories must include practically every teacher and student of philosophy in the universities of the Western world. If philosophy is to deal with matters that are relevant to both teachers and students, this is an issue that philosophers should discuss.

Discussion, though, is not enough. What is the point of relating philosophy to public (and personal) affairs if we do not take our conclusions seriously? In this instance, taking our conclusion seriously means acting upon it. The philosopher will not find it any easier than anyone else to alter his attitudes and way of life to the extent that, if I am right, is involved in doing everything that we ought to be doing.

At the very least, though, one can make a start. The philosopher who does so will have to sacrifice some of the benefits of the consumer society, but he can find compensation in the satisfaction of a way of life in which theory and practice, if not yet in harmony, are at least coming together.

So who provides the aid?

ONORA O'NEILL   Lifeboat Earth

If in the fairly near future millions of people die of starvation, will
those who survive be in any way to blame for those deaths? Is there
anything which people ought to do now, and from now on, if they
are to be able to avoid responsibility for unjustifiable deaths in famine
years? I shall argue from the assumption that persons have a right
not to be killed unjustifiably to the claim that we have a duty to try
to prevent and postpone famine deaths. A corollary of this claim is
that if we do nothing we shall bear some blame for some deaths.

JUSTIFIABLE KILLING

I shall assume that persons have a right not to be killed and a corresponding duty not to kill. I shall make no assumptions about the
other rights persons may have. In particular, I shall not assume that
persons have a right not to be allowed to die by those who could prevent it or a duty to prevent others' deaths whenever they could do
so. Nor will I assume that persons lack this right.

Even if persons have no rights other than a right not to be killed,
this right can justifiably be overridden in certain circumstances. Not
all killings are unjustifiable. I shall be particularly concerned with
two sorts of circumstances in which the right not to be killed is justifiably overridden. The first of these is the case of unavoidable killings; the second is the case of self-defense.

Unavoidable killings occur in situations where a person doing some
act causes some death or deaths which he could not avoid. Often such

deaths will be unavoidable because of the killer's ignorance of some relevant circumstance at the time of his decision to act. If B is driving a train, and A blunders onto the track and is either unnoticed by B or noticed too late for B to stop the train, and B kills A, then B could not have avoided killing A, given his decision to drive the train. Another sort of case of unavoidable killing occurs when B could avoid killing A or could avoid killing C, but cannot avoid killing one of the two. For example, if B is the carrier of a highly contagious and invariably fatal illness, he might find himself so placed that he cannot avoid meeting and so killing either A or C, though he can choose which of them to meet. In this case the unavoidability of B's killing someone is not relative to some prior decision B made. The cases of unavoidable killings with which I want to deal here are of the latter sort, and I shall argue that in such cases B kills justifiably if certain further conditions are met.

A killing may also be justifiable if it is undertaken in self-defense. I shall not argue here that persons have a right of self-defense which is independent of their right not to be killed, but rather that a minimal right of self-defense is a corollary of a right not to be killed Hence the notion of self-defense on which I shall rely is in some ways different from, and narrower than, other interpretations of the right of self-defense. I shall also assume that if A has a right to defend himself against B, then third parties ought to defend A's right. If we take seriously the right not to be killed and its corollaries, then we ought to enforce others' rights not to be killed.

The right of self-defense which is a corollary of the right not to be killed is a right to take action to prevent killings. If I have a right not to be killed then I have a right to prevent others from endangering my life, though I may endanger their lives in so doing only if that is the only available way to prevent the danger to my own life. Similarly if another has the right not to be killed then I should, if possible, do something to prevent others from endangering his life, but I may endanger their lives in so doing only if that is the only available way to prevent the danger to his life. This duty to defend others is *not* a general duty of beneficence but a very restricted duty to enforce others' rights not to be killed.

The right to self-defense so construed is quite narrow. It includes

no right of action against those who, though they cause or are likely
to cause us harm, clearly do not endanger our lives. (However, specific cases are often unclear. The shopkeeper who shoots a person
who holds him up with a toy gun was not endangered, but it may have
been very reasonable of him to suppose that he was endangered.) And
it includes no right to greater than minimal preventive action against
a person who endangers one's life. If B is chasing A with a gun, and
A could save his life either by closing a bullet-proof door or by shooting B, then if people have only a right not to be killed and a minimal corollary right of self-defense, A would have no right to shoot B.
(Again, such cases are often unclear—A may not know that the door
is bullet-proof or not think of it or may simply reason that shooting B
is a better guarantee of prevention.) A right of proportionate self-
defense which might justify A in shooting B, even were it clear that
closing the door would have been enough to prevent B, is not a corollary of the right not to be killed. Perhaps a right of proportionate retaliation might be justified by some claim such as that aggressors
lose certain rights, but I shall take no position on this issue.

In one respect the narrow right of self-defense, which is the corollary of a right not to be killed, is more extensive than some other
interpretations of the right of self-defense. For it is a right to take
action against others who endanger our lives whether or not they do
so intentionally. A's right not to be killed entitles him to take action
not only against aggressors but also against those "innocent threats"[1]
who endanger lives without being aggressors. If B is likely to cause
A's death inadvertently or involuntarily, then A has, if he has a right
not to be killed, a right to take whatever steps are necessary to prevent B from doing so, provided that these do not infringe B's right
not to be killed unnecessarily. If B approaches A with a highly contagious and invariably lethal illness, then A may try to prevent B
from getting near him even if B knows nothing about the danger he
brings. If other means fail, A may kill B in self-defense, even though
B was no aggressor.

1. Cf. Robert Nozick, *Anarchy State and Utopia* (New York, 1974), p. 34.
Nozick defines an innocent threat as "someone who is innocently a causal agent
in a process such that he would be an aggressor had he chosen to become such
an agent."

This construal of the right of self-defense severs the link between aggression and self-defense. When we defend ourselves against innocent threats there is no aggressor, only somebody who endangers life. But it would be misleading to call this right a right of self-preservation. For self-preservation is commonly construed (as by Locke) as including a right to subsistence, and so a right to engage in a large variety of activities whether or not anybody endangers us. But the right which is the corollary of the right not to be killed is a right only to prevent others from endangering our lives, whether or not they intend to do so, and to do so with minimal danger to their lives. Only if one takes a Hobbesian view of human nature and sees others' acts as always completely threatening will the rights of self-defense and self-preservation tend to merge and everything done to maintain life be done to prevent its destruction. Without Hobbesian assumptions the contexts where the minimal right of self-defense can be invoked are fairly special, yet not, I shall argue, rare.

There may be various other circumstances in which persons' rights not to be killed may be overridden. Perhaps, for example, we may justifiably kill those who consent to us doing so. I shall take no position on whether persons can waive their rights not to be killed or on any further situations in which killings might be justifiable.

JUSTIFIABLE KILLINGS ON LIFEBOATS

The time has come to start imagining lurid situations, which is the standard operating procedure for this type of discussion. I shall begin by looking at some sorts of killings which might occur on a lifeboat and shall consider the sorts of justifications which they might be given.

Let us imagine six survivors on a lifeboat. There are two possible levels of provisions:

(1) Provisions are on all reasonable calculations sufficient to last until rescue. Either the boat is near land, or it is amply provisioned or it has gear for distilling water, catching fish, etc.

(2) Provisions are on all reasonable calculations unlikely to be sufficient for all six to survive until rescue.

We can call situation (1) *the well-equipped lifeboat situation*; situation (2) *the under-equipped lifeboat situation*. There may, of course, be cases where the six survivors are unsure which situation they are in, but for simplicity I shall disregard those here.

On a well-equipped lifeboat it is possible for all to survive until rescue. No killing could be justified as unavoidable, and if someone is killed, then the justification could only be self-defense in special situations. Consider the following examples:

(1A) On a well-equipped lifeboat with six persons, A threatens to jettison the fresh water, without which some or all would not survive till rescue. A may be either hostile or deranged. B reasons with A, but when this fails, shoots him. B can appeal to his own and the others' right of self-defense to justify the killing. "It was him or us," he may reasonably say, "for he would have placed us in an under-equipped lifeboat situation." He may say this both when A acts to harm the others and when A acts as an innocent threat.

(1B) On a well-equipped lifeboat with six persons, B, C, D, E, and F decide to withhold food from A, who consequently dies. In this case they cannot appeal to self-defense—for all could have survived. Nor can they claim that they merely let A die —"We didn't *do* anything"—for A would not otherwise have died. This was not a case of violating the problematic right not to be allowed to die but of violating the right not to be killed, and the violation is without justification of self-defense or of unavoidability.

On an under-equipped lifeboat it is not possible for all to survive until rescue. Some deaths are unavoidable, but sometimes there is no particular person whose death is unavoidable. Consider the following examples:

(2A) On an under-equipped lifeboat with six persons, A is very ill and needs extra water, which is already scarce. The others decide not to let him have any water, and A dies of thirst. If A drinks, then not all will survive. On the other hand it is clear that *A* was killed rather than allowed to die. If he had received water he might have survived. Though some death was unavoidable, *A*'s was not and selecting him as the victim requires justification.

(2B) On an under-equipped lifeboat with six persons, water is so scarce that only four can survive (perhaps the distillation unit is designed for supplying four people). But who should go without? Suppose two are chosen to go without, either by lot or by some other method, and consequently die. The others cannot claim that all they did was to allow the two who were deprived of water to die—for these two might otherwise have been among the survivors. Nobody had a greater right to be a survivor, but given that not all could survive, those who did not survive were killed justifiably if the method by which they were chosen was fair. (Of course, a lot needs to be said about what would make a selection procedure fair.)

(2C) The same situation as in (2B) holds, but the two who are not to drink ask to be shot to ease their deaths. Again the survivors cannot claim that they did not kill but at most that they killed justifiably. Whether they did so is not affected by their shooting rather than dehydrating the victims, but only by the unavoidability of some deaths and the fairness of procedures for selecting victims.

(2D) Again the basic situation is as in (2B). But the two who are not to drink rebel. The others shoot them and so keep control of the water. Here it is all too clear that those who died were killed, but they too may have been justifiably killed. Whether the survivors kill justifiably depends neither on the method of killing nor on the victims' cooperation, except insofar as cooperation is relevant to the fairness of selection procedures.

Lifeboat situations do not occur very frequently. We are not often confronted starkly with the choice between killing or being killed by the application of a decision to distribute scarce rations in a certain way. Yet this is becoming the situation of the human species on this globe. The current metaphor "spaceship Earth" suggests more drama and less danger; if we are feeling sober about the situation, "lifeboat Earth" may be more suggestive.

Some may object to the metaphor "lifeboat Earth." A lifeboat is small; all aboard have equal claims to be there and to share equally in the provisions. Whereas the earth is vast and while all may have equal rights to be there, some also have property rights which give them special rights to consume, while others do not. The starving millions are far away and have no right to what is owned by affluent individuals or nations, even if it could prevent their deaths. If they die, it will be said, this is a violation at most of their right not to be allowed to die. And this I have not established or assumed.

I think that this could reasonably have been said in times past. The poverty and consequent deaths of far-off persons was something which the affluent might perhaps have done something to prevent, but which they had (often) done nothing to bring about. Hence they had not violated the right not to be killed of those living far off. But the economic and technological interdependence of today alters this situation.[2] Sometimes deaths are produced by some persons or groups of persons in distant, usually affluent, nations. Sometimes such persons and groups of persons violate not only some persons' alleged right not to be allowed to die but also their more fundamental right not to be killed.

We tend to imagine violations of the right not to be killed in terms of the killings so frequently discussed in the United States today: confrontations between individuals where one directly, violently, and intentionally brings about the other's death. As the lifeboat situa-

2. Cf. Peter Singer, "Famine, Affluence, and Morality," *Philosophy & Public Affairs* 1, no. 3 (Spring 1972): 229–243, 232. I am in agreement with many of the points which Singer makes, but am interested in arguing that we must have some famine policy from a much weaker set of premises. Singer uses some consequentialist premises: starvation is bad; we ought to prevent bad things when we can do so without worse consequences; hence we ought to prevent starvation whether it is nearby or far off and whether others are doing so or not. The argument of this article does not depend on a particular theory about the grounds of obligation, but should be a corollary of any nonbizarre ethical theory which has any room for a notion of rights.

tions have shown, there are other ways in which we can kill one another. In any case, we do not restrict our vision to the typical mugger or murderer context. B may violate A's right not to be killed even when

(a) B does not act alone.
(b) A's death is not immediate.
(c) It is not certain whether A or another will die in consequence of B's action.
(d) B does not intend A's death.

The following set of examples illustrates these points about killings:

(aa) A is beaten by a gang consisting of B, C, D, etc. No one assailant single-handedly killed him, yet his right not to be killed was violated by all who took part.
(bb) A is poisoned slowly by daily doses. The final dose, like earlier ones, was not, by itself, lethal. But the poisoner still violated A's right not to be killed.
(cc) B plays Russian roulette with A, C, D, E, F, and G, firing a revolver at each once, when he knows that one firing in six will be lethal. If A is shot and dies, then B has violated his right not to be killed.
(dd) Henry II asks who will rid him of the turbulent priest, and his supporters kill Becket. It is reasonably clear that Henry did not intend Becket's death, even though he in part brought it about, as he later admitted.

These explications of the right not to be killed are not too controversial taken individually, and I would suggest that their conjunction is also uncontroversial. Even when A's death is the result of the acts of many persons and is not an immediate consequence of their deeds, nor even a certain consequence, and is not intended by them, A's right not to be killed may be violated.

FIRST CLASS VERSUS STEERAGE ON LIFEBOAT EARTH

If we imagine a lifeboat in which special quarters are provided for the (recently) first-class passengers, and on which the food and water for all passengers are stowed in those quarters, then we have a fair, if crude, model of the present human situation on lifeboat Earth. For even on the assumption that there is at present sufficient for all to survive, some have control over the means of survival and so, indirectly, over others' survival. Sometimes the exercise of control can lead, even on a well-equipped lifeboat, to the starvation and death of some of those who lack control. On an ill-equipped lifeboat some must die in any case and, as we have already seen, though some of these deaths may be killings, some of them may be justifiable killings. Corresponding situations can, do, and will arise on lifeboat Earth, and it is to these that we should turn our attention, covering both the presumed present situation of global sufficiency of the means of survival and the expected future situation of global insufficiency.

Sufficiency Situations

Aboard a well-equipped lifeboat any distribution of food and water which leads to a death is a killing and not just a case of permitting a death. For the acts of those who distribute the food and water are the causes of a death which would not have occurred had those agents either had no causal influence or done other acts. By contrast, a person whom they leave in the water to drown is merely allowed to die, for his death would have taken place (other things being equal) had those agents had no causal influence, though it could have been prevented had they rescued him.[3] The distinction between killing and allowing to die, as here construed, does not depend on any claims about the other rights of persons who are killed. The death of the shortchanged passenger of example (1B) violated his property rights as well as his right not to be killed, but the reason the death was classifiable as a killing depended on the part which the acts of the other passengers had in causing it. If we suppose that a stowaway on a lifeboat has no right to food and water and is denied them, then clearly his property rights have not been violated. Even

3. This way of distinguishing killing from allowing to die does not rely on distinguishing "negative" form "positive" acts. Such attempts seem unpromising since any act has multiple descriptions of which some will be negative and others positive. If a clear distinction is to be made between killing and letting die, it must hinge on the *difference* which an act makes for a person's survival, rather than on the description under which the agent acts.

so, by the above definitions he is killed rather than allowed to die. For if the other passengers had either had no causal influence or done otherwise, his death would not have occurred. Their actions— in this case distributing food only to those entitled to it—caused the stowaway's death. Their acts would be justifiable only if property rights can sometimes override the right not to be killed.

Many would claim that the situation on lifeboat Earth is not analogous to that on ordinary lifeboats, since it is not evident that we all have a claim, let alone an equal claim, on the earth's resources. Perhaps some of us are stowaways. I shall not here assume that we do all have some claim on the earth's resources, even though I think it plausible to suppose that we do. I shall assume that even if persons have unequal property rights and some people own nothing, it does not follow that *B*'s exercise of his property rights can override *A*'s right not to be killed.[4] Where our activities lead to others' deaths which would not have occurred had we either done something else or had no causal influence, no claim that the activities were within our economic rights would suffice to show that we did not kill.

It is not far-fetched to think that at present the economic activity of some groups of persons leads to others' deaths. I shall choose a couple of examples of the sort of activity which can do so, but I do not think that these examples do more than begin a list of cases of killing by economic activities. Neither of these examples depends on questioning the existence of unequal property rights; they assume only that such rights do not override a right not to be killed. Neither example is one for which it is plausible to think that the killing could be justified as undertaken in self-defense.

Case one might be called the *foreign investment* situation. A group of investors may form a company which invests abroad—perhaps in a plantation or in a mine—and so manage their affairs that a high level of profits is repatriated, while the wages for the laborers are

4. The point may appear rather arbitrary, given that I have not rested my case on one theory of the grounds of obligation. But I believe that almost any such theory will show a right not to be killed to override a property right. Perhaps this is why Locke's theory can seem so odd—in moving from a right of self-preservation to a justification of unequal property rights, he finds himself gradually having to reinterpret all rights as property rights, thus coming to see us as the owners of our persons.

so minimal that their survival rate is lowered, that is, their expectation of life is lower than it might have been had the company not
invested there. In such a case the investors and company management do not act alone, do not cause immediate deaths, and do not
know in advance who will die; it is also likely that they intend no
deaths. But by their involvement in the economy of an underdeveloped area they cannot claim, as can another company which has
no investments there, that they are "doing nothing." On the contrary,
they are setting the policies which determine the living standards
which determine the survival rate. When persons die because of the
lowered standard of living established by a firm or a number of firms
which dominate a local economy and either limit persons to employment on 'their terms or lower the other prospects for employment
by damaging traditional economic structures, and these firms could
either pay higher wages or stay out of the area altogether, then those
who establish these policies are violating some persons' rights not
to be killed. Foreign investment which *raises* living standards, even
to a still abysmal level, could not be held to kill, for it causes no additional deaths, unless there are special circumstances, as in the following example.

Even when a company investing in an underdeveloped country
establishes high wages and benefits and raises the expectation of life
for its workers, it often manages to combine these payments with
high profitability only by having achieved a tax-exempt status. In
such cases the company is being subsidized by the general tax revenue of the underdeveloped economy. It makes no contribution to
the infrastructure—e.g. roads and harbors and airports—from which
it benefits. In this way many underdeveloped economies have come
to include developed enclaves whose development is achieved in part
at the expense of the poorer majority.[5] In such cases, government
and company policy combine to produce a high wage sector at the
expense of a low wage sector; in consequence, some of the persons
in the low wage sector, who would not otherwise have died, may die;

5. Cf. P.A. Baron, *The Political Economy of Growth* (New York, 1957), especially chap. 5, "On the Roots of Backwardness"; or A.G. Frank, *Capitalism and
Underdevelopment in Latin America* (New York, 1967). Both works argue
that underdeveloped economies are among the products of developed ones.

these persons, whoever they may be, are killed and not merely allowed to die. Such killings may sometimes be justifiable—perhaps, if they are outnumbered by lives saved through having a developed sector—but they are killings nonetheless, since the victims might have survived if not burdened by transfer payments to the developed sector.

But, one may say, the management of such a corporation and its investors should be distinguished more sharply. Even if the management may choose a level of wages, and consequently of survival, the investors usually know nothing of this. But the investors, even if ignorant, are responsible for company policy. They may often fail to exercise control, but by law they have control. They choose to invest in a company with certain foreign investments; they profit from it; they can, and others cannot, affect company policy in fundamental ways. To be sure the investors are not murderers—they do not intend to bring about the deaths of any persons; nor do the company managers usually intend any of the deaths company policies cause. Even so, investors and management acting together with the sorts of results just described do violate some persons' rights not to be killed and usually cannot justify such killings either as required for self-defense or as unavoidable.

Case two, where even under sufficiency conditions some persons' economic activities result in the deaths of other persons, might be called the *commodity pricing* case. Underdeveloped countries often depend heavily on the price level of a few commodities. So a sharp drop in the world price of coffee or sugar or cocoa may spell ruin and lowered survival rates for whole regions. Yet such drops in price levels are not in all cases due to factors beyond human control. Where they are the result of action by investors, brokers, or government agencies, these persons and bodies are choosing policies which will kill some people. Once again, to be sure, the killing is not single-handed, it is not instantaneous, the killers cannot foresee exactly who will die, and they may not intend anybody to die.

Because of the economic interdependence of different countries, deaths can also be caused by rises in the prices of various commodities. For example, the present near-famine in the Sahelian region of Africa and in the Indian subcontinent is attributed by agronomists partly to climatic shifts and partly to the increased prices of oil and hence of fertilizer, wheat, and other grains.

> The recent doubling in international prices of essential foodstuffs will, of necessity, be reflected in higher death rates among the world's lowest income groups, who lack the income to increase their food expenditures proportionately, but live on diets near the subsistence level to begin with.[6]

Of course, not all of those who die will be killed. Those who die of drought will merely be allowed to die, and some of those who die because less has been grown with less fertilizer will also die because of forces beyond the control of any human agency. But to the extent that the raising of oil prices is an achievement of Arab diplomacy and oil company management rather than a windfall, the consequent deaths are killings. Some of them may perhaps be justifiable killings (perhaps if outnumbered by lives saved within the Arab world by industrialization), but killings nonetheless.

Even on a sufficiently equipped earth some persons are killed by others' distribution decisions. The causal chains leading to death-producing distributions are often extremely complex. Where they can be perceived with reasonable clarity we ought, if we take seriously the right not to be killed and seek not merely to avoid killing others but to prevent third parties from doing so, to support policies which reduce deaths. For example—and these are only examples—we should support certain sorts of aid policies rather than others; we should oppose certain sorts of foreign investment; we should oppose certain sorts of commodity speculation, and perhaps support certain sorts of price support agreements for some commodities (e.g. those which try to maintain high prices for products on whose sale poverty stricken economies depend).

If we take the view that we have no duty to enforce the rights of others, then we cannot draw so general a conclusion about our duty to support various economic policies which might avoid some unjusti-

6. Lester R. Brown and Erik P. Eckholm, "The Empty Breadbasket," *Ceres* (F.A.O. Review on Development), March–April 1974, p. 59. See also N. Borlaug and R. Ewell, "The Shrinking Margin," in the same issue.

fiable killings. But we might still find that we should take action of certain sorts either because our own lives are threatened by certain economic activities of others or because our own economic activities threaten others' lives. Only if we knew that we were not part of any system of activities causing unjustifiable deaths could we have no duties to support policies which seek to avoid such deaths. Modern economic causal chains are so complex that it is likely that only those who are economically isolated and self-sufficient could know that they are part of no such systems of activities. Persons who believe that they are involved in some death-producing activities will have some of the same duties as those who think they have a duty to enforce others' rights not to be killed.

Scarcity Situations

The last section showed that sometimes, even in sufficiency situations, some might be killed by the way in which others arranged the distribution of the means of subsistence. Of far more importance in the long run is the true lifeboat situation—the situation of scarcity. We face a situation in which not everyone who is born can live out the normal span of human life and, further, in which we must expect today's normal life-span to be shortened. The date at which serious scarcity will begin is not generally agreed upon, but even the more optimistic prophets place it no more than decades away.[7] Its arrival will depend on factors such as the rate of technological invention and innovation, especially in agriculture and pollution control, and the success of programs to limit human fertility.

Such predictions may be viewed as exonerating us from complicity in famine deaths. If famine is inevitable, then—while we may have to choose whom to save—the deaths of those whom we do not or cannot save cannot be seen as killings for which we bear any responsibility. For these deaths would have occurred even if we had

7. For discussions of the time and extent of famine see, for example, P.R. Ehrlich, *The Population Bomb*, rev. ed. (New York, 1971); R.L. Heilbroner, *An Inquiry into the Human Prospect* (New York, 1974); *Scientific American*, September 1974, especially R. Freedman and B. Berelson, "The Human Population"; P. Demeny, "The Populations of the Underdeveloped Countries"; R. Revelle, "Food and Population."

no causal influence. The decisions to be made may be excruciatingly difficult, but at least we can comfort ourselves that we did not produce or contribute to the famine.

However, this comforting view of famine predictions neglects the fact that these predictions are contingent upon certain assumptions about what people will do in the prefamine period. Famine is said to be inevitable *if* people do not curb their fertility, alter their consumption patterns, and avoid pollution and consequent ecological catastrophes. It is the policies of the present which will produce, defer, or avoid famine. Hence if famine comes, the deaths that occur will be results of decisions made earlier. Only if we take no part in systems of activities which lead to famine situations can we view ourselves as choosing whom to save rather than whom to kill when famine comes. In an economically interdependent world there are few people who can look on the approach of famine as a natural disaster from which they may kindly rescue some, but for whose arrival they bear no responsibility. We cannot stoically regard particular famine deaths as unavoidable if we have contributed to the emergence and extent of famine.

If we bear some responsibility for the advent of famine, then any decision on distributing the risk of famine is a decision whom to kill. Even a decision to rely on natural selection as a famine policy is choosing a policy for killing—for under a different famine policy different persons might have survived, and under different prefamine policies there might have been no famine or a less severe famine. The choice of a particular famine policy may be justifiable on the grounds that once we have let it get to that point there is not enough to go around, and somebody must go, as on an ill-equipped lifeboat. Even so, the famine policy chosen will not be a policy of saving some but not all persons from an unavoidable predicament.

Persons cannot, of course, make famine policies individually. Famine and prefamine policies are and will be made by governments individually and collectively and perhaps also by some voluntary organizations. It may even prove politically impossible to have a coherent famine or prefamine policy for the whole world; if so, we shall have to settle for partial and piecemeal policies. But each person who is in a position to support or oppose such policies, whether global or local, has to decide which to support and which to oppose. Even for individual persons, inaction and inattention are often a decision—a decision to support the famine and prefamine policies, which are the status quo whether or not they are "hands off" policies. There are large numbers of ways in which private citizens may affect such policies. They do so in supporting or opposing legislation affecting aid and foreign investment, in supporting or opposing certain sorts of charities or groups such as Zero Population Growth, in promoting or opposing ecologically conservative technology and lifestyles. Hence we have individually the onus of avoiding killing. For even though we

(a) do not kill single-handedly those who die of famine
(b) do not kill instantaneously those who die of famine
(c) do not know which individuals will die as the result of the pre-famine and famine policies we support (unless we support something like a genocidal famine policy)
(d) do not intend any famine deaths

we nonetheless kill and do not merely allow to die. For as the result of our actions in concert with others, some will die who might have survived had we either acted otherwise or had no causal influence.

FAMINE POLICIES AND PREFAMINE POLICIES

Various principles can be suggested on which famine and prefamine policies might reasonably be based. I shall list some of these, more with the aim of setting out the range of possible decisions than with the aim of stating a justification for selecting some people for survival. One very general policy might be that of adopting whichever more specific policies will lead to the fewest deaths. An example would be going along with the consequences of natural selection in the way in which the allocation of medical care in situations of great shortage does, that is, the criteria for relief would be a high chance of survival if relief is given and a low chance otherwise—the worst risks would be abandoned. (This decision is analogous to picking the ill man as the victim on the lifeboat in 2A.) However, the policy of minimizing deaths is indeterminate, unless a certain time horizon is specified. For the policies which maximize survival in the short run—e.g. preventive medicine and minimal living standards—may also maximize population increase and lead to greater ultimate catastrophe.[8]

Another general policy would be to try to find further grounds which can justify overriding a person's right not to be killed. Famine policies adopted on these grounds might permit others to kill those who will forgo their right not to be killed (voluntary euthanasia, including healthy would-be suicides) or to kill those whom others find dependent and exceptionally burdensome, e.g. the unwanted sick or aged or unborn or newborn (involuntary euthanasia, abortion, and infanticide). Such policies might be justified by claims that the right not to be killed may be overridden in famine situations if the owner of the right consents or if securing the right is exceptionally burdensome.

Any combination of such policies is a policy of killing some and protecting others. Those who are killed may not have their right not to be killed violated without reason; those who set and support famine policies and prefamine policies will not be able to claim that they do not kill, but if they reason carefully they may be able to claim that they do not do so without justification.

From this vantage point it can be seen why it is not relevant to restrict the right of self-defense to a right to defend oneself against those who threaten one's life but do not do so innocently. Such a restriction may make a great difference to one's view of abortion in cases where the mother's life is threatened, but it does not make much difference when famine is the issue. Those who might be chosen as likely victims of any famine policy will probably be innocent of contributing to the famine, or at least no more guilty than others; hence the innocence of the victims is an insufficient ground for rejecting a policy. Indeed it is hard to point a finger at the guilty in famine situations. Are they the hoarders of grain? The parents of large families? Inefficient farmers? Our own generation?

In a sense we are all innocent threats to one another's safety in

8. See *Scientific American*, September 1974, especially A.J. Coale, "The History of the Human Population."

scarcity situations, for the bread one person eats might save another's life. If there were fewer people competing for resources, commodity prices would fall and starvation deaths be reduced. Hence famine deaths in scarcity situations might be justified on grounds of the minimal right of self-defense as well as on grounds of the unavoidability of some deaths and the reasonableness of the policies for selecting victims. For each famine death leaves fewer survivors competing for whatever resources there are, and the most endangered among the survivors might have died—had not others done so. So a policy which kills some may be justified on the grounds that the most endangered survivors could have been defended in no other way.

Global scarcity is not here yet. But its imminence has certain implications for today. If all persons have a right not to be killed and a corollary duty not to kill others, then we are bound to adopt prefamine policies which ensure that famine is postponed as long as possible and is minimized. And a duty to try to postpone the advent and minimize the severity of famine is a duty on the one hand to minimize the number of persons there will be and on the other to maximize the means of subsistence.[9] For if we do not adopt prefamine policies with these aims we shall have to adopt more drastic famine policies sooner.

So if we take the right not to be killed seriously, we should consider and support not only some famine policy for future use but also a population and resources policy for present use. There has been a certain amount of philosophical discussion of population policies.[10] From the point of view of the present argument it has two defects. First, it is for the most part conducted within a utilitarian framework and focuses on problems such as the different population policies required by maximizing the total and the average utility of a population. Secondly this literature tends to look at a scarcity of resources as affecting the quality of lives but not their very possibility. It is more

9. The failure of "right to life" groups to pursue these goals seriously casts doubt upon their commitment to the preservation of human lives. Why are they active in so few of the contexts where human lives are endangered?

10. For example, J.C.C. Smart, *An Outline of a System of Utilitarian Ethics* (Melbourne, 1961), pp. 18, 44ff.; Jan Narveson, "Moral Problems of Population," *Monist* 57 (1973): 62–86; "Utilitarianism and New Generations," *Mind* 76 (1967): 62–72.

concerned with the question, How many people should we add? than with the question, How few people could we lose? There are, of course, many interesting questions about population policies which are not relevant to famine. But here I shall consider only population and re-source policies determined on the principle of postponing and mini-mizing famine, for these are policies which might be based on the claim that persons have a right not to be killed, so that we have a duty to avoid or postpone situations in which we shall have to over-ride this right.

Such population policies might, depending upon judgments about the likely degree of scarcity, range from the mild to the draconian. I list some examples. A mild population policy might emphasize family planning, perhaps moving in the direction of fiscal incentives or mea-sures which stress not people's rights but their duties to control their bodies. Even a mild policy would require a lot both in terms of inven-tion (e.g. the development of contraceptives suitable for use in pov-erty-stricken conditions) and innovation (e.g. social policies which reduce the incentives and pressures to have a large family).[11] More draconian policies would enforce population limitation—for example, by mandatory sterilization after a certain number of children were born or by reducing public health expenditures in places with high net reproduction rates to prevent death rates from declining until birth rates do so. A policy of completely eliminating all further births (e.g. by universal sterilization) is also one which would meet the require-ment of postponing famine, since extinct species do not suffer famine. I have not in this argument used any premises which show that a complete elimination of births would be wrong, but other premises might give reasons for thinking that it is wrong to enforce sterilization or better to have some persons rather than no persons. In any case the political aspects of introducing famine policies make it likely that this most austere of population policies would not be considered.

There is a corresponding range of resource policies. At the milder end are the various conservation and pollution control measures now being practiced or discussed. At the tougher end of the spectrum are

11. Cf. Mahmood Mamdani, *The Myth of Population Control* (New York, 1972), for evidence that high fertility can be based on rational choice rather than ignorance or incompetence.

complete rationing of energy and materials consumption. If the aim of a resources policy is to avoid killing those who are born, and adequate policy may require both invention (e.g. solar energy technology and better waste retrieval techniques) and innovation (e.g. introducing new technology in such a way that its benefits are not quickly absorbed by increasing population, as has happened with the green revolution in some places).

At all events, if we think that people have a right not to be killed, we cannot fail to face up to its long range implications. This one right by itself provides ground for activism on many fronts. In scarcity situations which we help produce, the defeasibility of the right not to be killed is important, for there cannot be any absolute duty not to kill persons in such situations but only a commitment to kill only for reasons. Such a commitment requires consideration of the condition or quality of life which is to qualify for survival. Moral philosophers are reluctant to face up to this problem; soon it will be staring us in the face.

CHARLES R. BEITZ Justice and
International Relations

> Current events have brought into sharp
> focus the realization that . . . there is a
> close inter-relationship between the pros-
> perity of the developed countries and the
> growth and development of the developing
> countries. . . . International cooperation
> for development is the shared goal and
> common duty of all countries.[1]

Do citizens of relatively affluent countries have obligations founded on
justice to share their wealth with poorer people elsewhere? Certainly
they have some redistributive obligations, founded on humanitarian
principles requiring those who are able to help those who, without
help, would surely perish. But obligations of justice might be thought
to be more demanding than this, to require greater sacrifices on the
part of the relatively well-off, and perhaps sacrifices of a different kind
as well. Obligations of justice, unlike those of humanitarian aid,
might also require efforts at large-scale institutional reform. The
rhetoric of the United Nations General Assembly's "Declaration on the
Establishment of a New International Economic Order" suggests that
it is this sort of obligation which requires wealthy countries to substantially increase their contributions to less developed countries and
to radically restructure the world economic system. Do such obligations
exist?

This question does not pose special theoretical problems for the
utilitarian, for whom the distinction between obligations of humanitarian aid and obligations of social justice is a second-order distinc-

I am grateful to Huntington Terrell, who stimulated my interest in questions
of international ethics, for comments and criticisms on an earlier version and
to Thomas Scanlon, Richard Falk, and Dennis Thompson, for many helpful
discussions of earlier drafts.

1. "Declaration on the Establishment of a New International Economic
Order," Resolution No. 3201 (S-VI), 1 May 1974, United Nations General As-
sembly, *Official Records: Sixth Special Session*, Supp. No. 1 (A/9559) (New
York, 1974), p. 3.

tion. Since utility-maximizing calculations need not respect national boundaries, there is a method of decision available when different kinds of obligations conflict. Contractarian political theories, on the other hand, might be expected to encounter problems in application to questions of global distributive justice. Contractarian principles usually rest on the relations in which people stand in a national community united by common acceptance of a conception of justice. It is not obvious that contractarian principles with such a justification underwrite any redistributive obligations between persons situated in different national societies.

This feature of contractarian principles has motivated several criticisms of Rawls' theory of justice.[2] These criticisms hold, roughly, that it is wrong to take the nation-state as the foundation of contractarian principles, that, instead, such principles ought to apply globally.[3] I want to pursue this theme here, in part because it raises interesting problems for Rawls' theory, but also because it illuminates several important features of the question of global justice, a question to which too little attention has been paid by political philosophers. In view of increasingly visible global distributive inequalities, famine, and environmental deterioration, it can hardly be denied that this question poses a main political challenge for the foreseeable future.

My discussion has four parts. I begin by reviewing Rawls' brief remarks on international justice, and show that these make sense only on the empirical assumption that nation-states are self-sufficient. Even if this assumption is correct, I then claim, Rawls' discussion of international justice is importantly incomplete, for it neglects certain problems about natural resources. In part three, I go on to question the empirical foundation of the self-sufficiency assumption, and sketch the consequences for Rawlsian ideal theory of abandoning the assumption. In conclusion, I explore the relation of an ideal theory of

2. John Rawls, *A Theory of Justice* (Cambridge, Mass., 1972). Page references are given parenthetically in the text.

3. Such criticisms have appeared in several places. For example, Brian Barry, *The Liberal Theory of Justice* (Oxford, 1973), pp. 128–133; Peter Danielson, "Theories, Intuitions and the Problem of World-Wide Distributive Justice," *Philosophy of the Social Sciences* 3 (1973), pp. 331–340; Thomas M. Scanlon, Jr., "Rawls' Theory of Justice," *University of Pennsylvania Law Review* 121, no. 5 (May 1973), pp. 1066–1067.

international justice to some representative problems of politics in the nonideal world.

This is a large agenda, despite the absence of any extended consideration of the most familiar problems of international ethics, those concerning the morality of war, which I take up only briefly. While these are hardly insignificant questions, it seems to me that preoccupation with them has too often diverted attention from more pressing distributive issues. Inevitably, I must leave some problems undeveloped, and merely suggest some possible solutions for others. The question of global distributive justice is both complicated and new, and I have not been able to formulate my conclusions as a complete theory of global justice. My main concern has been to see what such a theory might involve.

I

Justice, Rawls says, is the first virtue of social institutions. Its "primary subject" is "the basic structure of society, or more exactly, the way in which the major social institutions distribute fundamental rights and duties and determine the division of advantages from social cooperation" (7). The central problem for a theory of justice is to identify principles by which the basic structure of society can be appraised.

Rawls' two principles characterize "a special case of the problem of justice." They do not characterize "the justice of the law of nations and of relations between states" (7–8) because they rest on morally significant features of an ongoing scheme of social cooperation. If national boundaries are thought to set off discrete schemes of social cooperation, as Rawls assumes (457), then the relations of persons situated in different nation-states cannot be regulated by principles of social justice. As Rawls develops the theory, it is only after principles of social justice and principles for individuals (the "natural duties") are chosen that principles for international relations are considered, and then only in the most perfunctory manner.

Rawls assumes that "the boundaries" of the cooperative schemes to which the two principles apply "are given by the notion of a self-contained national community" (457). This assumption "is not relaxed until the derivation of the principles of justice for the law of nations" (457). In other words, the assumption that national communities are self-contained is relaxed when international justice is considered. What does this mean? If the societies of the world are now to be conceived as open, fully interdependent systems, the world as a whole would fit the description of a scheme of social cooperation and the arguments for the two principles would apply, a fortiori, at the global level. The principles of justice for international politics would be the two principles for domestic society writ large, and their application would have a very radical result, given the tendency to equality of the difference principle. On the other hand, if societies are thought to be *entirely* self-contained—that is, if they are to have no relations of any kind with persons, groups, or societies beyond their borders—then why consider international justice at all? Principles of justice are supposed to regulate conduct, but if, ex hypothesi, there is no possibility of international conduct, it is difficult to see why principles of justice for the law of nations should be of any interest whatsoever. Rawls' discussion of justice among nations suggests that neither of these alternatives describes his intention in the passage quoted. Some intermediate assumption is required. Apparently, nation-states are now to be conceived as largely self-sufficient, but not entirely self-contained. Probably he imagines a world of nation-states which interact only in marginal ways; perhaps they maintain diplomatic relations, participate in a postal union, maintain limited cultural exchanges, and so on. Certainly the self-sufficiency assumption requires that societies have no significant trade or economic relations.

Why, in such a world, are principles of international justice of interest? Rawls says that the restriction to ideal theory has the consequence that each society's external behavior is controlled by its principles of justice and of individual right, which prevent unjust wars and interference with human rights abroad (379). So it cannot be the need to prohibit unjust wars that prompts his worries about the law of nations. The most plausible motivation for considering principles of justice for the law of nations is suggested by an aside regarding the difficulties of disarmament (336), in which Rawls suggests that state relations are inherently unstable despite each one's commitment to its own principles of justice. Agreement on regulative principles would then be a source of security for each state concerning each other's external behavior, and would represent the minimum conditions of peaceful coexistence.

For the purpose of justifying principles for nations, Rawls reinterprets the original position as a sort of international conference:

> One may extend the interpretation of the original position and think of the parties as representatives of different nations who must choose together the fundamental principles to adjudicate conflicting claims among states. Following out the conception of the initial situation, I assume that these representatives are deprived of various kinds of information. While they know that they represent different nations each living under the normal circumstances of human life, they know nothing about the particular circumstances of their own society. . . . Once again the contracting parties, in this case representatives of states, are allowed only enough knowledge to make a rational choice to protect their interests but not so much that the more fortunate among them can take advantage of their special situation. This original position is fair between nations; it nullifies the contingencies and biases of historical fate [378].

While he does not actually present arguments for any particular principles for nations, he claims that "there would be no surprises, since the principles chosen would, I think, be familiar ones" (378). The examples given are indeed familiar; they include principles of self-determination, nonintervention, the *pacta sunt servanda* rule, a principle of justifiable self-defense, and principles defining *jus ad bellum* and *jus in bello*.[4] These are supposed to be consequences of a basic principle of equality among nations, to which the parties in the reinterpreted original position would agree in order to protect and uphold their interests in successfully operating their respective societies and in securing compliance with the principles for individuals which protect human life (378, 115).

One objection to such reasoning might be that there is no guarantee that all of the world's states are internally just, or if they are, that they

4. These principles form the basis of traditional international law. See the discussion, on which Rawls relies, in J.L. Brierly, *The Law of Nations*, 6th ed. (New York, 1963), especially chaps. 3 and 4.

are just in the sense specified by the two principles. If some societies are unjust according to the two principles, some familiar and serious problems arise. In a world including South Africa or Chile, for example, one can easily imagine situations in which the principle of non-intervention would prevent other nations from intervening in support of an oppressed minority fighting to establish a more just regime, and this might seem implausible. More generally, one might ask why a principle which defends a state's ability to pursue an immoral end is to count as a moral principle imposing a requirement of justice on other states.

Such an objection, while indicating a serious problem in the real world, would be inappropriate in this context because the law of nations, in Rawls, applies to a world of just states. Nothing in Rawls' theory specifically requires this assumption, but it seems consonant with the restriction to ideal theory and parallels the assumption of "strict compliance" which plays a role in arguments for the two principles in domestic societies. It is important to see, however, that the suggested justification of these traditional rules of international law rests on an ideal assumption not present in most discussions of this subject. It does not self-evidently follow that these rules ought to hold in the nonideal world; at a minimum, an additional condition would be required, limiting the scope of the traditional rules to cases in which their observance would promote the development of just institutions in presently unjust societies while observing the basic protections of human rights expressed by the natural duties and preserving a stable international order in which just societies can exist.

Someone might think that other principles would be acknowledged, for example, regarding population control and regulation of the environment. Or perhaps, as Barry suggests, the parties would agree to form some sort of permanent international organization with consultative, diplomatic, and even collective security functions.[5] However, there is no obvious reason why such agreements would emerge from an international original position, at least so long as the constituent societies are assumed to be largely self-sufficient. Probably the parties, if confronted with these possibilities, would reason that fundamental questions of justice are not raised by them, and such issues of policy

5. Barry, *The Liberal Theory of Justice*, p. 132.

as arise from time to time in the real world could be handled with traditional treaty mechanisms underwritten by the rule, already acknowledged, that treaties are to be observed. Other issues that are today subjects of international negotiation—those relating to international regulation of common areas such as the sea and outer space—are of a different sort. They call for a kind of regulation that requires substantive cooperation among peoples in the use of areas not presently within the boundaries of any society. A cooperative scheme must be evolved which would create new wealth to which no national society could have a legitimate claim. These issues would be excluded from consideration on the ground that the parties are assumed not to be concerned with devising such a scheme. As representatives of separate social schemes, their attention is turned inward, not outward. In coming together in an international original position, they are moved by considerations of equality between "independent peoples organized as states" (378). Their main interest is in providing conditions in which just domestic social orders might flourish.

II

Thus far, the ideal theory of international justice bears a striking resemblance to that proposed in the Definitive Articles of Kant's *Perpetual Peace*.[6] Accepting for the time being the assumption of national self-sufficiency, Rawls' choice of principles seems unexceptionable. But would this list of principles exhaust those to which the parties would agree? Probably not. At least one kind of consideration, involving natural resources, might give rise to moral conflict among states and thus be a matter of concern in the international original position. The principles given so far do not take account of these considerations.

We can appreciate the moral importance of conflicting resource claims by distinguishing two elements which contribute to the material advancement of societies. One is human cooperative activity itself, which can be thought of as the human component of material advancement. The other is what Sidgwick called "the utilities derived from any portion of the earth's surface," the natural component.[7]

6. Trans. and ed. Lewis White Beck (Indianapolis, 1957), pp. 10–23.
7. Henry Sidgwick, *The Elements of Politics* (London, 1891), p. 242; quoted in S.I. Benn and R.S. Peters, *The Principles of Political Thought* (New York,

While the first is the subject of the domestic principles of justice, the second is morally relevant even in the absence of a functioning scheme of international social cooperation. The parties to the international original position would know that natural resources are distributed unevenly over the earth's surface. Some areas are rich in resources, and societies established in such areas can be expected to exploit their natural riches and to prosper. Other societies do not fare so well, and despite the best efforts of their members, they may attain only a meager level of well-being due to resource scarcities.

The parties would view the distribution of resources much as Rawls says the parties to the domestic original position deliberations view the distribution of natural talents. In that context, he says that natural endowments are "neither just nor unjust; nor is it unjust that men are born into society at any particular position. These are simply natural facts. What is just or unjust is the way that institutions deal with these facts" (102). A caste society, for example, is unjust because it distributes the benefits of social cooperation according to a rule that rests on morally arbitrary factors. Rawls' objection is that those who are less advantaged for reasons beyond their control cannot be asked to suffer the pains of inequality when their sacrifices cannot be shown to advance their position in comparison with an initial position of equality.

Reasoning analogously, the parties to the international original position, viewing the natural distribution of resources as morally arbitrary, would think that they should be subject to redistribution under a resource redistribution principle. This view is subject to the immediate objection that Rawls' treatment of natural talents is troublesome. It seems vulnerable in at least two ways. First, it is not clear what it means to say that the distribution of talents is "arbitrary from a moral point of view" (72). While the distribution of natural talents is arbitrary in the sense that one cannot deserve to be born with the capacity, say, to play like Rubinstein, it does not obviously follow that the possession of such a talent needs any justification. On the contrary, simply having a talent seems to furnish prima facie warrant for making use of it in ways that are, for the possessor, possible and

---

1959), p. 430. Sidgwick's entire discussion of putative national rights to land and resources is relevant here—see *Elements*, pp. 239–244.

desirable. A person need not justify his possession of talents, despite the fact that he cannot be said to deserve them, because they are already *his*; the prima facie right to use and control talents is fixed by natural fact.

The other point of vulnerability is that natural capacities are parts of the self, in the development of which a person might take a special kind of pride. A person's decision to develop one talent, not to develop another, as well as his choice as to how the talent is to be formed and the uses to which it is to be put, are likely to be important elements of his effort to shape an identity. The complex of developed talents might even be said to constitute the self; their exercise is a principal form of self-expression. Because the development of talents is so closely linked with the shaping of personal identity, it might seem that one's claim to one's talents is protected by considerations of personal liberty. To interfere with the development and use of talents is to interfere with a self. Or so, at least, it might be argued.

While I believe that Rawls' discussion of talents can be defended against objections like these, that is not my concern here. I want to argue only that objections of this sort do not apply to the parallel claim that the distribution of natural resources is similarly arbitrary. Like talents, resource endowments are arbitrary in the sense that they are not deserved. But unlike talents, resources are not naturally attached to persons. Resources are found "out there," available to the first taker. Resources must be appropriated before they can be used, whereas, in the talents case, the "appropriation" is a fait accompli of nature over which persons have no direct control. Thus, while we feel that the possession of talents confers a right to control and benefit from their use, we may feel differently about resources. Appropriation may not always need a justification; if the resources taken are of limited value, or if, as Locke imagined, their appropriation leaves "enough and as good" for everyone else, justification may not present a problem. In a world of scarcity, however, the situation is different. The appropriation of valuable resources by some will leave others comparatively, and perhaps fatally, disadvantaged. Those deprived without justification of scarce resources needed to sustain and enhance their lives might well press claims to equitable shares.

Furthermore, resources do not stand in the same relation to personal identity as do talents. It would be inappropriate to take the sort of pride in the diamond deposits in one's back yard that one takes in the ability to play the *Appassionata*. This is because natural resources come into the development of personality (when they come in at all) in a more casual way than do talents. As I have said, talents, in some sense, are what the self is; they help constitute personality. The resources under one's feet, because they lack this natural connection with the self, seem to be more contingent than necessary elements of the development of personality. Like talents, resources are used in this process; they are worked on, shaped, and benefited from. But they are not there, as parts of the self, to begin with. They must first be appropriated, and prior to their appropriation, no one has any special natural claim on them. Considerations of personal liberty do not protect a right to appropriate and use resources in the same way as they protect the right to develop and use talents as one sees fit. There is no parallel, initial presumption against interference with the use of resources, since no one is initially placed in a naturally privileged relationship with them.

I conclude that the natural distribution of resources is a purer case of something's being "arbitrary from a moral point of view" than the distribution of talents. Not only can one not be said to deserve the resources under one's feet; the other grounds on which one might assert an initial claim to talents are absent in the case of resources, as well.

The fact that national societies are assumed to be self-sufficient does not make the distribution of natural resources any less arbitrary. Citizens of a nation which finds itself on top of a gold mine do not gain a right to the wealth that might be derived from it *simply* because their nation is self-sufficient. But someone might argue that self-sufficiency, nevertheless, removes any possible grounds on which citizens of other nations might press claims to equitable shares. A possible view is that no justification for resource appropriation is necessary in the global state of nature. If, so to speak, social cooperation is the root of all social obligations, as it is on some versions of contract theory, then the view is correct. All rights would be "special rights" applying only when certain conditions of cooperation obtain.[8]

I believe that this is wrong. It seems plausible in most discussions of distributive justice because their subject is the distribution of the benefits of social cooperation. Appropriate distributive principles compensate those who are relatively disadvantaged by the cooperative scheme for their participation in it. Where there is no social cooperation, there are no benefits of cooperation, and hence no problem of compensation for relative disadvantage. (This is why a world of self-sufficient national societies is not subject to something like a global difference principle.) But there is nothing in this reasoning to suggest that our *only* moral ties are to those with whom we share membership in a cooperative scheme. It is possible that other sorts of considerations might come into the justification of moral principles. Rawls himself recognizes this in the case of the natural duties, which are said to "apply to us without regard to our voluntary acts" (114) and, apparently, without regard to our institutional memberships.

In the case of natural resources, the parties to the international original position would know that resources are unevenly distributed with respect to population, that adequate access to resources is a prerequisite for successful operation of (domestic) cooperative schemes, and that resource supplies are scarce. They would view the natural distribution of resources as arbitrary in the sense that no one has a natural prima facie claim to the resources that happen to be under his feet. The appropriation of scarce resources by some requires a justification against the competing claims of others and the needs of future generations. Not knowing the resource endowments of their own societies, the parties would agree on a resource redistribution principle which would give each national society a fair chance to develop just political institutions and an economy capable of satisfying its members' basic needs.

There is no intuitively obvious standard of equity for such matters; perhaps the standard would be population size, or perhaps it would be more complicated, rewarding nations for their efforts in extracting resources and taking account of the differential resource needs of

8. William N. Nelson construes Rawlsian rights in this way in "Special Rights, General Rights, and Social Justice," *Philosophy & Public Affairs* 3, no. 4 (Summer 1974): 410–430.

nations with differing economies. The underlying principle is that each person has an equal prima facie claim to a share of the total available resources, but departures from this initial standard could be justified (analogously to the operation of the difference principle) if the resulting inequalities were to the greatest benefit of those least advantaged by the inequality (cf. 151). In any event, the resource redistribution principle would function in international society as the difference principle functions in domestic society. It provides assurance to resource-poor nations that their adverse fate will not prevent them from realizing economic conditions sufficient to support just social institutions and to protect human rights guaranteed by the principles for individuals. In the absence of this assurance, these nations might resort to war as a means of securing the resources necessary to establish domestic justice, and it is not obvious that wars fought for this purpose would be unjust.[9]

Before turning to other issues, I must note two complications of which I cannot give a fully satisfactory account. The international original position parties are prevented by the veil of ignorance from knowing their generation; they would be concerned to minimize the risk that, when the veil is lifted, they might find themselves living in a world where resource supplies have been largely depleted. Thus, part of the resource redistribution principle would set some standard for conservation against this possibility. The difficulties in formulating a standard of conservation are at least as formidable as those of defining the "just savings rate" in Rawls' discussion of justifiable rates of capital accumulation. I shall not pursue them here, except to point

9. On this account, United Nations General Assembly Resolution 1803 (XVII), which purports to establish "permanent sovereignty over natural resources," would be prima facie unjust. However, there are important mitigating factors. This resolution, as the text and the debates make clear, was adopted to defend developing nations against resource exploitation by foreign-owned businesses, and to underwrite a national right of expropriation (with compensation) of foreign-owned mining and processing facilities in some circumstances. While the "permanent sovereignty" doctrine may be extreme, sovereignty-for-the-time-being might not be, if it can be shown (as I think it can) that resource-consuming nations have taken more than their fair share without returning adequate compensation. United Nations General Assembly, *Official Records: Seventeenth Session*, Supp. No. 17 (A/5217) (New York, 1963), pp. 15–16.

out that some provision for conservation as a matter of justice to future generations would be necessary (cf. 284–293).

The other complication concerns the definition of "natural resources." To what extent is food to be considered a resource? Social factors enter into the production of food in a way that they do not in the extraction of raw resources, so it may be that no plausible resource principle would require redistribution of food. A nation might claim that it deserves its abundant food supplies because of its large investments in agriculture or the high productivity of its farmers. On the other hand, arable land is a precondition of food production and a nation's supply of good land seems to be as morally arbitrary as its supply of, say, oil.[10] A further complication is that arable land, unlike iron ore or oil, cannot be physically redistributed to those nations with insufficient land, while food grown on the land is easily transportable. These dilemmas might be resolved by requiring redistribution of a portion of a country's food production depending on the ratio of its arable land to its total production; but the calculations involved would be complex and probably controversial. In the absence of a broader agreement to regard international society as a unified scheme of social cooperation, formulation of an acceptable food redistribution rule might prove impossible.

In failing to recognize resource problems, Rawls follows other writers who have extended the social contract idea to international relations.[11] Perhaps this is because they have attributed a greater symmetry to the domestic and international contracts than is in fact appropriate. Resource problems do not arise as distinct questions in the domestic case because their distribution and conservation are implicitly covered by the difference principle and the just savings principle. When the scope of social cooperation is coextensive with the territorial boundaries of a society, it is unnecessary to distinguish natural and social contributions to the society's level of well-being.

10. This statement needs qualification. After a certain point in economic development, a society could make good much of its apparently nonarable land, e.g. by clearing and draining or irrigating. So we ought not regard the total amount of arable land as fixed in the same sense as the total of other resources like oil. This was pointed out to me by Huntington Terrell.

11. Two classical examples are Pufendorf and Wolff. See Walter Schiffer, *The Legal Community of Mankind* (New York, 1954), pp. 49–79.

But when justice is considered internationally, we must face the likelihood of moral claims being pressed by members of the various social schemes which are arbitrarily placed with respect to the natural distribution of resources. My suggestion of a resource redistribution principle recognizes the fundamental character of these claims viewed from the perspective of the parties' interests in securing fair conditions for the development of their respective schemes.

III

Everything that I have said so far is consistent with the assumption that nations are self-sufficient cooperative schemes. However, there are strong empirical reasons for thinking that this assumption is no longer valid. As Kant notes in the concluding pages of *The Metaphysical Elements of Justice*, international economic cooperation creates a new basis for international morality.[12]

The main features of contemporary international interdependence relevant to questions of justice are the result of the progressive removal of restrictions on international trade and investment. Capital surpluses are no longer confined to reinvestment in the societies where they are produced, but instead are reinvested wherever conditions promise the highest yield without unacceptable risks. It is well known, for example, that large American corporations have systematically transferred significant portions of their capitalization to European, Latin American, and East Asian societies where labor costs are lower, markets are better, and profits are higher. A related development is the rise of an international division of labor whereby products are manufactured in areas having cheap, unorganized labor and are marketed in more affluent areas. Because multinational businesses, rather than the producing countries themselves, play the leading role in setting prices and wages, the international division of labor results in a system of world trade in which value created in one society (usually poor) is used to benefit members of other societies (usually rich).[13] It is also important to note that the world economy

12. Trans. John Ladd (Indianapolis, 1965), pp. 125ff.

13. Cf. Richard J. Barnet and Ronald E. Müller, *Global Reach* (New York, 1975), chaps. 2, 6, and passim. See also Stephen Hymer, "The Multinational Corporation and the Law of Uneven Development," in *Economics and World Order*, ed. J.N. Bhagwati (New York, 1972), pp. 113–141.

has evolved its own financial and monetary institutions that set exchange rates, regulate the money supply, influence capital flows, and enforce rules of international economic conduct.

The system of interdependence imposes burdens on poor and economically weak countries that they cannot practically avoid. Industrial economies have become reliant on raw materials that can only be obtained in sufficient quantities from developing countries. In the present structure of world prices, poor countries are often forced by adverse balances of payments to sell resources to more wealthy countries when those resources could be more efficiently used to promote development of the poor countries' domestic economies.[14] Also, private foreign investment imposes on poor countries patterns of political and economic development that may not be optimal from the point of view of the poor countries themselves. Participation in the global economy on the only terms available involves a loss of political autonomy.[15] Third, the global monetary system allows disturbances (e.g. price inflation) in some national economies to be exported to others that may be less able to cope with their potentially disastrous effects.[16]

Economic interdependence, then, involves a pattern of relationships which are largely nonvoluntary from the point of view of the worse-off participants, and which produce benefits for some while imposing burdens on others. These facts, by now part of the conventional wisdom of international relations, describe a world in which national boundaries can no longer be regarded as the outer limits of social cooperation. Note that this conclusion does not require that national societies should have become entirely superfluous or that the global economy should be completely integrated.[17] It is enough, for setting

14. Suzanne Bodenheimer gives an account of the role of foreign investment in exploiting the resources of Latin American countries in "Dependency and Imperialism: The Roots of Latin American Underdevelopment," *Politics and Society* 1 (1971): 327–357.

15. Peter B. Evans, "National Autonomy and Economic Development," in *Transnational Relations and World Politics*, ed. Robert O. Keohane and Joseph S. Nye (Cambridge, Mass., 1972), pp. 325–342.

16. See Richard N. Cooper, "Economic Interdependence and Foreign Policy in the Seventies," *World Politics* 24, no. 2 (January 1972): 159–181.

17. This conclusion would hold even if it were true that wealthy nations such as the United States continue to be economically self-sufficient, as Kenneth

the limits of cooperative schemes, that some societies are able to increase their level of well-being via global trade and investment while others with whom they have economic relations continue to exist at low levels of development.[18]

In view of these empirical considerations, Rawls' passing concern for the law of nations seems to miss the point of international justice altogether. In an interdependent world, confining principles of social justice to national societies has the effect of taxing poor nations so that others may benefit from living in "just" regimes. The two principles, so construed, might justify a wealthy nation's denying aid to needy peoples if the aid could be used domestically to promote a more nearly just regime. If the self-sufficiency assumption were empirically acceptable, such a result might be plausible, if controversial on other

---

Waltz has (mistakenly, I think) argued. A nation might be self-sufficient in the sense that its income from trade is marginal compared with total national income, and yet still participate in economic relations with less developed countries which impose great burdens on the latter. (See fn. 18, below.) To refute the claim I make in the text, it would be necessary to show that all, or almost all, nations are self-sufficient in the sense given above. This, plainly, is not the case. Waltz argues his view in "The Myth of National Interdependence," *The International Corporation,* ed. Charles P. Kindleberger (Cambridge, Mass., 1970), pp. 205–226; he is effectively refuted by Richard Cooper, "Economic Interdependence . . ." and Edward L. Morse, "Transnational Economic Processes," in *Transnational Relations and World Politics,* pp. 23–47.

18. The situation is probably worse than this. A more plausible view is that the poor countries' economic relations with the rich have actually worsened economic conditions among the poor. Global trade widens rather than narrows the rich-poor gap, and harms rather than aids the poor countries' efforts at economic development. See André Gunder Frank, "The Development of Underdevelopment," in James D. Cockcroft et al., *Dependence and Underdevelopment* (Garden City, N.Y., 1972), pp. 3–18. This raises the question of whether interdependence must actually benefit everyone involved to give rise to questions of justice. I think the answer is clearly negative; countries *A* and *B* are involved in social cooperation even if *A* (a rich country) could get along without *B* (a poor country), but instead exploits it, while *B* gets nothing out of its "cooperation" but exacerbated class divisions and Coca-Cola factories. If this is true, then Rawls' characterization of a society as "a cooperative venture for mutual advantage" (4) may be misleading, since everyone need not be advantaged by the cooperative scheme in order for requirements of justice to apply. It would be better to say that such requirements apply to systems of economic and social interaction which are nonvoluntary from the point of view of those least advantaged (or most disadvantaged) by them, and in which some benefit as a result of the relative or absolute sacrifices of others.

grounds.[19] But if participation in economic relations with the needy society has contributed to the wealth of the "nearly just" regime, its domestic "justice" seems to lose moral significance. In such situations, the principles of domestic "justice" will be genuine principles of justice only if they are consistent with principles of justice for the entire global scheme of social cooperation.

How should we formulate global principles? As several others have suggested, Rawls' own two principles, suitably reinterpreted, could themselves be applied globally.[20] The reasoning is as follows: if evidence of global economic and political interdependence shows the existence of a global scheme of social cooperation, we should not view national boundaries as having fundamental moral significance. Since boundaries are not coextensive with the scope of social cooperation, they do not mark the limits of social obligations. Thus, the parties to the original position cannot be assumed to know that they are members of a particular national society, choosing principles of justice primarily for that society. The veil of ignorance must extend to all matters of national citizenship. As Barry points out, a global interpretation of the original position is insensitive to the choice of principles.[21] Assuming that the arguments for the two principles are successful as set out in Rawls' book, there is no reason to think that the content of the principles would change as a result of enlarging the scope of the original position so that the principles would apply to the world as a whole.[22]

Rawls' two principles are a special case of the "general conception" of social justice.[23] The two principles hold when a cooperative scheme

19. For example, on utilitarian grounds. See Peter Singer, "Famine, Affluence, and Morality," *Philosophy & Public Affairs* 1, no. 3 (Spring 1972): 229–243.

20. For example, Barry, *The Liberal Theory of Justice*, pp. 128–133; and Scanlon, "Rawls' Theory of Justice," pp. 1066–1067.

21. Barry, *The Liberal Theory of Justice*, p. 129.

22. David Richards also argues that the principles apply globally. But he fails to notice the relationship between distributive justice and the morally relevant features of social cooperation on which its requirements rest. It is this relationship, and not the simpler, blanket assertion that the original position parties are ignorant of their nationalities, which explains why Rawlsian principles of social justice should be thought to apply globally. See David A.J. Richards, *A Theory of Reasons for Action* (Oxford, 1971), pp. 137–141.

23. The general conception reads as follows: "All social primary goods— liberty and opportunity, income and wealth, and the bases of self-respect—are to

has reached a level of material well-being at which everyone's basic needs can be met. The world, conceived as a single cooperative scheme, probably has not yet reached this threshold. Assuming that this is the case, on Rawls' reasoning, we should take the general conception, which does not differentiate the basic liberties from other primary goods, as the relevant standard for assessing global economic institutions. In conditions of underdevelopment or low-average levels of well-being, he argues, rational people might opt for a principle allowing rapid growth at the expense of some personal liberties, provided that the benefits of growth and the sacrifices of liberty are fairly shared and that the bases of self-respect relevant to such background conditions are not undermined (see 152, 298–303). The argument is that the prospects of the least advantaged would be less advanced, all things considered, by observing the lexical priority of liberty than by following the general conception of social justice.[24]

The globalization of the two principles (or of the general conception, if appropriate) has the consequence that principles of justice for national societies can no longer be viewed as ultimate. The basic structure of national societies continues to be governed by the two principles (or by the general conception), but their application is derivative and hence their requirements are not absolute. A possible view is that the global principles and the principles applied to national societies are to be satisfied in lexical order. But this view has the consequence, which one might find implausible, that national policies which maximize the welfare of the least-advantaged group within the society cannot be justified if other policies would be more optimal

---

be distributed equally unless an unequal distribution of any or all of these goods is to the advantage of the least favored" (303).

24. It must be noted that the question whether the general conception is more appropriate to developing societies turns heavily on empirical considerations. In particular, it needs to be shown that sacrifices of liberty, equally shared, really do promote more rapid advances in average levels of well-being than any other possible development strategy not involving such sacrifices. After considering the evidence, it might seem that an altogether different conception of justice is more appropriate to such societies than either of Rawls' conceptions. Perhaps, in the end, the general conception will turn out to be the best that can be advanced, but it would be interesting to canvass the alternatives. See Norman Bowie's attempt to do this in *Towards a New Theory of Distributive Justice* (Amherst, Mass., 1971), pp. 114ff.

from the point of view of the lesser advantaged elsewhere. Further-more, no society could justify the additional costs involved in moving from the general to the special conception (for example, in reduced productivity) until every society had, at least, attained a level of well-being sufficient to sustain the general conception.

These features of the global interpretation of Rawlsian principles suggest that its implications are quite radical—considerably more so even than their application to ational societies. While I am not now prepared to argue positively that the best theory of global justice consists simply of Rawls' principles interpreted globally, it seems to me that the most obvious objections to such a theory are not valid. In the remainder of this section, I consider what is perhaps the leading type of objection and suggest some difficulties in giving it theoretically compelling form.

Objections of the type I have in mind hold that considerations of social cooperation at the national level justify distributive claims capable of overriding the requirements of a global difference principle. Typically, members of a wealthy nation might claim that they deserve a larger share than that provided by a global difference principle because of their superior technology, economic organization, and efficiency.

Objections of this general sort might take several forms. First, it might be argued that even in an interdependent world, national society remains the primary locus of one's political identifications. If one is moved to contribute to aggregate social welfare at any level, this level is most likely to be the national level. Therefore, differential rates of national contribution to the global welfare ought to be re-warded proportionally. This is a plausible form of the objection; the problem is that, in this form, it may not be an objection at all. The difference principle itself recognizes the probability that differential rates of reward may be needed as incentives for contribution; it re-quires only that distributive inequalities which arise in such a system be to the greatest benefit of the world's least-advantaged group. To the extent that incentives of the kind demanded by this version of the objection actually do raise the economic expectations of the least advantaged without harming them in other ways, they would not be inconsistent with the difference principle.

Such objections count against a global difference principle only if they hold that a relatively wealthy nation could claim more than its share under the difference principle. That is, the objection must hold that some distributive inequalities are justified even though they are not to the greatest benefit of the world's least-advantaged group. How could such claims be justified? One justification is on grounds of personal merit, appealing to the intuition that value created by someone's unaided labor is properly his, assuming that the initial distribution was just.[25] This sort of argument yields an extreme form of the objection. It holds that a nation is entitled to its relative wealth because each of its citizens has complied with the relevant rules of justice in acquiring raw materials and transforming them into products of value. These rules might require, respectively, that an equitable resource redistribution principle has been implemented and that no one's rights have been violated (for example, by imperial plunder) in the process of acquisition and production leading to a nation's current economic position. (Note that my arguments for a resource principle are not touched by this sort of objection and would impose some global distributive obligations even if the personal merit view were correct in ruling out broader global principles.)

This interpretation of the objection is strictly analogous to the conception of distributive justice which Rawls calls the "system of natural liberty." He objects to such views that they allow people to compete for available positions on the basis of their talents, making no attempt to compensate for deprivations that some suffer due to natural chance and social contingency. These things, as I have said, are held to be morally arbitrary and hence unacceptable as standards for distribution (cf. 66–72). I shall not rehearse this argument further here. But two things should be noted. First, the argument seems even more plausible from the global point of view since the disparity of possible starting points in world society is so much greater. The balance between "arbitrary" and "personal" contributions to my present well-being seems decisively tipped toward the "arbitrary" ones by the realization that, no matter what my talents, education, life goals, etc., I would have been virtually precluded from attaining my present level

25. This, roughly, is Robert Nozick's view in *Anarchy, State, and Utopia* (New York, 1974), chap. 7.

of well-being if I had been born in a less developed society. Second, if Rawls' counterargument counts against natural liberty views in the domestic case, then it defeats the objection to a global difference principle as well. A nation cannot base its claim to a larger distributive share than that warranted by the difference principle on factors which are morally arbitrary.

A third, and probably the most plausible, form of this objection holds that a wealthy nation may retain more than its share under a global difference principle, provided that some compensation for the benefits of global social cooperation is paid to less fortunate nations, and that the amount retained by the producing nation is used to promote domestic justice, for example, by increasing the prospects of the nation's own least favored group. The underlying intuition is that citizens owe some sort of special obligation to the less fortunate members of their own society that is capable of overriding their general obligation to improve the prospects of lesser advantaged groups elsewhere. This intuition is distinct from the intuition in the personal desert case, for it does not refer to any putative individual right to the value created by one's labor. Instead, we are concerned here with supposedly conflicting rights and obligations that arise from membership in overlapping schemes of social cooperation, one embedded in the other.

An argument along these lines needs an account of how obligations to the sectional association arise. One might say that the greater degree or extent of social cooperation in national societies (compared with that in international society) underwrites stronger intranational principles of justice. To see this objection in its strongest form, imagine a world of two self-sufficient and internally just societies, *A* and *B*. Assume that this world satisfies the appropriate resource redistribution principle. Imagine also that the least-advantaged representative person in society *A* is considerably better off than his counterpart in society *B*. While the members of *A* may owe duties of mutual aid to the members of *B*, it is clear that they do not have parallel duties of justice, because the two societies, being individually self-sufficient, do not share membership in a cooperative scheme. Now suppose that the walls of self-sufficiency are breached very slightly; *A* trades its apples for B's pears. Does this mean that the difference principle suddenly applies to the world which comprises A and B, requiring A to share all of its wealth with B, even though almost all of its wealth is attributable to economic interaction within A? It seems not; one might say that an international difference principle can only command redistribution of the benefits derived from international social cooperation or economic interaction. It cannot touch the benefits of domestic cooperation.

It may be that some such objection will turn out to produce modifications on a global difference principle. But there are reasons for doubting this. Roughly, it seems that there is a threshold of interdependence above which distributive requirements such as a global difference principle are valid, but below which significantly weaker principles hold. I cannot give a systematic account of this view here, but perhaps some intuitive considerations will demonstrate its force.

Consider another hypothetical case. Suppose that, *within* a society, there are closely-knit local regions with higher levels of internal cooperation than the level of cooperation in society as a whole. Certainly there are many such regions within a society such as the United States. The argument rehearsed above, applied to closely-knit localities within national societies, would seem to give members of the localities special claims on portions of their wealth. This seems implausible, especially since such closely-knit enclaves might well turn out to contain disproportionate numbers of the society's most advantaged classes. Why does this conclusion seem less plausible than that in the apples and pears case? It seems to me that the answer has to do with the fact that the apples and pears case looks like a case of voluntary, free-market bargaining that has only a marginal effect on the welfare of the members of each society, whereas we assume in the intranational case that there is a nonvoluntary society-wide system of economic institutions which defines starting positions and assigns economic rights and duties. It is these institutions—what Rawls calls "the basic structure" (7–11)—that stand in need of justification, because, by defining the terms of cooperation, they have such deep and pervasive effects on the welfare of people to whom they apply regardless of consent.

The apples and pears case, of course, is hardly a faithful model of the contemporary world economy. Suppose that we add to the story to make it resemble the real world more closely. As my review of the current situation (above, pp. 373–375) makes clear, we would have to add just those features of the contemporary world economy that find their domestic analogues in the basic structure to which principles of justice apply. As the web of transactions grows more complex, the resulting structure of economic and political institutions acquires great influence over the welfare of the participants, regardless of the extent to which any particular one makes use of the institutions. These features make the real world situation seem more like the case of subnational, closely-knit regions.

These considerations suggest that the amount of social and economic interaction in a cooperative scheme does not provide a straightforward index of the strength of the distributive principle appropriate to it. The existence of a powerful, nonvoluntary institutional structure, and its pervasive effects on the welfare of the cooperators, seems to provide a better indication of the strength of the appropriate distributive requirements. This sort of consideration would not necessarily support a global difference principle in the apples and pears case; but it does explain why, above a threshold measure of social cooperation, the full force of the difference principle may come into play despite regional variations in the amount of cooperation.[26]

Proponents of this objection to a global difference principle might have one last resort. They might appeal to noneconomic features of national societies to justify the special obligations that citizens owe to the less fortunate members of their own societies. On this basis, they could claim that the difference principle applies to national societies despite regional variations in cooperation but not to international society. Probably the plausibility of this sort of argument will depend on the degree to which it psychologizes the ties that bind

26. I do not claim to have resolved the problem which underlies this objection, although I believe that my remarks point in the right direction. It should be noticed, however, that what is at issue here is really a general problem for any theory which addresses itself to institutional structures rather than to particular transactions. One can always ask why institutional requirements should apply in full force to persons who make minimal use of the institutions they find themselves in. This point emerged from discussions I have had with Thomas Scanlon.

the members of social institutions.[27] There are problems, however. First, it needs to be shown that psychological ties such as national loyalty are of sufficient moral importance to balance the international economic ties that underwrite a global difference principle. Second, even if this could be persuasively argued, any account of how institutional obligations arise that is sufficiently psychological to make plausible a general conflict of global and sectional loyalties will probably be too psychological to apply to the large modern state (cf. 477).

Perhaps this line of objection can be made good in some way other than those canvassed here. If this could be done, it would not follow that there are no global distributive obligations but only that some portion of a nation's gross product would be exempt from the requirements of the global standard provided that it were used domestically in appropriate ways. The question would not be whether there are global distributive obligations founded on justice, but rather to what extent considerations relevant to the special features of cooperation within national societies modify the egalitarian tendencies of the global standard.

IV

We have now reached two main conclusions. First, assuming national self-sufficiency, Rawls' derivation of the principles of justice for the law of nations is correct but incomplete. He importantly neglects resource redistribution, a subject that would surely be on the minds of the parties to the international original position. But second, the self-sufficiency assumption, upon which Rawls' entire consideration of the law of nations rests, is not justified by the facts of contemporary international relations. The state-centered image of the world has lost its normative relevance because of the rise of global economic interdependence. Hence, principles of distributive justice must apply in the first instance to the world as a whole, then derivatively to nation-states. The appropriate global principle is probably something like Rawls' general conception of justice, perhaps modified by some provision for intranational redistribution in rela-

27. For a suggestive account of a similar problem, see Michael Walzer, "The Obligation to Disobey," *Obligations: Essays on Disobedience, War, and Citizenship* (Cambridge, Mass., 1970), pp. 3–23.

tively wealthy states once a threshold level of international redistributive obligations has been met. Rawls' two principles become more relevant as global distributive inequalities are reduced and a higher average level of well-being is attained. In conclusion, I would like to consider the implications of this ideal theory for international politics and global change in the nonideal world. In what respects does this interpretation of the social contract doctrine shed light on problems of world order change?

We might begin by asking, in general, what relevance social ideals have for politics in the real world. Their most obvious function is to describe a goal toward which efforts at political change should aim. In Rawls' theory, a very important natural duty is the natural duty of justice, which "requires us to support and to. comply with just institutions that exist and . . . constrains us to further just arrangements not yet established, at least if this can be done without too much cost to ourselves" (115). By supplying a description of the nature and aims of a just world order, ideal theory "provides . . . the only basis for the systematic grasp of these more pressing problems" (9). Ideal theory, then, supplies a set of criteria for the formulation and criticism of strategies of political action in the nonideal world, at least when the consequences of political action can be predicted with sufficient confidence to establish their relationship to the social ideal. Clearly, this task would not be easy, given the complexities of social change and the uncertainties of prediction in political affairs. There is the additional complication that social change is often wrongly conceived as a progressive approximation of actual institutions to ideal prescriptions in which people's welfare steadily improves. An adequate social theory must avoid the pitfalls of a false incrementalism as well as what economists call the problem of the second best.[28] But a coherent social ideal is a necessary condition of any attempt to conquer these difficulties.

Ideal justice, in other words, comes into nonideal politics by way of the natural duty to secure just institutions where none presently exist. The moral problem posed by distinguishing ideal from nonideal theory is that, in the nonideal world, the natural duty of justice is like-

28. On the problem of the second best, see Brian Barry, *Political Argument* (London, 1965), pp. 261–262.

ly to conflict with other natural duties, while the theory provides no
mechanism for resolving such conflicts. For example, it is possible
that a political decision which is likely to make institutions more
just is equally likely to involve violations of other natural duties,
such as the duty of mutual aid or the duty not to harm the innocent.
Perhaps reforming some unjust institution will require us to disappoint legitimate expectations formed under the old order. The principles of natural duty in the nonideal world are relatively unsys-
tematic, and we have no way of knowing which should win out in
case of conflict. Rawls recognizes the inevitability of irresolvable conflicts in some situations (303), but, as Feinberg has suggested, he
underestimates the role that an intuitive balancing of conflicting
duties must play in nonideal circumstances.[29] Rawls says that problems of political change in radically unjust situations must rely on a
utilitarian calculation of costs and benefits (352–353). If this is true,
then political change in conditions of great injustice marks one kind
of limit of the contract doctrine, for in these cases the principles of
justice collapse into utilitarianism. It seems to me, however, that this
conclusion is too broad. At least in some cases of global justice, nonideal theory, while teleological, is not utilitarian. I shall try to show
this briefly with respect to questions of food and development aid,
the principle of nonintervention, and the obligation to participate in
war on behalf of a nation-state.

The duty to secure just institutions where none exist endows certain political claims made in the nonideal world with a moral seriousness which does not derive merely from the obligations that bind
people regardless of the existence of cooperative ties. When the contract doctrine is interpreted globally, the claims of the less advantaged
in today's nonideal world—claims principally for food aid, development assistance, and world monetary and trade reform—rest on
principles of global justice as well as on the weaker duty of mutual
aid. Those who are in a position to respond to these claims, despite
the absence of effective global political mechanisms, must take account of the stronger reasons provided by the principles of justice in
weighing their response. Furthermore, by interpreting the principles

29. Joel Feinberg, "Duty and Obligation in the Nonideal World," *Journal of
Philosophy* 70 (10 May 1973): 263–275.

globally, we remove a major source of justifying reasons for not responding more fully to such claims. These reasons derive from statist concerns, for example, a supposed right to reinvest domestic surpluses in national societies that are already relatively favored from a global point of view. The natural duties still require us to help members of our own society who are in need, and a wealthy nation would be justified on this account in using some of its resources to support domestic welfare programs. What cannot be argued is that a wealthy nation's general right to retain its domestic product always overrides its obligation to advance the welfare of lesser-advantaged groups elsewhere.

An ideal theory of global justice has implications for traditional doctrines of international law as well. Consider, as a representative example, the rule of nonintervention. It is often remarked that this rule, which is prominently displayed in a number of recent authoritative documents of international law, seems inconsistent with the international community's growing rhetorical commitment to the protection of human rights, which is also prominently displayed in many of the same documents.[30] The conflict can be illustrated with reference to South Africa: the doctrine of nonintervention seems to prevent other states from giving aid to local insurgent forces explicitly committed to attaining recognition of basic human rights for the vast bulk of the South African population. Ordinarily, such conflicts are regarded as simple matters of utilitarian balancing, but the global interpretation of social contract theory shows that more can be said. The global interpretation introduces an asymmetry into the justification of the rules of international law. These rules impose different obligations depending on whether their observance in particular cases would contribute to or detract from a movement toward more just institutions.

The nonintervention rule is to be interpreted in this light. When it would demonstrably operate to advance or protect just arrange-

30. For example, the U. N. Charter, articles 2(4) and 1(3), and article 1 of the "Declaration of Principles of International Cooperation . . . ," approved by the General Assembly on 24 October 1970. Both are reprinted in *Basic Documents in International Law*, ed. Ian Brownlie, 2nd ed. (Oxford, 1972), pp. 1–31 and 32–40.

ments, it furnishes a strong reason not to intervene. In the absence
of compelling reasons to the contrary, it imposes a duty to comply.
This is typically the case when intervention would interfere with a
people's right of self-determination, a right which protects the fair
exercise of political liberty. Thus, American intervention in Allende's
Chile certainly violated a basic requirement of global justice. But
sometimes, as in South Africa, observing the nonintervention rule
cannot be justified in this way. Rather than resting on considerations
of justice, which give strong reasons for compliance, it rests on considerations of natural duty—such as protection of the innocent against
harms that might be suffered if large-scale military intervention
occurred—and of international stability. These are certainly not negligible reasons for nonintervention, but, from the standpoint of global
justice, they are weaker reasons than those provided by global justice
itself. Obviously, peaceful resolution of cases such as that of South
Africa is to be preferred. But when this goal cannot be attained, or
when insurgent forces fighting for human rights request foreign assistance, intervention cannot be opposed as a matter of justice (as it
could be on the traditional interpretation of this international rule,
preserved in Rawls' own brief discussion), for its effect would be to
help secure rights, including the right of self-determination, protected
by the global principles. Again, in the absence of compelling reasons
to the contrary (of which, certainly, a great number can be imagined),
there might be an international duty to intervene in support of insurgent forces. I say that there may be an *international* duty because
it seems clear that unilateral intervention can almost always be successfully opposed on grounds of international stability. But a decision
by the international community to enforce principles of justice would
be less susceptible to this sort of objection. Here I note what has too
often been overlooked (except, perhaps, by American multinationals),
that intervention in another country's internal affairs can take many
nonviolent forms, including economic blockades, nonmilitary aid to
insurgent forces, diplomatic pressure, etc. While such forms of intervention obviously carry no guarantee of success, it is fair to say
that their potential effectiveness has been widely underestimated.[31]

31. See Gene Sharp, *The Politics of Non-violent Action* (Boston, 1973).

Finally, what are the implications of global justice for participation in a nation's military forces? From what I have said thus far, it should be clear that the global interpretation supplies reasons for acting or not acting which are capable of overriding the reasons provided by traditional rules of international law. These reasons are also capable of overriding the rule that demands compliance with internally just domestic regimes. One important consequence is that conscientious refusal to participate in a nation's armed forces would have far broader possible justifications than on the account given in Rawls (cf. 377–382), assuming for the moment that, given the great destructiveness of modern weapons and war strategies, participation in national armed forces could ever be justified at all. For instance, in some circumstances, a war of self-defense fought by an affluent nation against a poorer nation pressing legitimate claims under the global principles (for example, for increased food aid) might be unjustifiable, giving rise to a justified refusal to participate in the affluent nation's armed forces.

These three examples show that the contract doctrine, despite limitations noted here, sheds light on the distinctive normative problems of the shift from statist to global images of world order. The extension of economic and cultural relationships beyond national borders has often been thought to undermine the moral legitimacy of the state; the extension of the contract doctrine gives a systematic account of why this is so, and of its consequences for problems of justice in the nonideal world, by emphasizing the role of social cooperation as the foundation of just social arrangements. When, as now, national boundaries do not set off discrete, self-sufficient societies, we may not regard them as morally decisive features of the earth's social geography. For purposes of moral choice, we must, instead, regard the world from the perspective of an original position from which matters of national citizenship are excluded by an extended veil of ignorance.

I do not believe that Rawls' failure to take account of these questions marks a pivotal weakness of his theory; on the contrary, the theory provides a way of determining the consequences of changing empirical circumstances (such as the assumption of national self-sufficiency) for the concept of justice. The global interpretation is the result of recognizing an important empirical change in the structure of world political and social life. In this way the theory allows us to apply generalizations derived from our considered judgments regarding familiar situations to situations which are new and which demand that we form intelligent moral views and act on them when action is possible and appropriate. This is no small achievement for a moral theory. Some might think, however, that our moral intuitions are too weak or unreliable to support such an extension of the theory. I doubt that this is true; rather, it often seems to be a convenient way to beg off from unpleasant moral requirements. But if I am wrong about this—if we cannot expect moral theory to provide a firm guide for action in new situations—one might wonder whether moral theory has any practical point at all.

THE CONTRIBUTORS

LAWRENCE A. ALEXANDER is Professor of Law at the University of San Diego. He is a frequent contributor to both legal and philosophical journals on various topics in legal and moral theory.

CHARLES R. BEITZ is Associate Professor of Political Science at Swarthmore College. He is the author of articles on topics in international ethics, human rights, and democratic theory, and of the book, *Political Theory and International Relations* (Princeton, NJ: Princeton University Press, 1979).

MARSHALL COHEN is Professor of Philosophy and Law and Dean of Humanities at the University of Southern California; he is the Editor of *Philosophy & Public Affairs*.

ROBERT K. FULLINWIDER is Research Associate at the Center for Philosophy and Public Policy of the University of Maryland at College Park. He has written on a variety of issues in moral philosophy and public policy and is the author of *The Reverse Discrimination Controversy: A Moral and Legal Analysis* (Totowa, NJ: Rowman & Littlefield, 1980).

GREGORY S. KAVKA is Professor of Philosophy at the University of California, Irvine, where he teaches political philosophy and ethics. He has written a number of articles on moral issues concerning nuclear deterrence, and is currently completing a book on Hobbesian moral and political philosophy.

DOUGLAS P. LACKEY is Professor of Philosophy at Baruch College of the City University of New York, where he teaches courses in philosophy and in business policy. He is the author of *Moral Principles and Nuclear Weapons* (Totowa, NJ: Rowman & Allanheld, 1984).

DAVID LUBAN is Research Associate at the Center for Philosophy and Public Policy of the University of Maryland at College Park and Lecturer at the Maryland Law School. He has published articles on political philosophy and lawyers' ethics and has edited *The Good Lawyer: Lawyers' Roles and Lawyers' Ethics* (Totowa, NJ: Rowman & Allanheld, 1983). Professor Luban is currently completing a book on the legal profession.

GEORGE I. MAVRODES is Professor of Philosophy at the University of Michigan. He is the author of *Belief in God: A Study in the Epistemology of Religion* (New York, 1970), the editor of *The Rationality of Belief in God* (New York, 1970), and coeditor (with Stuart C. Hackett) of *Problems and Perspectives in the Philosophy of Religion* (Boston, 1967).

THOMAS NAGEL is Professor of Philosophy at New York University and author of *The Possibility of Altruism* (1970; reprint, Princeton, NJ: Princeton University Press, 1979) and *Mortal Questions* (Cambridge: Cambridge University Press, 1979).

ONORA O'NEILL is Reader in Philosophy at the University of Essex. She is the author of *Acting on Principle* (New York: Columbia University Press, 1975) and a variety of recent papers on Kantian ethics. Her other writing on the subject of world hunger includes "Moral Perplexities of Famine Relief," in *Matters of Life and Death*, ed. T. Regan (New York: Random House, 1980) and *Faces of Hunger* (forthcoming, George Allen & Unwin).

PETER SINGER is Professor of Philosophy and Director of the Centre for Human Bioethics at Monash University, Melbourne, Australia. His books include *Animal Liberation, Practical Ethics, The Expanding Circle,* and (with Deane Wells) *The Reproduction Revolution.*

MICHAEL WALZER is Professor of Social Science at the Institute for Advanced Study in Princeton, New Jersey. He is the author of *Just and Unjust Wars* (New York: Basic Books, 1977) and *Spheres of Justice* (New York: Basic Books, 1983).

Library of Congress Cataloging in Publication Data

Main entry under title:

International ethics.

(A Philosophy & public affairs reader)
Most of the essays included were previously
published in Philosophy & public affairs.
Includes bibliographies.
1. International relations—Moral and ethical
aspects—Addresses, essays, lectures.   I. Beitz,
Charles R.   II. Alexander, Lawrence A.
III. Philosophy & public affairs.   IV. Series.
JX1255.I67 1985   172'.4   84-42938
ISBN 0-691-07683-9
ISBN 0-691-02234-8 (pbk.)